OTHER BOOKS BY MISHA HA BAKA

Poetry

CONFESSIONS OF A LONELY MYSTIC small talk

Short Stories

CONFESSIONS OF A LONELY MYSTIC short talk

Art and Humor

TWO WOMEN CONTEMPLATING THE NATURE OF THE UNIVERSE Print Operas BW

TWO WOMEN CONTEMPLATING THE NATURE OF THE UNIVERSE Print Operas

TWO WOMEN, THREE FLAMINGOES AND A POOCH Print Operas

TWO WOMEN, THREE FLAMINGOES AND A POOCH Print Operas BW

TWO MEN CONTEMPLATING THE NATURE OF WOMEN AND THE UNIVERSE Print Operas

PORTRAITS OF A LONELY MYSTIC IN 3D

PORTRAITS OF A LONELY MYSTIC IN 3D

Misha Ha Baka

PORTRAITS OF A LONELY MYSTIC IN 3D

Copyright © 2017 Misha Ha Baka.
All rights reserved.

ISBN-13: 978-0-9987941-7-4
ISBN-10: 0-9987941-7-1

Published by Ha Baka Book

Although every precaution has been taken to verify the accuracy of the information contained herein, the author and publisher assume no responsibility for any errors or omissions. No liability is assumed for damages that may result from the use of information contained within.

No part of this book may be reproduced, stored in a retrieval system, or transmitted in any form or by any means, electronic, mechanical, photocopying, recording, or otherwise without the prior written permission of the copyright owner except in the case of brief quotations embodied in critical reviews and certain other noncommercial uses permitted by copyright law. Contact www.mishahabaka.com for permission requests or other inquiries.

This is a work of fiction. Names, characters, businesses, places, events and incidents are either the products of the author's imagination or used in a fictitious manner. Any resemblance to actual persons, living or dead, or actual events, or actual places is purely coincidental. However, all references to God and Spirit are real and true.

First edition paperback 2017

DEDICATION

To my Mother and Beloved Father

PROLOGUE

No animals were abused or insulted during the writing of this volume.

Yours truly,

The Lonely Mystic

Table of Contents

1 Horizon-Visions 1

2 Tiny Tyke-And So It Starts 2

3 Soda Pop? – Fashion Skills 5

4 Escape Artist - The Quest Begins! 7

5 The Prophecy – The Black-Cap Kid 9

6 Premonitions-Attitude Dude 11

7 Barn Boy - The Horsey 12

8 Sherpa Boy - The Journey 14

9 Katmandu Via Lhasa – Three Wise Guys 20

10 Answer Man – Tao Guy 25

11 Back to the Country - The Fool 27

12 Are We There Yet? – Siberia 30

13 Bandanarama – Finger Walking 33

14 Camper Guy – Circular Reasoning 38

15 Rain, Rain Go Away – The Calypso Kid 40

16 Rock Star – Lift Off! 43

17 Out of Body - Captain Cosmos 45

18 The 70's - Cool Dude 48

19 The Symbol - Some Piece 51

20 The Wise One – The Pit and The Pee 53

21 I Do - Do You Do Too? 55

22 Bad Hair Days - Handle Bar Man 60

23 Look Into My Eyes - Svengalli Guy 62

24 Revelations – Mysteries Explained 66

25 The Great Escape – Nurse Bitemei 70

26 Loosing It - Crew Cut Guy 73

27 The Gym - The Excersist 74

28 The Escapist - El Sicko 78

29 The Genealogist - The Relatives 81

30 The Gynecologist - Safe Sex 84

31 The Messenger – Divine Directions 86

32 The Community - Rituals 88

33 The Mystic – Religious Experiences 91

34 Shades - De Ja Views 93

35 Heavenly Bodies – Astronomy Guy 96

36 What Did You Say? – Can You Hear Me? 102

37 Music of the Spheres - Music Man 105

38 Wrong Numbers – The Answer Man 108

39 Can You See Me Now? – Serious Dude 110

40 Bad Hairma - Unsure Guy 114

41 What a Bod! – The Visible Man 118

42 Salon – The Mechanics of Genealogy 121

43 Sunglasses – ICMEUCUWECUS 125

44 Taxidermist - Unforeseen Events 128

45 Foreign Tongues – The i-Diot 133

46 Relatives - The Commuter 135

47 Rush Hour – A OK 139

48 Beautiful Dreamer – Umbrella Man 141

49 Dinosaur – The Lonely Mistress 144

50 Angel Rays – A Glimpse of Heaven 146

51 Only the Plumbing – New Beginnings 148

52 Dog Gone It – Man's Best Friend 153

53 Ivy Leaf School – The Graduate 155

54 Live Wire – Mr. Seltzer 158

55 Best Friends – Irving & Shirley 161

56 Eye To Eye - Night At The Opera 167

57 Mr. Fashion - Guitar Man 170

58 Out of This World - Head Start 172

59 Take Me To Your Leader - The Alien 174

60 Ancient Dancer – Dressed In Drag 177

61 The Adjustment – Ido Everythink 182

62 The Hitch Hiker – Destiny Calls 187

63 Frenchie – The Gendarme 189

64 Odd Lot – The Neighbors 192

65 Man of Many Hats - Mr. Wardrobe 197

66 I Am 4 U – Dream Lover 200

67 Knee Deep – Can You Hear Me Now? 202

68 More Than One – Juggle My Balls 207

69 Circus, Circus – Dancing With Animals 209

70 All Wet – A Midnight Swimmer's Song 215

71 Strung Out – All Hung Out to Dry 218

72 All Aboard – Night Ladies & Mr. Pick 221

73 La Tub – Music To My Ears 225

74 All Boxed In – Repeat Offender 229

75 Room Service – Origin of a Species 231

76 Stiff Upper Lip – All Around Town 235

77 Au Naturalé – Father T and Bi Bi 239

78 It's Good To Be King – Small Fry 243

79 The Reader - I Made It Up 246

80 The Reading – The Troupe 248

Epilogue 252

List of Illustrations 253

Additional Books by Misha Ha Baka 255

MiKeigh Music 256

About the Author & Artist 257

PORTRAITS OF A LONELY MYSTIC IN 3D

Portraits of a Lonely Mystic is an unbridled, irreverent, unauthorized pictorial and quasi-autobiographical exposition of events in the life of The Lonely Mystic written by none other than The Lonely Mystic, himself. All persons, events or places referenced, or depicted are figments of a very fertile imagination and although they may bear semblances to known or unknown personages, places or events, such resemblances are purely coincidental, unintentional and definitely unpremeditated. This holds true for The Lonely Mystic himself, who although is depicted as various personas, is actually a gorgeous, blond haired, blue eyed muscular giant of a man standing 6'5" tall in his sandals, which he always wears so not to further intimidate others. Of course, this is due to mystical reasons, which can't be divulged at the moment. All art and prose presented herein was written and created by yours truly, The Lonely Mystic. This is Volume 1; there are other volumes...

Misha Ha Baka 2017

1   HORIZON-VISIONS

Mount Everest, Tibet, China
Tears of Joy, Tears of Sadness
"Is it me, or is it them?"

MOUNT EVEREST, TIBET—DECEMBER 12, 2012

The Lonely Mystic stared at the skies and went into a visionary trance. The present, past and future started to swirl around him. The skies were filled with iconic symbols of the country and the world. Some of which he recognized while others seemed quite strange to him. He saw presidents, countries, vehicles, and people from here and elsewhere living in cities in the sky. The images shifted and changed, ebbed and flowed, and rose and fell. He didn't know how long he was in this mystic trance, but when he came to, he noticed that tears were flowing abundantly from his eyes. He then began to ponder whether those tears were tears of joy, or tears of sadness. But before delving too far into his future, let's begin with his glorious past.

2   TINY TYKE-AND SO IT STARTS

Wallabout Street, Brooklyn—1953
Hi Roller
"Get that camera out of my face!"

WALLABOUT STREET, BROOKLYN—1953

The Lonely Mystic has rarely been photographed, or for that matter ever been drawn. That is one of the reasons for the rarity of this volume. The other reason is he has yet to find a publisher for it. If you are lucky enough to have a copy, please place it in a safe place. It is sure to be sought after by all your neighbors when they find out you are hoarding, hiding and coveting it. That being said, above is one of the only early surviving pictures of The Lonely Mystic. We find him wrapped up in a mystical Chinese blanket. This blanket, which by the way he named "Na, Na, Nah" and its various incarnations, has accompanied him throughout all of his life. It was tattered, fur-balled pink cotton with a border of silky-smooth shiny, pink satin sheen. It was only later in life that he discovered its transcendental nature. This became transparently vivid to him; upon the discovery of its true origin.

On that fateful day and upon close and careful examination, a mysterious note, which was attached to the blanket, caught his discerning eye. It read: *Made in China*. This one event influenced him greatly. It was the source of inspiration that prompted him to travel the far corners of the earth in search of a replacement: For in a fit of jealousy due to lack of attention, his guard dog, *The Tiger* decided the *Nah*, would also make an excellent watering hole. The Tiger then proceeded to tear it to shreds in order to cover up his dastardly deed. He was severely devastated when he discovered his missing *Nah*. This was only the first of many traumatic experiences that would mold his life in inexplicable ways.

Even though the *Nah* was rumpled, soiled, and ripped to shreds, he still faithfully carried his first possession with him wherever he went. He had a reverence for the finer things in life. There was nothing finer than his pink blanky and the touch of its smooth, satin border trim pressed against his cheeks.

On the very same day of this photo, Mom had accidentally let loose the stroller, or at least she thought she did, inaugurating his future love of fast cars and protective headgear. Fortunately, he was wearing his lucky cap. It prevented a nasty bang to his noggin. Mom picked him up, wrapped him in his security blanket, held him high up to the sky and said to him, "Don't worry, everything will be all right. Everything is as it should be."

Her comforting declaration became ingrained in his memory as his first life-affirming mantra. Of course, since he was crying at the moment, he couldn't imagine everything would ever be all right. This dichotomy confused him. He couldn't tell as to whether he was crying tears of joy, or tears of sadness. This confusion regarding his inability to interpret his feelings vs. another's accompanied him throughout life. Later he realized this was actually an empathic, psychic ability, which still sometimes confuses him until this very day. He learned several things that day:

LIFE LESSONS
1	You can overcome adversity by rising above it.
2	Running away from where you are doesn't get you farther away from it anyway. Usually, it puts you back right to where you started from with even more problems.
3	If you are going for a ride, at least be dressed for the occasion. You might as well travel fast if you are going to the wrong place. This way you won't waste time coming back to where you originally were.
4	Leaving home without your parents' permission doesn't get you any place since they bring you back to where you started from anyway.
5	And most importantly, smile when you are in public. You never know when the paparazzi are going to photograph you.

He always thought he looked angry in this shot. In actuality, he was. The guy taking the picture didn't count to three, and he said, "Cheese." He thought *everyone knew I hated cheese unless it was soy cheese*. His Mom had to breastfeed him soy milk since he was lactose intolerant even as a child. As you can only well imagine, this was no small feat. Of course, at that time, you couldn't even buy soy milk. She had to put soy beans in a large vat. Then with her bare feet; she danced around on them until they gave up the goods. Her favorite tune to dance to was *Have a Some Milka* and *Oh Soy La Meo*. Of course, soy milk wasn't going to be invented until several decades later, but he came from a family of visionaries. They knew way in advance what was going to occur.

He was actually trying to get out of the stroller to grab the camera from the photographer when he realized his father was taking the picture. *Pop*, the name he later gave him, was rarely fully present with them, so he had forgotten what he looked like. He was always somewhere else, even though he was always there. He inherited this uncanny capability. Later on in life, he transformed it into being able to be in two or even three places at the same time. But at that very moment, through sheer willpower, he tipped the balance of the stroller and well, rolled into history. He was to find out each of his extraordinary experiences enabled him to obtain and develop special mystical abilities and powers:

MYSTIC POWERS
Visionary: An uncanny ability to see.
Stationary: An uncanny ability to remain motionless even when mobile.
Presence: What you get when you are there, not what you get for your birthday.

3 SODA POP? – FASHION SKILLS

Brooklyn, New York—1954
The Soda Pop Kid
"Who says thin is in?"

LIFE LESSONS
1 Always wear protective gear when sleeping.
2 Always dress for the occasion.
3 Excess weight has its purpose.
4 Pop might pop you if you pop his pop.

MYSTIC POWERS
4 **Dreaming:** The ability to dream with no effort at all, especially strong during the night hours. Eyes move even when closed.

BROOKLYN, NEW YORK—1954

As a result of his downhill adventure, The Lonely Mystic learned the valuable lesson of the first fall was always the hardest. Consequently, for added protection, he always dressed in layers, especially when going to sleep. Even at an early age, he knew you never know what dreams might cause you to jump out of bed. So, as a protective measure, from then on he decided to always dress for sleep. He found a sleeping cap with a pompom on it. When Pop wasn't looking, he drank lots of Pop's soda to toughen up and put on padding like the Sushi wrestlers do. Because of the bubbles, he developed a love affair with seltzer. Of course, he also had to wear earmuffs given the possibility of his head slipping off the pillow. Matching gloves and slippers completed the outfit; he got those from his mom's walk-in closet. Her closet was really a second bedroom that his father had converted for her. His legendary fashion skills originated from Mom's influence upon him. She was a Fashion Consultant. Needless to say, he mediated all of this with seasoning.

In the summer he didn't wear gloves. In the fall he wore double everything because even the seasons gave you clues about impending events. After the winter, he wore sneakers so he could spring back, should he fall out of bed. In the fifth seasoning, salt and pepper, he wore a mask. He had allergies and a way with words.

4   ESCAPE ARTIST - THE QUEST BEGINS!

Canarsie Beach, Brooklyn, New York
Runaway Kid
"I'm an Old Soul."

LIFE LESSONS

1 Old Souls may have premature hair growth on their upper lip.
2 Grass is a superfood!
3 God is good.
4 If you are going to leave, then do it fast before they catch you.
5 Don't cut your hair because they may get angry and run away from home.
6 Smoking animals can be hazardous to your health.

MYSTIC POWERS

5 **Youthful:** The ability to stay young even when old. The ability to look like a kid even when old. The ability to be clueless and yet very deep.

CANARSIE BEACH, BROOKLYN—1954

The Lonely Mystic left home soon after he was able to walk. He wore his trusty multi-color hat and backpack. He sported a mustache, which had appeared at a very early age. Later in life, he was often told he was an Old Soul. He attributed his premature hair growth to that very fact. But he was to discover the body has a finite number of hairs and *what grows prematurely, leaves prematurely*. He intuitively knew the value of going green. This greatly contributed to his college education. For him, this meant since he didn't have any money, he might have to live on grass. He had heard cows live on eating only grass. He knew he was smarter than a cow, so he figured he too could biologically transmutate grass into calcium and all the other nutrients he would need.

A friend of his at school also told him if you burn grass it could make you happy. The friend even offered to sell him a bag of it for five dollars. Can you imagine, before that he thought the guy was actually a friend of his? Now he thought *how could a friend want to charge me money for something I can easily get from my front lawn?* He was ready to leave home and cut some grass. He never got to smoke or eat it since he never even got out of the door. The effort prepared him for his life-long journey of searching for God. Of course, at that time, he was on a quest for some *good* food. Later he learned *good* was an extension of God and the unity of God when manifested became dual, hence two "oo"s came together to form: "good." This confirmed the reason why he instinctively went, "Oo" when he saw something that was really good. Just as you do, "Right?" He was really deep for his age.

5 THE PROPHECY – THE BLACK-CAP KID

East New York, Brooklyn—April 1955
The Black Cap Kid
"Ben do dis!"

LIFE LESSONS
1 If you get caught, shave your mustache.
2 Listen to your elders, even if you have no clue as to what they mean.
3 Assume the role.
4 Dress the part.
5 Poetry can be useful.
6 The universe is synchronistic.
7 Zen Ben one liners cure ITF.

MYSTIC POWERS
6 **Ancestry:** The ability to have relatives that are older than oneself. The ability to hear elders and have no clue as to what they are saying.

EAST NEW YORK, BROOKLYN—1955

After having grown teeth, The Lonely Mystic tried to escape from home again. This time he shaved off his mustache and turned his cap around. He figured this way no one would recognize him as he exited the building. This event marked the beginning of his ability to disguise himself and transform into other personages, as will be quite evident throughout the remainder of these manuscripts. He almost made it out the door. However, his bright yellow shirt caught the watchful eye of his grandfather. He was promptly grabbed by the collar and told, "One day you will learn that short, yellow caps fly off in the wind."

He was in awe. *I have never heard a mystical statement from my grandfather Zen Ben before.* He thought *it was rather serendipitous my grandfather is named after a branch of a Japanese mystical school called, Ben Do Dis.* His grandfather's real name was Ben. It was mistakenly misspelled when he arrived at *Tellus Island* from Europe. It was called Tellus Island because the clerks asked everyone their names and being immigrants themselves, had difficulty understanding and spelling what they heard. So as not to lose their jobs, they either misspelled it or changed it. Ben became Zen, and his wife's name became Hitou, which was very poetic.

One of Ben's favorite one-liners was "The sound of one hand slapping." Ben's wife would often tell him, "Ben do dis" and then give him a slap on his rear to get him going. The Lonely Mystic's early life was filled with these synchronistic occurrences.

Another example can be culled from his elementary school years. His favorite teacher, Mrs. Paradox as he called her, would read him poems called *Ben Kohan's*. (He thought it was a remarkable coincidence too! Later he was to learn there were no coincidences, only unexplained events.) They were a collection of one-liners. He had ITF, so his inability to focus prevented him from comprehending more than one sentence at a time. He swore his grandfather had something to do with all those poems.

6   PREMONITIONS-ATTITUDE DUDE

Mill Basin, Brooklyn—1956
Attitude Dude
"Oh Yeah?"

LIFE LESSONS
1 Never give up. Doing so would only let you down.
2 Stick to the plan.
3 Don't hesitate.
4 Also don't dilly-dally if you do hesitate.
5 Don't get caught.
6 Three strikes don't necessarily get you out.

MYSTIC POWERS
7 **Transfixiation:** The ability to escape without having to really go anywhere. A genetic acquisition from his father who developed it because of Mom.

MILL BASIN, BROOKLYN—1956

The Lonely Mystic was determined to leave home; two prior failed attempts did not thwart his resolute, unswerving determination and focused spirit. By then he had developed quite an escapist attitude. He purchased a three-tier hat to commemorate his third attempt at freedom. Of course, between his second and his third contemplation of leaving, a lot had transpired. He stood there for a moment transfixed. This was an early form of his mystical intuitiveness. He began to recollect some of the events that had transpired in his life: Both present and to be since time had no boundaries for him. Due to the voluminous nature of the experiences, he remembered, his cap twisted around on his head. He was just about ready to set one foot forward ahead of the other and leave the door when his parents informed him they were all moving to the *country*. The picture portrays how he felt about that.

7 BARN BOY - THE HORSEY

Liberty, New York—June 1957
Farm Boy
"A *Jack* what?"

LIFE LESSONS
1 Cats eat lice and make mounds.
2 Although unconfirmed, mountains can arise due to these mounds.
3 Be careful what you say with your hands.
4 People don't always get your name right; make sure you confirm it with them.

MYSTIC POWERS
8 **Dislocation:** The ability to change locations and still have no idea where you are. Similar to walking in your sleep, only you are awake.

LIBERTY, NEW YORK—SUMMER, 1957

The Lonely Mystic easily got used to living in the country. Although he thought it a permanent move, of course, it was just a temporary relocation. It was the start of the annual summer vacation in the *Cats Kill Mountains*, a name that always confused him. He could never understand how a cat could kill a mountain or anything other than lice. He knew cats love to chase lice. He often pondered it and thought *the name was derived from the common knowledge that cats like making a mound after they defecated. But it would take a lot of cats and a lot of poop to make a mound large enough to be able to hold Zen Ben "Kohan's" entire tribe and all of their friends for the summer. How was that possible? Besides, how could they tolerate that pungent aroma?* He decided *there must be another hysterectomy for the name Cats Kill.*

In this picture, taken by Hitou Kohan, Ben's wife, he is pointing to his *horsey*. Ben's wife only spoke in three line sentences. Ben referred to it as Hitou poetry since it was music to his ears. She often began speaking by saying: "Hi-to-u." She could tell a complete story using only three lines.

The horse was not really a horse. It was a jackass. Due to an animated manner of speaking with his hands, Jack Ash, the property owner pointed to the animal in the barn when telling them his name. His parents misunderstood what Jack Ash was trying to convey to them.

Later he had asked his parents the name of the horse; they told him it was "Jack Ass's horse." They meant *Jack Ash's horse*, but due to their heavy accent, it just sounded that way. Later in life, he found some people often called him by the horse's name. He never could quite figure out why these people called him so and more importantly, he thought *how did they know the horse was called* Jack Ass? This became a tough, sweaty acorn for him to swallow. Eventually he needed to come to terms with this.

8   SHERPA BOY - THE JOURNEY

Lhasa, Tibet—June 1968
Sherpa Boy
"If the hat fits, wear it."

LIFE LESSONS

1 Don't allow anyone to make a jackass out of you unless you know why.
2 If you have no money, someone took it. Ask your significant other, perhaps they know.
3 If you are filthy, you may be rich.
4 Wear protection when you sleep.
5 All Fools Day is on April 1st.
6 Planets make music; listen carefully.
7 Take out the garbage before you are snagged.
8 Dictionaries are not best sellers.
9 KUS is not a theory, but a fact.

MYSTIC POWERS

9 **Transiteration:** The ability to say a lot and mean nothing. Genetic predisposition. Often rephrased as: You are talking a lot and saying nothing.

LIBERTY, NEW YORK—SUMMER, 1968

As a result of the *Jack Ash* incident, The Lonely Mystic traveled to Lhasa in his late teens. He asked the holy men, "Why did some people occasionally call me by the horse's name?" However, for now, he was still in New York. Of course, we know it wasn't really a horse, but a jackass. He didn't. His parents never corrected him when he called the animal a *horsey*. For them, "horsey" sounded so much nicer than calling it by the owner's name.

One day he saw his mother, with her arms wide open, twirling around and yelling, "Tis's mine, Tis's all mine." He thought his parents had purchased the entire farm. Of course, she was referring to the air and clouds. Even though perhaps you might be unaware, it is owned by everyone and is free. But now you have been duly notified.

He was also under the impression his father was filthy and rich. Every time his mother asked his father for some money, his father would always say, "Money, what money? You need money? You already took it all."

She would then quickly retaliate and say, "You dirty bum! You good for *notin."*

Since his father didn't need any money and his mother had all of it, he figured *she was rich too*. But he did wonder *why Pop didn't shower more often? Why else would she say he was dirty?* He also couldn't figure out what *good for notin* meant since his father was good at several things. For example, he owned a farm and had a child, him. Everyone knows you have to be able to afford a child and know how to make one. He was alive, so obviously Pop knew what he was doing.

The Lonely Mystic once had his chart done by a professional *gastrologer*. The practitioner was able to pinpoint exactly where his parents were on the night he was concocted. The gastrologer told him, "On that night, three planets were in the sky and there were millions of stars behind them." The gastrologer also said, "The sun used to spin around the earth, but stopped one day when a Polish guy by the name of *Caphernius* dropped his hat and consequently felt a pull in his intestines."

Caphernius yelled out, "Stop everything! I have seen the light, and it doesn't revolve around me. I am not the center of the known universe, but a mere shell for the divine to fill." Everything around Caphernius stopped. The clouds stopped moving, the Earth stopped spinning, and the waters stopped flowing. So potent and mystical was his specific declarative exclamation. Somehow, he had hit upon one of the primal formulas of the universe with that mystical incantation. The force of him holding everything still was far too great for him. It caused him to rupture his intestines. As a result, this condition was named after him and his cap. The back lag of the Earth stopping on its axis caused everyone to pass gas and belch at the same time since everyone was sick to their stomachs. It was a foul day in *Hysterectomy*, the town that Caphernius lived in. Later, that anonymous day was to be commemorated every year as *All Fools Day*. It was April 1st. At the time people actually believed the Sun revolved around the Earth, but that was finally disproven by Caphernius.

Circumstantial evidence can be quite incriminating. What really happened was, at the very moment Caphernius had uttered his mystical words, the local garment workers, transportation workers, policemen, firemen and sanitation workers unions simultaneously declared a strike. As everyone well knows, when this happens even singly, all things come to a dead halt, but the rare astronomical conjunction of all five unions caused the entire known world and the Sun to come to a halt. This caused the Earth to start spinning around the Sun and not vice versa. Since the other planets didn't want to play second fiddle to the Earth, they did the same. The other planets, by the way, didn't know how to play a fiddle; the fiddle was the Earth's specialty. Venus was into harps, Jupiter – trombones, Saturn – tambourines, Mercury – glockenspiels, Neptune – xylophones and Pluto, since it was still a planet then, was into tympani. In a sense, you could call it the *Music of the Spheres*, which, by the way, was coined by none other than Caphernius.

The Lonely Mystic's penchant for hats started growing on him from an early age. He loved wearing the kind that had a sock and bell sticking out from the top of it. This type of hat always reminded him of Caphernius and his musical spheres. He felt quite close to him. A closeness that later on in life was explained to him when he visited a genealogist. He was told he was an actual descendant of Capherinius and his wife, Maria Intonets, the great fishing mogul's daughter. This elucidated why he was conceived in *Tahtent*.

According to his gastrologer, his parents celebrated their love in a tent one night. His father offered his mother a glass of wine.

His mother refused and said, "No, you have to shave first." She was an *elegant lady*, even when she was young.

His father said, "OK. Man, I shave its. So drink?"

A traveling merchant from the Sand people tribe, outside of the tent, heard this and thought *what a remarkable name for a new wine!* His mother eventually took a sip and fell promptly asleep and *there ya' go*, he was a dream child!

He knew this because his father often said to his mom, "Man, I often dream of makin' babies with youz, but youz iz alwayz too tired or sleeping." That is one of the reasons why he always dressed when he went to sleep. He never knew when he and his dream lover would make a baby.

His father always started a sentence with "Man." His mother didn't think his father did much of anything, but he knew his father was a real *much* of everything man. They even wrote a song about his father. One day, he had heard it on the Sand People radio station. It was playing loud and clear on the radio he was still building. He was into experimental, futuristic, electronics and swore that radio could tune into alternate realities and futures. *If only I can get it to turn on.* But how they, the future knew about his father's vocabulary choices was a mystery to him.

His father read the *New York Minutes* regularly in order to increase his vocabulary. He figured the radio disc jockey somehow got hold of his father's newspaper and saw all the circled words on it. His father circled the words he didn't know. Of course, the entire newspaper contained circled words that were all NEWS to his father; which was why they called it a *Newspaper*. Some people think NEWS stands for the directions. But that is incorrect. It stands for *new* words in the plural. His father wasn't big on grammar either; he followed in his father's footsteps on both accounts, which is why later in life, he became a writer. Writers don't have to know how to spell or be grammatically correct; they just need to be able to tell a good story. How many dictionaries, the epitome of being able to spell 100% accurately and the paragon of grammatical, political correctness, are on the *New York Minutes* bestseller list? *None.* "Ta-dah!"

Although his father was excellent at N.E.W.S, namely, the directions, which is different from NEWS, new words, (Yes, he repeats himself, ((Bet you never saw that before in a book-just goes to show how deep this exposition truly is))) if you asked Mom, she would say, "He didn't have a clue as to where he was going." His mother often said to his father, "Woo, man, you have no idea where you are going and you will amount to nothing!" His mother always prefaced her remarks with "Woo." She had tried riding the jackass, A.K.A. the *horsey* one time, and it didn't want to move, so she yelled, "Woo! Woo! Woo!" Since the jackass was stubborn, it started to run just to spite her. Everyone on the farm thought it was something short of a miracle. Since then she always has yelled, "Woo" when she has wanted someone or something to stop because she too was stubborn and more often than not, had done the exact opposite of what you had expected.

Of course, his father would always try proving to his mother he was an expert at directions. He wouldn't stop and ask someone for help even if it took three days to get around the block. If he had stopped, it wouldn't have mattered. They initially wouldn't have understood him, since he hadn't had time to look up all those circled words in the newspapers. Which by now were piling up by the stack full.

One day his mother decided to do spring-cleaning, in the middle of the winter, nonetheless. She told The Lonely Mystic to take all of his father's newspapers out and throw them into the garbage. Ten large garbage bags of newspapers were piled up by the door. He was only three at the time and didn't even know how to spell the word door, let alone take something to it. He had a bad back since early childhood. He figured it was a bad back since he was always laying around on it. Later in life, he realized it was bad because people with bad backs lie around and do nothing. He often lay around at night doing nothing when he slept. He figured *either this was a hereditary trait culled from my father, who according to my mother also did the same thing, or it was a symptom shared with back injury patients. They also were on their backs.*

He tried lifting one of the bags. It ripped apart. All the newspapers fell out. At that point, his father walked into the room. He saw him with the newspaper in his hand and said, "Man, am I proudz of youz!" Youz taken za bullz by za nose and pullin' his chainz! Man, I can teach youz to read, youz don't need to organize all myz papers." (Pop lost his accent later in life.) His father knew exactly what order he had put them in. Pop had actually invented the *Kus Theory*. Scientists later renamed it the *Chaos Theory be-kus* they didn't understand his accent. They secretly wanted to steal the glory, but we know better. "Right?"

His mother often asked his father, "Why are the papers just laying around randomly and in no order?"

His father would answer, "Kus, that's the wayz I want it and them to liez around, if they could standz, they would walk into a neat pilez, but they can't so letz them be, don't make them feelz bad because theyz are handicapped."

His mother was very compassionate and started to cry, it could have been tears, but he swears he heard her walk away saying something about his horsey and a hole? Because of her accent, he couldn't quite make it out.

Pop continued, "I know howz to read wellz, understanding is the hard partz." In truth, his father knew how to read well, as did many people, who came through Tellus Island at the time. Understanding what they read, well that was a horsey of another color.

His father went to get his wife to show her how proud he was of the little mystic and his organizational skills. When his father returned with Mom, she looked at him and put her finger to her mouth and said, "Woo!" Later on in life, this single act contributed to reinforcing his *horsey/jackass complex*. He figured Mom always knew best, but if he wasn't a jackass, why did she yell, "Woo" at him? His father unpacked the newspapers and to this day they are still in the crawl space if the local inhabitants haven't eaten them.

LHASA, TIBET—SUMMER, 1968

Living in the Cats Kill Mountains wetted his appetite for natural surroundings. Asia was also abundant in snow-covered greenery. The cold climate gave him occasion to develop a love for fur coats. Lhasa gave him ample opportunity to add to his already large collection of unusual ones. He loved going to the Barkhor Bazaar and to the local caravans. He bought a beautiful one there. The animal rights activists were well established there as everyone who was a member of note wore one. He was happy the cold climate prompted him to wear it, even when he slept. He was well dressed and ready to embark upon his quest in search of holy men who might explain the mystery of his horsey to him. If he was lucky, perhaps they might even be able to explain some of Zen Ben's one-liners too.

      He put an ad on the local donkey. The service was called, "Pin-the-Ad-On-The-Donkey." Unbeknownst to most, later, he brought this to America. It soon after became a party game. You must have heard of it, for sure. The donkey traveled around the countryside. People would then ride it back to whoever had placed the ad. This was kind of like a moving billboard and homing pigeon tied together in one. There was a pigeon tied to the back of the donkey, which is how it knew how to always come home. Brilliant. "Right?" The ad he had placed was for a group of wise guys to guide him. He needed someone who would be able to answer all of his questions. It only took three weeks and then one cold and windy morning some people showed up at the opening of his tent.

9 KATMANDU VIA LHASA – THREE WISE GUYS

Gyantsie, China—1968
Wise Guys
"We already took out the garbage."

LIFE LESSONS

1 Lhasa was once in Tibet, and then it moved to China.
2 Long beards get dirty.
3 Yellow caps fly off in the wind.
4 You only need to take out the garbage one time.
5 To thine own self be too.
6 If you fantasize for more than twenty minutes and don't recognize anyone, then it isn't your fantasy.
7 Farts echo in canyons.
8 If someone calls you an asshole, then you have secretly been indoctrinated into the Assoterical Society. If it was your wife, and she is hysterical at the time, then she already joined the Hysterical Disorder.

MYSTIC POWERS

10 **Clairesaudiance:** The ability to hear gongs, especially when they hit you in the head and there are others present to hear them.

GYANTSIE, CHINA—1968

While he was in Lhasa, The Lonely Mystic met several people, who taught him many things. Of course, at that time, the country was still called Tibet. He learned *long beards get dirty and short yellow caps fly off in the wind.* Something about that saying sounded vaguely familiar, but *dysexlia* had set in right after he reached *pubabee*. As hard as he tried, he couldn't remember. More importantly, his guru, a member of the Polyandry tribe, told him to travel to Nepal. It would be there that he would find out how to deal with his horsey issues. Later that guru went on to discoverer a country in Europe.

One day his guru was kicked out of Lhasa for marrying two women. It was considered a big mess. Later this *big mess* evolved into *bigamist*. Since he was a *polyandryizing bigamist*, he was all washed up there. As a result, he left there to dry out somewhere else. That *somewhere else* finally brought him to a land where he felt he could comfortably settle. But let's not jump ahead, yet again.

The Lonely Mystic had just opened his eyes and was still dreaming of some nice hot, buttered cha when he heard scraping at his tent. He opened up the entranceway fold and saw two guys with glasses, and a third sported a very long beard and wore a yellow cap. They were staring at him. It was the yellow-caped, bearded one who spoke first. He said, "Short, yellow caps fly off in the wind." Something about this sounded vaguely familiar. Try as he might, he couldn't remember.

He was aware of his dysexlia, but thought he was over it since at school he had been told he was *oversexed*. The doctor or nurse (He couldn't figure out which it was so he called them *they*. Perhaps *they* were *both*.) had told him it was due to him excessively fantasizing. He asked *them*, "What *does fantasizing* mean?" *They* then spent about twenty minutes telling him about an escapade *they* had last night in their mind with someone. *They* didn't spare any of the details.

When *they* had finished, he said, "I believe your diagnosis is completely wrong. I have never visited the place you just described either during the day, during the night, or at any time in between. I don't fantasize either mildly or excessively."

He had *them* almost convinced until he said, "Can you please give me the phone number of the fantasy girl you just described to me?"

As a result, he was sent home for the day and was told he had a fever.

He felt his head, and it felt fine to him. Of course, *they* were telling him he was a hot head, but he didn't catch the drift. He also was hard of hearing. Yet another family malady.

It was then he noticed the yellow-capped guy had a *dirty beard*. He had an epiphany and remembered Zen Ben's very same words. It was as if the heavens had opened up and spoke directly to him. He felt he was in the right place and at the right time. He felt this was a confirmation for his entire journey across the world. He asked the yellow caped one, "Are you and your two partners here in answer to my traveling donkey ad?"

In unison, they answered: "We are members of the Polyandry tribe. We all have the same wife and due to that, we all know the one who asks the question already knows the answer. If that weren't so how could the *asker* recognize the answer as being true? Unless of course, they already knew and heard it before?"

They knew this since their wife would often say to them, "How many times do I have to tell you to take out the garbage?"

They all would look at one another and they would repeat in unison, as if they were reciting some holy mantra, "Only once, dear." They knew better than to upset their lovely, lovely.

The very first time this happened, they still all answered in unison. This confirmed to them their answer was a universal one and they were cosmically connected to one another. Later, when any one of them had a question, then the other two always had the answer. So their answer rang true as a bell for him. He actually heard a bell ring when they said it to him. He was about to attribute it to some mystic experience when he realized the bell he had heard was his head hitting the gong that hung over his tent's entrance. He took a deep breath; he was skilled in spasmodic breathing and asked his new teachers, "Where can I find the answer to my identity crises?"

Each one of them pointed in a different direction. In unison, they told him: "To thine own self be too." This was unusual for them because until now, they had always had the same answer. This apparently contradictory event caused them to be profoundly disturbed. Each one of them started walking in the direction they were pointing to. They hoped to find out why they were no longer connected to one another in the uniting "assoteric" manner that had connected them before.

As for him, he thought deeply about their response and realized *the only direction to go in was the one direction they weren't pointing to.* That was his direction. He thought *the universe was so intimately interconnected. How wonderful it was that a rare group of three men could unite and give me a meaningful clue into the nature of myself. After all, they could have been bigamists and then the two of them would have pointed in two different directions. This would have resulted in me not knowing which of the two other directions to go in.* He was very humbled, appreciative, and decided to give thanks. He pulled down his pants, squatted and blessed the ground he stood upon; letting go a big one. It echoed through the canyons of Gyanste, China where he had reached and each of the polyandryists heard the sound. Upon hearing it they realized they had given him the correct unified answer and the *many* are *one*. *All Is One*. All three reversed their directions and eventually met up at the tent. He, on the other foot, had already left for Kathmandu. They headed there too. They didn't want to abandon their new teacher. Yes, the student became the teacher.

This is the way with "assoteric" communities, their common link being, an *asinus holeus* (asshole). This was why The Lonely Mystic was called a *jackass* (Equus Asinus) occasionally; he was destined to be a regal member of the *Assoterics*, a new world organization. Nothing happens without a reason, and destiny always gives you clues about your future. They may not be understood or interpreted correctly, but they are there. One thing was for sure, the *Asinus'* or what the Assoterics' members were called had three sacred doctrines:

The Assotericical Sacred Doctrines
1. If it goes in, it comes out.
2. If it stinks, then it isn't yours.
3. If it weren't for asinus holeus',
   Then we'd all be full of it.

The third was a unifying link for all of humanity. Of course, Assoterics was only for men.

The other half of the mystical equation was the women, who just happened to have their own order. The female version of the Assoterical order was called: *Hysterics* or the *Hysterical Disorder*. It was *Assotericisim's* antagonistic and complementary opposite. Most people knew this intuitively. It also explained why some women were prone to hysterical outbreaks. They blamed the cause of these on their men, whom they affectionately called asinus holeus'. It was the way the universe worked, the *Him and the Hung*, as the Chinese put it before they became Asians. Two sides of the same manhole cover, no pun intended.

The American version of this saying was *he is hung*. Things get lost in the translation. The American version of this symbol was a picture of a snake eating its tale and dumping baby snakes, which turn into baby eagles, that start crying hysterically and fly around banging into the walls of the hut they were in until they bang their heads repeatedly, causing a hole to develop, through which they escape, only to fly in again, this time fully grown through the front door, which was open in the first place, and eat the snakes and then dump them out so the cycle can continue.

He also thought *it was too complicated a symbol.* Later he simplified it with two curves that interconnect with a ball in each of their centers. He figured *the two balls represented the Assoterics. And since one could look at it also as one hole and one hole,* he figured *it also indicated the Hysterics too.* He further colored it in using his favorite two colors namely, black and white. He intentionally left out the gray because that color, of course, wasn't invented until later on. The Chinese (Yes, they hadn't moved to Asia yet. Tibet hadn't moved yet, either. Tibet was still in China.) called the symbol *T'ai Chi*, or the *Great Extremes*. It was a symbol for the entire universe and yes, he drew it.

Due to his dysexlia he didn't remember it was the very same symbol etched into the gong he had banged his head on. The same one still impressed on his forehead; both figuratively and literally. But minor details aren't that important, what counts is the intent. His was a cosmic destiny, although he didn't know that until later on in life. He had a history of royalty in his blood. After all, his mother treated him as if he were a prince. So what more important and noble a distinction could he hope for other than being indoctrinated into his order as a "Royal Asinus Holeus." But let's not jump ahead, again.

10 ANSWER MAN – TAO GUY

Great Kumbum Stupa,
China (Nganyang Valley)—1969
Ding-Ah-Ling
"You try eating with only one chopstick."

LIFE LESSONS
1 The answer is within your grasp. Pay attention to what you are holding.
2 Eating with one chopstick may pose problems.
3 Casual comments can cause headaches. Think before you speak.
4 Animals understand.
5 Animals are man's best friend and they like women too.

MYSTIC POWERS
11 **Animalistic:** The ability to communicate with animals without words or motions.

GREAT KUMBUM STUPA, CHINA—1969

The direction The Lonely Mystic pointed to was toward Nepal. To get there, he rented the donkey and pigeon from the *Have-Donkey-Will-Travel Agency*. After visiting the Great Kumbum Stupa in Gyantse, he learned of yet another one of his many Chinese names, *Ding-Ah-Ling* and more importantly that:
1   The answer is always right in front of you.
2   The answers are always within your grasp.

He was holding and looking at the bridle of the donkey. He then experienced a flash of *knowingness*, realizing if he substituted *donkey* for *Jack Ash*, he would be cured! His logic being *who would ever call him a donkey?* Fate works in mysterious ways: Contrary to some popular beliefs, you can't escape your destiny.

That afternoon, he was calmly sitting at the local noodle shop eating white rice with one chopstick. He was focused on appreciating the bountifulness of Creation. With gratitude, he was lifting one kernel of rice at a time; he was deeply spiritual. Of course, with only one chopstick, it is difficult to do more than one kernel at a time. The man sitting next to him watched his every move. Finally, his neighbor turned to him and said: "Man what is wrong with you? You are eating as slow as a donkey!" Then the neighbor let out the nasal sound donkeys make. You can only imagine how devastated The Lonely Mystic was when he heard the word *donkey* and heard that sound.

    The points of his new hat, which had been pointing up, did an inverse turn and flopped down ringing the bells that were attached to their ends. He thought *music was God's gift to elevate us in times of great disaster.* He looked over to his donkey. The donkey must have understood what he was thinking. The donkey walked right up to the noodle shop, shook his head once. It was rather large. The bells on its bridle rang in unison to his caps bells. At the very same time, it raised its hind legs and kicked his neighbor. The very same one who poorly commented on his eating skills. The kick struck him right in his asinus holeus. He thought *how head to toe! That guy wasn't making an asinus out of me and my donkey again!* His donkey bellowed the loudest donkey bellow he had ever heard, "He haw!" He smiled, big time. The asinus hobbled away. Karma had been served and dished out, one kernel at a time.

11 BACK TO THE COUNTRY - THE FOOL

Kathmandu, Nepal—1969
The Fool
"Of course I want to hear the truth. Do I look like a fool?"

LIFE LESSONS
1 *Animal Sense* is universal.
2 *Commons Sense* is uncommon.
3 The whole truth is better than half a lie.
4 A whole lie is better than half a lie.
5 If you are going to lie, don't ask for permission.
6 Carry your own mirrors; it will keep you out of trouble.
7 If you hear a jackass laughing, it must be the wind.

MYSTIC POWERS
12 **Deception:** The ability to fool yourself into thinking that you are something different then you truthfully are.

KATHMANDU, NEPAL—1969

After being humiliated by the stranger, The Lonely Mystic visited Shigatse. He retreated deep into the countryside near the Buddhist monasteries of Tashilungpo. Near Turquoise Lake he surrounded himself with all kinds of animals, including a donkey. He felt animals understood him better than people. They had animal sense, while only some people had common sense. Everyone knows animal sense is a highly, fine-tuned mechanism that directs birds in the winter and enables dogs to find their home, despite great distances. It enables fish to stay in the water and prompts them not jump too high. He could go on and on, but the publisher of this manuscript has limited the number of words he can use here, so he is using them sparingly. (Please contact the publisher if you wish this embargo removed from future volumes.)

While animals had this innate *animal sense*, people either had or didn't have *common sense*. He had always heard people say, "That person has no common sense." Hence, he deduced common sense was not a common attribute. He went so far as to think not everyone had it. So, for the time being, he was going to stick to the animals. For additional therapy, he would visit the local bazaars like the Ason Tole and the Panuti to do some shopping. Of course, his favorite hunt was the one for the perfect hat or coat. The hat he had been wearing on that regrettably memorable night of the *One Chopstick Trauma* never recovered from the event and consequently always drooped.

One day he was truly fortunate, at a local haberdashery he happened upon another hat, which was similar to it. It was made of socks and bells, his favorite. He was ecstatic. He immediately picked it up and tried it on. He looked around for a mirror to see what it looked like on him. There were none to be found in the shop. He thought *that is strange?* So he asked the shopkeeper, "How come there aren't any mirrors?"

The shopkeeper said, "It's a long story."

He asked him to keep it short, only because he knew he had a limited number of words to use. Yes, he could see the future, even then.

So the shopkeeper told him he was an immigrant from Brooklyn. He felt an immediate kinship with the man. He asked him to please continue, even at the cost of aggravating the word counters. The shopkeeper said, "My father had recently died. According to my faith, I needed to keep the mirrors covered as part of observing the Jewish ritual for the dead, called *sitting shiva*. I remorsefully didn't have anything to cover them with so I just removed them."

The Lonely Mystic totally understood. "I deeply express my condolences to you and your family. May your father find a better place in the high heavens." He then asked the shopkeeper, "How do I look in my new hat?"

"Do you want me to tell you the truth, or do you want me to tell you a lie?"

That type of remark always perplexed him. What did the person who asked a question like expect for an answer? Did that person really expect someone to say, "Hey, who wants to hear the truth? Just lie to me." Of course not. He wanted to hear the truth, the whole truth, and nothing, but the truth. He had always wanted to say that.

So he said, "Yes, please tell me the truth, the whole truth and nothing but the truth."

The shopkeeper smiled and told him, "You look absolutely, unequivocally and undeniably like a complete, unadulterated fool!"

The Lonely Mystic was beside himself upon hearing this response; of course, in this instance, he wasn't literally beside himself, that wasn't to occur until later in life. He was figuratively beside himself and was filled with amazement. Here and now, someone had specifically delineated a superlative, exclamatory definition of the nature of his being. He had identifiably categorized and characteristically determined definitive qualities about his persona. His quest was over, he was no longer a *Jack Ash*, and for now, without question, he finally felt he had reached the zenith of his self-discovery. He was now a *Fool*. He even swore to himself he heard *Mymama the Carneedsbrakes* playing in the distance, but he knew hearing things like that were just his imagination playing tricks on him. He was in Asia and not in Brazil. He knew for sure if he were going to hear things, they would definitely be in Asian, not in Brazilian. He looked around. He could swear, *I think I hear a donkey laughing in the wind,* but "*Nahhhhhh,*" that wasn't really happening. "Was it?"

12 ARE WE THERE YET? – SIBERIA

Novosibrisk, Siberia (Russia)
Ice Cold Kid
"Dreaming is easy, life is hard."

MILL BASIN,
BROOKLYN—1967

LIFE LESSONS
1 Dream travel is cheap but it has no frequent flyer miles.
2 If you are going to hold your breath, make sure you eventually let it go or it will permanently escape.
3 Contrary to popular opinion, Siberia is not a vacation spot.
4 Bodies in motion, stay in motion until you are tired and need to go to sleep of course.
5 Physics isn't always right because it is all theoretical.
6 Physicists are *wanna* be psychics.
7 Lightning is faster than thunder unless it isn't raining.

MYSTIC POWERS
13 **Clairsaiciance:** The ability to know before you can prove it with a theory. Often accompanied with the ability to tell fact from fiction or cow from bull.

Dreaming was an early love for The Lonely Mystic. He found it amazing he had to do nothing for dreams to occur. Well, *almost* nothing, other than falling asleep, of course. In the beginning, sleep was easy. He could close his eyes and wake up hours later having dreamt dreams that dreamers only dream about dreaming when they are dreaming dreams dreamt. Becoming less young, sleeping was sometimes a bit more difficult to catch. Almost caught, and then lost by the slightest outside interference: Train-of-thought, broken. It might have been a hair falling off his pillow and landing on the mattress or a crumb being blown off the kitchen table and landing on the floor. He was hypersensitive, over-active, and just plain wired: The way it often is with mystical beings.

To him dreaming was like breathing. He didn't have to do anything about this too, well, almost. But one day, he was lying down and decided to see whether he could control his breathing. So he did just that. He inhaled slowly, he exhaled slowly. He inhaled slowly, he exhaled slowly. He did this for quite a while and then decided, experiment finished. Wrong. He may have been finished with his experiment, but his experiment wasn't finished with him yet.

He was to learn everything has an aim and purpose and something set in motion, continues in motion. This was a basic law of physics. He understood this because when he lay in bed, he stayed in bed. Of course, the guy who invented this physical law must not have been an insomniac or sleepwalker, since everyone knows sleepwalkers don't stay in bed, which of course disproves this theory. And even more so, when they are finished walking, they return to bed. *So how do bodies in motion stay in motion and bodies at rest, stay at rest?* He was no rocket scientist, but he knew logic when he heard it and he recognized faulty logic as sure as he could see the sun was falling from the sky at night.

When he thought about it *the difference between physics and psychics was only a few letters. More importantly,* psychics *has more of them. Therefore, psychics is more inclusive. Physics is theoretical whereas psychics is actual. One can't be born a physicist, but one can be born a psychic.* He decided physics was derived from psychics and that physicists really wanted to be psychics, but didn't have the abilities to do so; hence, they fabricated theories about things to compensate for their shortcomings.

For example, you didn't even have to be psychic to know light travels across the room. But it took physics *several* centuries to realize that, and it took a genius, nonetheless to discover it. He and everyone else, however, knew that light is faster than sound. Even a fool, although there weren't any around, could tell you lightning is seen before thunder is heard. But it took our friendly physicist a long time to figure out the details. Elements have been around forever, how long did it take for them to be counted? Centuries. Any psychic could have told you there were elements. Even British detectives and their doctor friends knew that was *elementary*. Physicists, however, were always the last to know. And what was worse was they didn't always agree. So, one minute, a planet is a planet and then the next it isn't! *Think about it!* We are talking about a planet, not a mountain or a lake! *How could they mistake a planet?* He could continue with example upon example. When he got worked up like this it affected his breathing, which was still recovering from the time he decided to investigate its physics.

As soon as he consciously stopped controlling his breath, he stopped breathing. He started getting panicky and his heart started racing. He didn't have a clue as to where it was racing, who it was racing away from and what it was racing against, but he knew it was doing a great job, going pretty fast and winning. So now he was trying to slow down his heart rate and remember to breathe. The effort was strenuous enough to cause him to pass out. When he awoke, he forgot what he had been doing because he was focused on remembering a dream. Dreaming, for him, was significantly easier than breathing or heart rates. He just closed his eyes and *presto*: He was either dreaming or in a trance.

He often dreamed of remote locations and envisioned himself at these locales. He even swore he actually was there. *Was that possible?* This gave him an opportunity to add to his immense hat collection without even spending a single penny! In dream-state, he could get as many hats as he wanted to and more importantly, when he awoke, they didn't even need to be dusted off! He was especially fond of sleeping caps and had a huge collection.

He often dreamed of visiting the Siberia because he had heard stories that during World War Two, people had traveled long distances to get there. They were, of course, fleeing from the Nazis, but he thought it was a resort area since these people traveled from Europe to get there. He had figured they were traveling there for a vacation since it was a long distance from their home. He knew people usually travel long distances to go away on vacation, so the conclusion was a logical one, although much to his cleft chin, a very, very wrong one.

In his dream, he was able to purchase an unusual hat, and in Red Square he purchased a red coat. His penchant for red coats continued all throughout his life. The day his parents broke the news to him his horse wasn't really a horse, was also the day they also told him Siberia was not a vacation spot. He remembered the day very clearly because it was his favorite day of the year. April 1st. So many good things happened to him on that day. He thought it was a personally lucky one for him. When his parents told him Siberia wasn't a vacation spot, he was so confused, he never knew what vacation spots to pick in the future and always wound up staying home alone.

13 BANDANARAMA – FINGER WALKING

Lake George, New York—1967
Mr. Vacation
"Every solution originally had a problem."

LIFE LESSONS
1 Be careful where you place your hands.
2 Check your cookware for holes regularly.
3 Check your roads for black holes, the fabric of the universe may be unwinding.
4 Don't drive blindfolded.
5 Don't get naked in front of cops.
6 If your maid is British, grill her about being a mistress or a madam too.

MYSTIC POWERS
14 **Transportation:** The ability to rise after one has fallen. The ability to logically move from one point to another and physically do so by following GPS directions.

LAKE GEORGE, NEW YORK—1967

The Lonely Mystic would often place a bandana around his eyes, put on his mystic, multicolor hat, and then do twirls while facing in front of a map. He did this when he was unable to decide upon a vacation place. While blindfolded, although he often cheated, he would then attempt to finger a spot on the map. Several times he wound up with his finger stuck in the faucet and had to call a plumber. One time he wound up with his finger stuck somewhere else and had to call a proctologist. He eventually got the hang of it, but couldn't understand why he always wound up only a few blocks away.

Then one day he realized, the reason for this was the map he was using, was a survey map of his property. With the advent of GPS, he was sort of able to overcome this handicap later on in his life. Once a location was selected, he would know how to get there. But that wasn't the problem; the problem, of course, was how to select the location in the first place. So instead, he bought a vacation home and traveled there weekly, avoiding the whole issue of having to try to figure out where to go. Luckily for him, he didn't need to wear his bandana around his eyes when he drove. Although, with his psygonic senses, he most probably could still have gotten there even with it on. He figured the local law enforcement wouldn't have understood. *I needed to wear glasses when I drove. What good would a pair of glasses be if they were resting over a bandana around my eyes?*

NEW YORK CITY—WINTER, 1968

There was one time he did have an out-of-body experience when he was driving, or rather when he wasn't. He had driven over a pothole. He never did quite understand why they were always called *potholes*. "Did you ever see any cookware on the road when you drive with holes in them?" Then he thought *perhaps the spelling of the name was wrong and, it ought to be spelled* Pot Whole. *Perhaps there was a full set of cookware laying around somewhere on the road, and the box had holes in it, as a result of so many cars bumping into it. Maybe, it referred to people who smoked grass? These people, by doing so, were creating holes in the very fabric of our society. These holes then ripped into the fabric of reality and manifested themselves on the highways and roads as black holes of destruction.* Although he himself was more of a psychic than a physicist, he did have many theories about many things. Theories were just that and the fabric of reality can change. What previously was ill-considered, could soon become considered as helping the ill. But, in this specific regard, after he went over the pothole, he awoke with his car on its side precariously balanced on the edge of a ravine.

He gingerly got out of the automobile, although it wasn't mobile at the time, stood up, only to witness people running over to him, to see whether he was all right. He checked himself and there wasn't even one scratch. Of course, he had to strip so he could conduct a thorough examination of himself.

An officer came over asked him, "Are you crazy?"

"No, I was just in an automobile accident, why are you asking?"

"Because you are naked."

He pointed to the sweet old man and his young daughter. (He figured she was a young daughter since she kept calling the old man, "My *Suga' Daddy*." The *young daughter* gave him a card, which he promptly had put into his pocket before he undressed.) He said, "They asked me if I was injured, so I undressed to check."

The policeman said, "Yes, I see."

"Then if you see, why are you asking me?"

"Do you have your license on you?"

"No, I'm naked, I have nothing on me, can't *you* see?"

"OK. Where is your wallet?"

"In my pants, isn't that where you keep yours?"

The policeman was about to refer to a wise part of his anatomy, a place he had heard mentioned many times before, but the officer restrained himself. The policeman picked his pants up, took out his wallet, gave him his pants and underwear and then told him to put them on. He complied with the long arm of the law. The officer was a giant.

He asked the policeman, "Can you also hand me my shirt?"

"Do I look like your maid?"

"I don't have a maid. I had a house cleaner once, but she was an alien, at least she said she was, but I didn't believe her. You are not getting me to admit that. I'm no fool and, besides, 'No,' you don't look like her either. She had beautiful blonde hair, ruby red lips, and great legs. I asked her whether she was really a house cleaner, and she said, 'Yes' and then she said, 'I am going to take you to the cleaners.' Followed by, 'Men always fall all over me due to my looks.' "

He thought for a moment, *hey, I just realized I never fell on her or even fell close to her when she worked for me that one time.* He had called up a service that had advertised for *cleaners*. He knew this because it said: "We are what you want us to be: Maids, Mistress', and Madams." He figured *they were a British service from their choice of language.* He needed a maid so he called them.

When she arrived he asked, "What price do you charge for your services?"

"$200.00 a pop."

"My Pop is not here right now. Can you do it for me instead?"

"Sure."

"OK then, let's start."

"Where do you want me to begin?"

"In the shower."

"OK. Do you want to undress, or do you want me to undress, or do you want to undress me?"

"Why, my clothes were just cleaned and don't you know how to undress by now?"

He figured *maybe she wanted to undress so she didn't get her nice new maid outfit dirty or wet from the shower?*

"Don't matter, but you need to be undressed."

He thought *for sure, she is nuts.* "You don't have to clean me! Please clean my bathroom."

She said, "Are you crazy? Do I look like a cleaner? I'm a maid!"

He knew he had called the wrong number and said, "Please leave."

She said, "Not until I finish what I came here to do."

"If you didn't come here to clean, then what exactly did you come here to do?"

"I came here to *do* you."

He thought *perhaps she was a hairdresser who is out of work and is masquerading as a house cleaner?* He felt bad she needed to give up her profession and resort to a secondary job. But that wasn't his problem. Besides he had just gotten a new *do* yesterday and didn't need to be *do-doed* again today. He decided not to reveal that he knew her true identity and said, "I'm not in the mood to play, and I needed my apartment cleaned. So please leave before I call the cops."

The minute she heard that she tore asinus out of the apartment.

He went to close the door and as she was walking down the hall he could see all his male neighbors were opening their doors and saying, "Hello" to her by name.

He couldn't figure out, *how did they know her? She had never even told me her name. But now I know: It was Miss Hooka.*

Of course, the policeman ignored the story. The policeman knew if he took him to the police station there would be an inordinate amount of paperwork to fill out. Considering it was Friday night and he had the weekend off, he wasn't about to let a naked crazy man spoil any of his plans. The policeman said, "I'm going to let you slide."

He looked around and said, "I hope not, I just got out of an automobile accident and I have no intentions of hitting the sidewalk."

"Not slide, but *slide*. I am going to let you go."

He looked around and saw the policeman wasn't holding him. *Why would he want to let me go?* He figured he didn't want to have a brush-in with the law, so he thanked the officer, whose name was Ike.

"Thank you, Officer Ike." He picked up his shirt, as the *daughter* handed him his jacket, winked and blew him a kiss. A tow truck arrived and offered him a ride back to the train station; as he needed a way to get home since his car was totaled. While getting into it, he slipped, fell and hit his head on the asphalt. He then had an epiphany and realized why it was called *asphalt*. He had fallen on his *ass*, and it was definitely his *fault*. Sometimes his brilliance was blinding.

He took out the card that was given to him by the *young daughter*. Much to his amazement, it read: *Maids, Mistresses and Madams, We are what You Want Us to Be*. He smiled. He knew the old man was going to be taken to the cleaners, a place he had almost visited. He sincerely felt bad for him.

It was at that moment he promised himself the next car he would buy would have the GPS system built into it. From then on he was going to rely on it to get him where he needed to go, and he would also allow it to pick his vacation spots. "See how difficult vacation planning was even for someone one as logical as him.*"*

14   CAMPER GUY – CIRCULAR REASONING

Glenn Falls, New York—1967
Mr. Directions
"Before you get to the right place,
You had to be in the wrong one."

GLENN FALLS,
NEW YORK—1967

LIFE LESSONS
1 Use a map for directions, or have large hands.
2 Make sure you know where you are going otherwise you won't recognize it when you get there.
3 Since it's not where you are going, but the trip to it that counts, then prolong the trip by forgetting where you are going.
4 It doesn't matter when you get there because how you got there is more important.
5 When you get there you might as well go somewhere else because where you are is unimportant.
6 Stay in motion otherwise, how would you eventually arrive at your destination?

MYSTIC POWERS
15 **Fasting:** The ability to eat nothing and still never quickly arrive at where you are going to

Although The Lonely Mystic developed a fondness for rapidly moving vehicles when his stroller first rolled downhill, he consequently developed an aversion for them as well. This dichotomy of feelings was to permeate his emotional life. Here is a picture of him hiking to his local supermarket. He felt the fifteen-mile *green* walk was a good form of exercise. It also served to preserve the planet's oil reserves. But he suffered from *STML* (Short Term Memory Loss). When he got to a corner, he frequently circled the same block several times, forgetting where it was he had started from. The only way he could get out of this endless loop was due to an off chance someone would be waiting on the corner to also cross.

He would then have to ask, "Which way should I turn?" Of course, the first question the stranger would ask in return was, "Where do you want to go?" Sometimes he remembered and would say he wished to go to the food store. Of course, this didn't help him at all: On his small hands, he could only write a limited portion of the lengthy directions to the food store a stranger would give him. He eventually ran out of space and was at a loss for words. That is if he had happened to bring along a pen that worked. He had many pens. However, he was convinced the Pen Guardian had a huge sense of humor. This sense manifested itself as his pen running out of ink after the first letter. Sometimes he had to take along twenty or more pens to be able to write a complete sentence. As a result, he wound up eating infrequently and required very little. He thought *this was the universe's way of telling me to shape up.* These long walks to nowhere gave him an opportunity to wear another one of his many caps.

15 RAIN, RAIN GO AWAY – THE CALYPSO KID

Tashkent, Uzbekistan—1970
Calypso Kid
"If the hat fits, wear it even if it's wet."

LIFE LESSONS
1 If you don't know where you are going then you don't have to worry about how you are going to get there.
2 Look around; your ideal vacation spot may be closer than you think!
3 Sometimes destiny calls while you are on a different track.
4 When you least expect it, surprises happen.
5 Keep shampoo out of your eyes, or it will cause you to tear and you will get wet!

MYSTIC POWERS
16 **Aqueousistic:** The ability to make water by causing someone to cry. Beware of flying animals if they are in the vicinity.

TASHKENT, UZBEKISTAN—1970

Even though The Lonely Mystic had a tough time picking vacation spots, he eventually got out in the sun and into the water. One day, while wandering around in the old city of Tashkent, near the Kudeldas Madrassa, he found the Chorsu Bazaar. There he discovered the *perfect hat*. He had never ever seen, nor would ever see its equal. It was sheer beauty, elegance, and functionality all wrapped up into an inspired artistic and technological marvel. He figured *what more perfect a hat could I find then this* umbrella *hat to wear when I go swimming? After all, umbrellas keep the water off of you, and I wouldn't want to get wet when I got into the water, would I? It was truly perfect.* He took it with him all the time when he traveled to the Caribbean, which by the way was located in Brooklyn, New York.

BROOKLYN, NEW YORK—1970

Every year he took a trip to the Caribbean festival there. Of course, he always wore this hat. Though, he felt a little guilty when he did so. Since it had a propeller and was waterproof, he secretly wished for it to rain on his parade. He knew it was a selfish thought, but somewhere inside of him, he felt he had the capability of influencing the heavens to make it rain. He felt this ability was somehow tied to his destiny, in some inexplicable way. Strange as it sounded, that was how he felt. Needless to say, no matter how many times he went, that was how many times it didn't rain. He guessed his mystical abilities to influence the skies hadn't matured yet; after all, he was still a young man.

He did feel some water on his trousers one time and got excited. So he looked up and all around. He held his hands out at both sides of his body, with palms up. "Nope, no rain in them there skies." Then he looked down. There was a pack of stray dogs standing at his feet. One of them somehow mistook him for a fire hydrant. All of them started barking and rubbing themselves against his legs. As he walked, they walked. And so on that fateful day, the *Legend of the Dog Walker* began. He had heard *if you don't find life, it finds you.* So here was proof of the cosmic order of things. He now knew one day he would both make rain and walk dogs, not necessarily at the same time. He spun his propeller around counter-clockwise with jubilant happiness and yelled to the skies, "Rain, Rain, go away, come again another day. Who needs you anyway?"

Although he didn't know it, a few seconds after he got into the subway, it started to pour not only the dogs that adopted him but cats too! There was a torrential downpour. What he didn't know at the time was that *Rain* was female. The moment he told her, "Go away" and he didn't *need* her; she *wanted* him and started to shower her affections upon him. Since he continued ignoring her, she started crying. Her pets, she had many, started to lick the tears from her eyes and slipped while doing so, since it was wet up there. They started falling from the heavens: One big hairy *wet* mess in those normally soft, white billowy *dry* clouds.

Cats, dogs, and tears all flowing onto the very spot his dog had marked the night when he had accidentally peed on his leg. To this day, dogs commemorate this event. They psychically share the *One Hundred Dog Syndrome* with their monkey siblings. He was standing next to a fire hydrant. Once one dog saw it rain, and then all the dogs were able to see it rain. It was a religious experience for the dogs because they witnessed heavenly dogs come raining down and more importantly, those dogs were dancing with cats! It was as if peace had broken out in the Land of the Sand. Two archrivals were swimming around in divine waters. Dogs weren't chasing cats and, cats weren't hissing at dogs.

Rain realized he hadn't really *dis'd* her, but instead he was just overcompensating for his disappointment and her poor timing. Yes, she was able to admit mistakes or rather omissions. She was one smart cookie and looked great in a wet T-shirt, her signature look. She promised herself one day she would find a way for him to have the opportunity to stand in the limelight and let the heavens open up and pour down on his parade. Of course, he knew nothing about any of this, as was usually the case when destiny comes to call and one is in a rush to go somewhere else. Sometimes, although no one really knows it, he wears that hat in the shower, so his eyes wouldn't get filled with shampoo. "Please don't tell anyone."

16 ROCK STAR – LIFT OFF!

Niagara Falls, New York—1970
Star Man
"Don't play in the shower
Or your strings will get rusty."

LIFE LESSONS
1 Water is conducive to wet dreams.
2 Playing guitar in the shower will cause your strings to rust.
3 Watch out for hot air balloons while meditating.
4 Bling may elevate you, but it is a short-lived experience.
5 Only go out with women who know how to untie knots if you are going to travel by air.
6 And conversely, if you are tying the knot, make sure you can easily get out of it.

MYSTIC POWERS
17 **Fantastical:** The ability to a star in your dreams and have fans.

NIAGARA FALLS, NEW YORK, 1970

One of The Lonely Mystic's favorite elements was water. He often pondered about its varied uses. The shower was where he did the majority of his pondering. The natural dance and flow of the spitter spattering hot spray streaming on him was a natural inducement for him to enter a lucid dreaming state, even while he was still standing and wide awake. He was a purist and often went to the source, instead of using cheap imitations. Since he loved the flow of water as much as he did, he decided to visit the *Mother of Waterfalls*: Niagara Falls.

Upon arriving and when the water police weren't looking, he climbed to the bottom of the falls, took his clothes off, and stood under the raging waters. Under the influence of these mystic, ancient waters, he saw himself as myriad aspects of his being. These took form as manifold personages. Some would even go so far as to say all the personages in this *Tell-all* were washed up from a wet dream he had one day in his shower. Often, he would come out of his wet dreams in a trance and embark upon a new project. On that fateful day, he decided to play guitar, which immediately resulted in fantasies of him being a rock star. His long blond hair looked great wild and windblown. "Don't you think?"

There must have been some animals showering at the falls that day too since he could hear a man yelling. "Hey, everybody focus your binoculars on that naked jackass showering down below." He looked around, but of course, he didn't see any animals and figured *the man was having hallucinations.* These often happen when you are around nature's high-energy power spots and vortexes. It even happened to him once when he was visiting Sedona and meditated at one of the power points.

He started levitating on the vortex and was hovering above the rock. His companion at the time had to call the Air Traffic Controllers for them to guide him back down to safety. Luckily for him, they were able to easily disentangle his *Bling* necklace from the runaway hot air balloon above. Somehow, they had both become entangled during his meditation. Originally he hadn't noticed it due to his head being somewhere else. His companion had an opinion as to where his head was, *but* she was too polite to mention it to the Air Traffic Controllers. We have our suspicions too, "Don't we?"

17 OUT OF BODY - CAPTAIN COSMOS

The Bronx, New York—1963
Captain Cosmos and the Magic Cape
"You don't have to look before you leap,
If you know where you are going to land."

THE BRONX, NEW YORK—1963

During a different wet dream, The Lonely Mystic thought about how wonderful it would be to soar above the planets and enter the heavenly mythic, mystical realms and beyond. When he was a child, he had often fantasized about being an astronaut. He ran around the house flying his trusty paper plane. Times were tough then. The folks couldn't even afford to buy him a plastic one. Mom had spent all her money buying plastic to cover the entire house and didn't have a single penny left over for any toys, let alone spaceships. He dreamed of meeting the inhabitants of those realms and having communion and communication with them. He knew about them because one night before he was going to bed, he had asked his mom to tell him a bedtime story. Every word she said was golden to him.

That night, she told him of a time when she had a dream, right about the time when she was his age. She had never ever heard about flying saucers or space people. The first time she did was when she took him to see one of the first released matinee space films. She said, "I was standing in a field. There were flying ships and these elongated ships were shooting rays of fire down upon the ground. There

LIFE LESSONS
1 Don't use plastic for everything, or you will wind up penniless.
2 If you see a red cape, snag it. It is magical.
3 Pay attention or you will fail the tests.
4 Be focused and aware, or pay the consequences.
5 You don't always have to look before you leap.
6 But if you don't look before you leap, first check that the coast is clear.
7 If you are like your mom, you fell out of a pear tree.
8 Sci-fi movies were invented by The Lonely Mystic's mom.

MYSTIC POWERS
18 **Somnambulism:** The ability to walk around in your dreams without waking yourself. The ability to walk around yourself while dreaming. The ability to still be dreaming and also be walking.

were many of them." She never understood how she could have a dream of this nature. TVs weren't invented yet, plus she had never gone to the movies. She wasn't able to read and no one had read anything to her about these things.

Later on, he was to realize futuristic dreaming was a family trait. But more importantly, that he wasn't the only *space cadet* in his family. He hadn't fallen far from the pear tree. He knew it was a pear tree since he was nothing like his father. His father liked eating apples. His mom liked pears and was always saying, "What a pear she and her husband made; a real sweat *compote*." Compote was Yiddish for a cooked fruit dessert. She went on saying, "It must have been a match made in Heaven because no one on Earth, in their right mind, could have brought your father and me together!"

This was the role model for love he grew up with: Women complained about their men. Men complained about their woman. Men who bonded because of their dislike of their wives and woman who bonded because of their complaints about their men. This, of course, never even in the slightest way influenced him, or was any reason why he chose to stay single. His quest: A mystical one. His path: Lonely. It was then when he decided to call himself, The Lonely Mystic and to *dream dreams that are only dreamt of being dreamed,* even while being awake.

After his dreams, he dreamed of returning back to us to tell us all about the wondrous and magical worlds he had contacted, visited and experienced. Of course, this was only a dream because who can actually experience these kinds of things? One could wish couldn't one? At the very least he had his trusty *Na, Na, Nah*: His magic pink security blanky. It also doubled as a protective cape. He thought *I would have to dye my hair pink to match.* Then he did so. One result was the Punk hair movement. He thought *you always needed to dress the part.* "Right?"

He didn't want to enter the Celestial Spheres inappropriately dressed. After all, they all had wings and at the very least he needed some sort of flying apparatus. One night he stood up on his bed with his nightcap and sleepy-time sneakers on and held his red cape (it was really pink, but only looked red in the dark) spread out wide and jumped with his eyes closed. This way he was doing it with complete trust in the beneficence of the universe. He believed in blind faith. He believed in Providence and destiny, even at an early age. Old Soul, "Remember?"

He instantly opened his eyes, only to find he landed on his night table and hadn't gotten very far at all. He thought *how lucky can a guy get?* He could have jumped and landed on the floor, but that wouldn't have been as exciting. He figured *the floor was lower than his bed* and he wanted to soar to the heights, not the depths. So in reality, he had achieved his purpose and had landed at a new level. He was proud of his expansion into beingness and he commemorated the moment with the self-portrait shown herein.

He was an excellent portrait artist even from early on. His scribbles were often attributed to setting the stage for the abstract movement. Being modest, later in life, he never claimed credit for the achievement and decided to let posterity decide. By the way, if you are friendly with posterity, please put in a good word for him. He will send you a check letting you know he thinks you are A-OK. Check is pass, "X" is fail. He likes checks versus "X"s. "X"s indicate you can't spell or write your own name, or even worse that you are playing games, especially when they are next to "O"s. Of course, he likes it when there are lots of "X"s and "O"s in a row because it means you are sending him a kiss and he likes being kissed. Something that is only known by people he knows.

18 THE 70'S - COOL DUDE

Sheepshead Bay, Brooklyn—1975
Cool Dude and the Magic Specs
"Did you say something?"

SHEEPSHEAD BAY,
BROOKLYN—1975

LIFE LESSONS

1 Watch out for continental shifts and name changes.
2 Try not to forget what STML is or you might have caught it.
3 "Forgetaboutit" is not a cannoli or other Italian dessert pastry.
4 Destiny, cause and effect, and time are somehow interconnected.
5 You can be totally in the dark during the day if you black out your glasses. Very cool!

MYSTIC POWERS

19 **Concatenation:** The ability to combine seemingly unconnected words into new ones and only you know what they really mean. A form of invisible writing only it is visible, but the meaning is invisible to others when they see it and becomes understandable only when they hear it said slowly and spoken in syllables.

In the seventies, The Lonely Mystic returned to the states from Asia. His adventures in Nepal, China, and Central Asia were now long forgotten. Cigarettes and small eyeglasses were still in vogue then. His love of the cold made him a natural for chilin' out and being the cool dude he already was.

Asia was a different place then. First, it was still called "the Orient." Then, all of a sudden, it stopped being what it was and became something else. He didn't mind because *Orient* was three syllables and Asia was one long one. He was always taught to be succinct, so shorter words were an integral part of his vocabulary. He used them frequently.

Some of his favorites short words were *of*, *a*, *is* and *o*. Sometimes, to mix it up a bit, he combined them. (He was so, so, creative.) He was also innovative and dysexlic, so sometimes he mixed up the order of the syllables. Having STML, he often couldn't find examples of what he had just said because he couldn't remember what he had just said. Unless, of course, he had just said it before he forgot what he had forgotten. This confused the conversation quite often, but then again, he didn't have a significant amount to say anyway, so there wasn't much to be confused about. He was always taught the *Mom Rule*, which was, *Silence Is Golden*. Mom taught him and his brother, the "Boychickle," about cause and effect and the finality of the universe. After all, she was a space cadet too and understood these things well.

CANARSIE, BROOKLYN—1960

One day when his brother was talking a lot, (He always talked a lot when he was a kid.) she told him, "Stop talking so much. One only has a limited number of words to say and if you use them up now you will have nothing to say later."

His brother bit his lip, started crying and ran to his father and said, "Mom told me to stop talking."

"What were you saying when she told you this?"

"Nothing."

"If you weren't saying anything, which by the way is the same as nothing, then how could you stop saying what you weren't saying to begin with?"

"That's what I said when Mom said, 'See, you are doing it again.' I then told Mom, 'My back is against the wall, and your back is against the wall, so we are definitely not talking back to anyone.' Mom got very agitated at this point, and said, 'That's enough. If you want to talk, go talk to your father.' What should I do Pop?"

This back-and-forth went back-and-forth for quite a while. He had overheard the whole conversation. From his mom's comments, he induced *a person has a destiny and there are cause and effects that rule the universe. Talking about it won't change this. The more you talk about it, the fewer things will change, other than you being told to stop talking about it. If you talk about it too much, you will have nothing more to say about it. You will have used up your words and thoughts talking about something, which you couldn't change in the first place since it was destined to be anyway.* This explained a lot to him. From then on he was very sparse with his words and decided not to be a writer since writers need words and couldn't afford to be stingy.

As a result, he decided to become a musician instead. Musicians need music and can improvise their way to greatness. But, as his mom had taught him, he wound up being both. But before he realized this, he contracted his words so he wouldn't use them all up. People would think he had an accent when he spoke. This was far from the truth. It was a conscious decision to concatenate and be sparse and sparing.

"Getotahhere" was one of his favorites, but due to his memory issues and maladies; "fahgetaboutit" was more of an appropriate example. A good thing he even remembered that one.

19   THE SYMBOL - SOME PIECE

Sheepshead Bay, Brooklyn—1967
Pieceman and the Magic Omuelette
"If the crepe looks good, wear it."

LIFE LESSONS
1 Peace is really spelled piece, or is it the other way around?
2 Be careful what you say to your girlfriends if you want to keep them.
3 Don't wear your food unless you are French.
4 Follow directions herein if you wish to see stars.

MYSTIC POWERS
20 **Idiosyncrasitus:** The ability to be remarkably connected to events that to the ordinary person would make one look like an idiot.

SHEEPSHEAD BAY, BROOKLYN—1967

The Lonely Mystic became fixated on and obsessed with, the concept of peace because he misunderstood what the peace symbol really symbolized. He thought *it was a sex symbol*. He looked at it as a body with legs spread wide apart. He had an *omuelette* custom made for him without the protruding piece on the lower half since he felt the actual symbol was quite discriminatory. His version was more androgynous. He even spelled the name of the symbol correctly while everyone else had it wrong. To him peace was spelled "p-i-e-c-e" and he made it his life's mission to find some. As he was fated to be The Lonely Mystic, this posed some real destiny issues. He remembers referring to one of his girlfriends as a *piece symbol*. Of course, she was only his girlfriend for about three seconds: A record for him.

His chances of finding that elusive *piece* were slim to none. Eventually, he learned how to spell the word correctly and his quest was then diverted to obtaining *peace* as well. Some will say he delivered a series of books devoted to that very same theme. If you ask him he would only say, "Cool man! If you say so, then that's what it is." This photo shows him wearing one of his favorite hats, the *French Crepe*.

He loved to cook. One time, he tossed his crepe up in the air and believe it or not (Sometimes it is difficult to believe *idiotsyncrasies* do occur.) the crepe landed on his head. He raced to a mirror. He had brought this particular mirror back from his trip to Tibet. The shop owner who sold him the hat also insisted he take the mirror as a gift. This way he could constantly see how truly ridiculous he looked in the hat. He was so thankful for the gift. When he looked in the mirror, he thought, *Woo! That would make a great hat!* The crepe was burned charcoal black, one of his favorite colors. On that very day, the French Crepe hat was created! He was so innovative.

To commemorate his love of that elusive and often sought after *piece,* he sewed two small legs onto the French hat. He then hit himself over the head, so he would see stars. In the picture, you can see the whole story in an acorn shell; a wet, salty one with the nut still intact.

20 THE WISE ONE – THE PIT AND THE PEE

Iri City, South Korea—1971
The Wise One
"I need to go now!"

LIFE LESSONS
1 Pack your waterproof undies; you never know when you might need them.
2 Don't believe everything you see in other peoples mirrors.
3 Read the labels before you take the stuff in those little bottles.

MYSTIC POWERS
21 **Entrancement:** The ability to enter mystic visions aided or unaided by mysterious liquid substances. Often accompanied by frequent visits to the Pee Pee Palace.

IRI CITY, SOUTH KOREA—1971

The Lonely Mystic had many experiences in Asia. Much of his time there was often spent entranced in mystic visions. He always made it a point to visit the local shaman and holy men of whatever town he visited. One night during an excursion in South Korea, he was led to a house across a moonlit rice field. He could hear wolves howling in the background. (They may have been a pack of Chihuahuas, but wolves sound so much better.) He and his guide, Mr. Allsmiles, as he called him, wadded knee-deep through the rice paddies. A good thing he was wearing his waterproof underwear, a habit he had picked up during early childhood.

When they arrived at the house of Venerated Teacher, he was given a drink and told it was not only delicious but also delirious. He, of course, mistook the word *delirious* for the word *mysterious* and proceeded to gulp it down. It was a special ancient herbal and medicinal blend, later to become popular in the states. After a while, he stood up and announced to everyone nothing had happened to him. To be sure, he wanted to see for himself, so he got up and looked at himself in the mirror. There he saw an old wise man. He then asked Venerated Teacher, "Dear Venerated Teacher, when did *Old Fartz*' show up?"

"A few minutes after you drank the brew." The teacher was trained in the *Mystic Fartz'* and was able to see the visions he was experiencing.

"Good timing wasn't it?"

"Yes, very *propitious*."

He thought the teacher was asking him whether he needed to go pee pee so he said, "Yes where can I go?"

"Go? You are ready here. You don't need to go any place."

"But Venerated Teacher, I must insist, I need to go now!"

"That wouldn't be good for your health since you have just started your mystical journey."

"No, I don't want to end my journey; I just want to make a pit stop."

Venerated Teacher thought he had said he had a pit stuck, so he and Faithful Guide, Mr. Allsmiles threw him on to the ground stomach up. They both started pounding his chest alternately in unison. They do it differently in Asia. It is called *Ah Gitta Zetz* there.

No longer being able to hold it in anymore, he yelled, "I have to go now!"

Faithful Guide and Venerated Teacher in unison yelled, "Pit Out!" They were into positive affirmations and forceful mental programming.

Of course, to him, it sounded like "piss off." He smiled and let it rip! He felt so relieved. He yelled, "Ahhhhh!"

Both Faithful Guide and Venerated Teacher looked around for the pit. They figured it had popped out, otherwise, why would he be sighing and ahhing?

He stood up and visited the mirror again. This time he saw several other people in it: One was a naked man with a huge staff, and another was dressed all in black who wore a religious looking black hat. As he was reaching for the staff, he heard Venerated Teacher yell, "Don't touch the big stick!" Of course, he heard it differently and looked away embarrassed.

He never could quite figure out what the letters on the side of the bottle, standing next to the drink they had given him were. What was even more astounding was the letters weren't even written in Chinese. He was able to make out the first two, and the third one had worn off. It read, "LS_." To this very day, he still doesn't know what "LS_" stands for. At first, he thought it stood for some religious order, but it was only his dysexlia kicking in. If you know what it stands for, by all means, please drop him a *letter*. The missing one, of course. He looks cute with a long stash, "Don't you think?"

21   I Do - Do You Do Too?

Las Vegas, Nevada—1973
The Do Do Man
"Do me!"

LIFE LESSONS
1 Don't try to find yourself in Vegas, you will get lost.
2 Make sure you get a haircut before you travel.
3 Don't "I Do" unless you are ready to *tie the knot*.
4 Don't tell your wife you are going to the barber.
5 Accents are contagious, carry Echinacea with you at all times.
6 If you only have three hairs left, try a crew cut.

MYSTIC POWERS
22 **Multiligualitis:** The ability to speak in languages that don't even exist yet and will not be discovered until the next century. Being able to say things no one understands.

LAS VEGAS, NEVADA—1973

During the seventies, The Lonely Mystic had an identity crisis. He couldn't decide on how to cut his hair, so he traveled to Las Vegas to find out everyone there looked the same. He checked into a hotel, and the entire lobby was filled with men wearing the same *Do*. They all had the same accents, mannerisms', dressed the same and spoke the same phrases in a Texas sort of way. They even had a convention named after themselves. All of them walked around with guitars strapped around their shoulders and a slick black curl hanging over their forehead.

He thought *perhaps that was how I should look too?* He felt so out of place that he promptly walked into the nearest hair salon and said, "Can you *Do me*, please?"

The hairdresser was dressed like all the rest of them, he said, "I can do. Do you want the *Do* or do you want me to do the *Do* that is you?"

He thought *I must be on a planet that only speaks Hairese*, which was a distant cousin of *Fairese*, the language lawyers used in mediation cases. Fairese had the most words you could find in any language for saying nothing in so many different ways and still come to the same *just* conclusion: *My Side Is Always Right*. Often the outcome of the mediation was, *just pay me!* The recipient always thought it was just and fair. Fairese was a second cousin to *Obesitese*. This was the language Personal Trainers used to communicate with their clients. It contained the greatest quantity of words in any language that could be used to tell someone how wonderful they looked and how they had made such significant progress. (It could also have been called, *Suckitup*.) In reality, their trainees had gained ten pounds and looked like, well you know.

He was linguistically a marvel. It all started with the single fact that he didn't speak English until he went to kindergarten. He was multilingual before that. Yes, hard to believe for so small a toddler, but he was different even then. This information was only recently discovered inside an oatmeal can, which had lain buried in Brooklyn for who knows how long? It was accidentally dug up by a squirrel looking to bury his batch of salty, sweaty acorns. A passerby noticed the can, opened it and sent its contents over to the *Jonesonian Institute*, the archrival of the Mythsonian Institute which was constantly trying to keep up with the Jonesonian. The Jonesonian published the autobiographical piece in their Sunday Blog, which was called "Being Assoterically and Hysterically Correct According to Prior Undisclosed Facts about Historical Peoples." Apparently, that particular squirrel was quite busy digging up oatmeal cans all over the world.

Since by then The Lonely Mystic was already a well-known personage, the website took so many hits it brought down the server and eventually even brought down the whole Net for a short time. The Net goes down a lot; only most people don't realize it. When you have to wait for a web page to load, the Net is down. They tell you it is your computer and blame it perhaps on some spyware. Nope, that is just a worldwide cover-up for the truth, which is: There aren't enough patches in production to be able to supply the whole Internet community with protection.

Patches stopped being produced in bulk when they came up with something called *hand sanitizer*. He always thought *for most people, if you kept your hands clean, then why cover them with a dirt-attracting patch?* The problem with the biographical snippet that was published on the Net about him was, it was written in his first language, *Scribbilese. Scribbilese is* the language of immigrant parent's children. Most other children would write using *ABC*, but not him, he wrote using cryptic wavy lines and punctuation points; lots of punctuation points and holes.

His editor for this book returned his manuscript to him with the very same editorial marks he had used as a child. He instantly felt a kinship and was amazed at how he knew Scribbilese too! His doctor knew it also and wrote him prescriptions using it. It wasn't until the twenty-second century that computers were smart enough to interpret what this young avant-garde toddler had written in the twentieth century.

After exhaustive computing, that would have taken the original basketball field sized sixties' computer a century to code-crack, the futuristic supercomputer which fit on the head of a pin (just like angels) only took twenty years. Finally, on April 1 (Amazingly synchronistic, *don't you think?*) it spit out a piece of paper that said: "I knowz nothing! Butz, what I doez knowz iz, I knowz how to wrightz!" The prevailing society at the time took that to mean The Lonely Mystic was a descendant of the original *Spellink B* founders and history was changed forever.

Meanwhile, back in Vegas, he thought for a minute and said, "Why don't you do what you do and do the *Do'* for me that does me best!"

The hairdresser smiled. "Ah," he said, "You recognize I am 'ze artiste!'"

"Yes, I do."

"Buddyez, you have to be very careful about how you use the woidz *I do* around here."

Now he was really worried about the sanity level of this hotel. The hairdresser looked both ways, put his finger over his mouth and made a *sushi sound*. Now he was sure he was hallucinating and was also having a flashback from his South Korean daze.

Doman said, "Only say, 'I do' if you are getting married mize a friend. If you want a *Do*, then usea, Do me pleasza." He didn't want The Lonely Mystic to wind up married before he got his hair cut because if you're married, everyone knows your wife will *comment* on how you look and dress. This would put him out of business if he had to wait for the *wife* to formulate The Lonely Mystic's mind up for him.

The Lonely Mystic thanked him and asked, "Will it take the rest of my visit to Las Vegas for me to get my hair cut?"

"Only if you wantz to. You are freeze to come here and let me do the *Do* as many times as you do wish of couresa."

"No pleasa, do me now." He was starting developing a slight accent from listening to the man who came from the South Bronx originally but migrated to Vegas. He was eager to find out *what Do he would* do *for him*.

Doman started doing his thing. While he was doing it, he said, "Thanks Godz you gotta some haira."

"Whyza that?"

"Becausza, if youza nota hada haira, meza would havea had to do a 'big ado about nothing.' " He then proceeded to tell The Lonely Mystic about a previous customer who happened to only have three hairs on the top of his head: One up front in the middle, one in the middle on the left side, and one in the back on the right side. That customer wanted a *Do* like the rest of the people in the lobby. Doman wanted to tell him what to do, but he was a polite person, so he teased his hair.

The Lonely Mystic felt so badly upon hearing the story he burst into tears.

"Why isa youza crying? Did I doa somethinga?"

"Yes and no."

"Pleasza, makea upa you minda."

"My mind isn't confused. I was sad because you teased that man. I hate being teased. I think it is a cruel thing to do."

"Don't be sadda. The man was very happy. I made a *Do* for him and he looka just like the others doa."

"How did you doa that?" His language was shot to Vegas by now and had become Accent City.

"I usea *Doa Dough*."

"What was thata?"

The Lonely Mystic listened to the tale intently and repeats it now, sans accent otherwise; you might *doa* something to this *booka*.

Doman said:

> I heard from a friend, who heard from a mutual friend about someone who had used dough to bread eyelashes in the sixties. So I went around the corner to the bakery and borrowed some pumpernickel dough. I threaded the pumpernickel with some of the threads from a black towel. Before you could say, 'I do.' The bald-headed man had a *much ado about a nothing*.

The Lonely Mystic stopped listening to the Do Do man before he even started speaking about the pumpernickel dough. He didn't even want to look in the mirror after his *Do*. He just cut out of there figuring *I can't change my haircut without also changing my overall appearance.* You see this every day, "Right?" Certain cut's go with specific personalities and outfits. Every time he tried a different one, his entire persona, demeanor, personality, and clothing changed. For example, when he got a crew cut, he became short with people and made pointed remarks. People accused him of being rigid and he walked around in shorts even if it was the middle of winter. Long hair produced the opposite. He became garrulous, loquacious and long-winded. He was lackadaisical and wore his shirt over his pants, even when he was wearing a suit. His fascination with hair was a major transformational event, which he pursued later on. The constant changes in hairstyles caused his hair to suffer and they, like him, left home at an early age.

22 BAD HAIR DAYS - HANDLE BAR MAN

The Bronx, New York—1966
Mustache Man
"Some dough, my dear?"

LIFE LESSONS
1 Dough is for baking, not eyelashes.

MYSTIC POWERS
23 **Inventitus:** The ability to discover unique and original solutions for pre-existing problems. The ability to take seemingly disconnected and utterly impossibly related objects and string them together into a cohesive fabric. Doing so alters the perception of how one perceives what one has previously looked at. Sometimes even many times before and have not been able to see what one now sees after they look at it with this new perspective. A close cousin to:

24 **Conjunctivitius:** The ability to connect apparently disconnected junk into something else.

THE BRONX, NEW YORK—1966

The Lonely Mystic tried many things to compensate for his losing battle with his hair. Here we see him with a huge handlebar mustache and superthick eyebrows. He was the one who actually invented *eyelash-breading* in the sixties. You, of course, have heard of it, but no one knows about it except us. (Being the modest inventor that he was.) He was the one that the Do Do man was previously talking about. He had a beautician interweave bread dough with threads from his favorite towel. The finger action created heat, which allowed the bread to rise and expand. This caused eyelashes to look thicker. Of course, they felt soft and cushiony when he slept on them was merely an added perk. What was even more important for people, who eat when they sleep, was they didn't have to go too far for a snack. They could always break a piece of bread off from their eyelashes and nibble away in the comfort of their own bed! Of course, they had to be extra careful not to get hair in their mouth or crumbs on their beds.

In addition, he had heard rumors about people who actually fell asleep when they were in bed. Being the cautious and circumspect individual that he was, he took out an umbrella policy. This covered the possible loss of his vacation hat and sleeping outfits in the event they somehow got lost if he fell out of bed. *Now, I could have even more hair on my face since women like to see lots of hair on a man, even if it isn't on the top of their head.* He knew this because his girlfriend, the one with the mustache had told him so.

23 LOOK INTO MY EYES - SVENGALLI GUY

London, England—1972
Deep Dude
"How do you spell American Greyhounds?"

LONDON, ENGLAND—1972

LIFE LESSONS
1 Certain colors are more radioactive than others.
2 British cars break down.
3 American cars can be boring.
4 London Bridge may be falling down.
5 Make sure there is no metal in your Swiss cheese.
6 Make sure the chocolate wrapper is dry before you remove it.
7 Make sure that time doesn't run out for you before you are finished aging.

MYSTIC POWERS
25 **Psycholadelic:** The ability to spin around in circles and mystically wind up at a Kosher Deli thinking you are nuts because you have no idea how you got there and what is worse, they are out of seedless rye bread.

During a flight to London, The Lonely Mystic pondered on how old age would affect his superlong eyebrows and large mustache. He even thought *how would they look when they changed seasons and entered winter? I would have to dispose of all my colorful clothes and only buy the three basics: black, white and the middle color.* This caused him great trepidation because he never remembered how to spell the *middle* color.

He was concerned about how that color was manufactured. Its origin was unbeknownst to most, but he had very good reasons to be concerned. He knew *1gray* was the equivalent of one *jewel* of irradiated energy. Most people don't know *gray* is produced by being radiated. *Yes!* That's how they manage to manufacture it out of the black and the white colors. They send the black and white colors into a *psycholatron* and with atomic bombardment the color is manufactured.

The psycholatron is powered by millions of gerbils or hamsters, depending upon which part of the world it is located in. They cause the psycholatron to spin around. This is similar to the hamster wheels which many children love. Their toys were modeled after these mega-wheels. One of these resides in America at *Area 52*, and the other is located in England, underneath the London Bridge. Sometimes the psycholatron shakes so violently, it prompts people to start yelling, "London Bridge is falling down, falling down, falling down." The confusion as to the spelling of the word occurs because, after irradiation, the colors produced in America are different from the colors that come out of Great Britain.

The Brits use gerbils to do their colorizing. The USA'ers uses hamsters. The American version of the mix is spelled *gray* while the British version is spelled *grey*. One summer, at the *Helstinki* ICNC (International Color Naming Conference) both countries decided to use the second letter of the animal engaged in producing the color. Most people don't know both of these colors are actually different shades of the same color. The *American Gray* was almost the middle of black and white since America is democratic and wanted a balanced color. The *British Grey* is silver colored since Britain is a monarchy and is currently ruled by a woman. Women like lighter pastel colors and gemstones, so she had the Earl put some of her crown jewels into the psycholatron mix in order to brighten it up a bit and turn it to a silvery color. The Brits then used their version of the color on their cars. Of course, since the color was irradiated and radioactive, (Please don't tell anyone it would cause a panic.) their vehicles often broke down. Just ask anyone who owns one. America's gray, on the other hand, was a more stable isotope of bombarded atoms and molecules. Consequently, when used in cars, although being stable, it was also drab and boring. Hence, people preferred the British cars even though they were high maintenance.

The original inventor of the British process, an Earl, had a tea named after him to commemorate his service for this project. Of course, it was named, *Earl Grey*. As he was getting knighted the silver plating on the sword that was being used for ceremony started to peel. They had to send it back down under the bridge to be refinished. They are still waiting for it to come back up. This is expected to occur as soon as the labor disputes with the GU (Gerbil Union) are worked out. They are demanding sweatier, salty nuts.

The Swiss also came up with their own version of the color. They called it *Metallic Silver Gray*. Their process involved bombarding the British and American colors with some hard cheese; the soft kind didn't work, then milking the new color for everything it had. It was a cross between Cream de la Crème and Black Forest Cake. It was a milky grey-gray. The Swiss being highly efficient used the same vats that were used to produce their national cheese to manufacture these colors, only at night. They didn't use a psycholatron; instead, they used alternating movements of centrifugal and centripetal force. They trained trillions of ants to pull a string, which spun the vats one way. When they wanted it to spin the other way, they put sugar behind the last ant. They kept reversing the process until the black and white colors became so car sick, they just had to spit the grey-gray out. Of course, they didn't want you to know about the vats never being cleaned all that well. But everyone knows paint is hard to get off, and the *Metallic Silver Gray* color, which was produced at night, got into the cheese during the day. Big holes had to be cut into the cheese in order to remove it. These cutouts were then used to market a new type of chocolate. These chocolate coins had metallic grey-gray foil around them, which was actually the *Metallic Silver Gray* paint that had dried. The expression *that looks cheesy* was first *coined* in response to a batch of this new color.

Most people also don't know the original settlers, who left Britain, did so over a dispute about how to spell the *color*. Some people are passionate about their *spellink*. These *lexiconic* settlers formed the first law enforcement agency in The Americas called, The *Spellink Police*. It still exists today, albeit clandestinely. Their motto was *Be Write, Be Coreckt, Be Accurit*. Since they didn't want to speak like the Brits, they created their own words. *Three Be* events to educate the recent arriving immigrants arriving at Tellus Island were organized. These eventually came to be known as *Spellink Be's*. This name was eventually shortened and altered by the clandestine members of a factionalist group within the Original *Spellers*.

Because of The Lonely Mystic's remarkable ability to spell so well, he was convinced somehow he was related to the original *Spellers*. Of course, this wasn't possible since his parents came from Europe. But he secretly harbored the thought the founder of the *Spellink Police* was a Polish descendant. After all, how far is *police* from *polish*? Only two letters, which is an easy slip of the pen or tongue, for that matter. He knew he was *write, correckt and accurit* about this, his psychogenic senses told him so.

His knowledge of word events and hysteria was short of being uncanny and even phenomenal. He just knew all about this stuff, intuitively. When he didn't, he had the remarkable ability of being able to use his imagination to just make it up. He often went into these hysterical and philosophical reveries at the drop of a hat, as he had many hats and dropped them often. Sometimes they turned into deep meditations where he explored the nature of time, time travel, shape-shifting and why his DVR never seemed to record the right channel. He often thought *why was the space between my eyebrows decreasing with time?* He had several theories about this:

He figured *when I was young; I felt I had all the time in the world. Then as I aged, I had less and less time since the time I had left to live was less then I had when I was young. Time speed up as I aged.* Everyone I know is always saying, "Gee, where did the time go, I ran out of time or why do I never have enough time?" So I figured *since time is getting faster and faster it takes less time to arrive at where you are going. That is also why they only use old gerbils and old hamsters and old ants in the psycholatron and vats for color mixing.* But this caused him to be perplexed and when he was perplexed, he scrunched his eyebrows together and voila! The distance between his two eyebrows consequently decreased. So, this one event inspired him to develop his monumental theory of the Time-Space Continuum.

Space compresses and time slows down. Under extreme pressure, things come to a complete standstill and it takes forever to cause things to start moving again. *I often felt this on my way to work, especially during rush hour in the morning, when I had a regular job.* These phenomena enabled him to have a penetrating gaze and stare. When he looked at something long enough it started to move around. Amazing to you too, "Right?" But it's true, just ask any Quantum Mechanic at your local dealership. They will explain *spooky action* to you.

After starring at something for a long period, about five seconds, he got so dizzy everything started to spin. He attributed this to the centrifugal motion of the planet and how in touch he became with it when he went into his mini-mediations. This, however, caused him further concern because after awhile the visions of everything spinning stopped. He now worried somehow this would affect the planet from spinning on its back. He didn't want to interfere with the cosmic process. He thought *if the planet stopped spinning then because of the law I had discovered earlier, it would take a long time for it to start up again. Besides, who would be stupid enough to go outside into the coldness of space and give it a push? Not me, I would lose a good hat to the cosmic winds that blow around out there, otherwise, where would all the dust come from?*

He was all for global consciousness and caretaking, but he didn't want to injure himself. Everyone knows, if you try moving a heavy object beyond your abilities, you'll surely wind up with a *hysterectomy*. He surely didn't want another ailment that he would have to take any additional pills for. He took too many pills already. He, however, was quite sure that none of them began with an L and S.

24 REVELATIONS – MYSTERIES EXPLAINED

Gordonsville, Virginia—1975
Crypto Man and the Mystic Specs
"You got to have balls,
If you are having some chicken soup."

LIFE LESSONS
1 Friendship outlasts the grave.
2 Chocolate and peanut butter make an excellent conductor for transcendental messages.
3 Applesauce was not invented by Newton when he discovered gravity.
4 When something is upside down, then turn it over or stand on your head.
5 Walking backward slows down time.
6 **Bonus Mystery explained**: Which came first, the chicken or the Matzah Ball?

MYSTIC POWERS
26 **Extrapolation:** The ability to decipher and interpret seemingly incongruous and disconnected otherworldly events.

GORDONSVILLE, VIRGINIA—1975

During a bicycle ride through Gordonsville, Virginia, The Lonely Mystic discussed a few of the global and comic revelations he had been thinking about with some of his friends. He only had two. They told him he was looking at the world upside down. Of course, his two best friends were Rabbit, who was like a sister to him and Golf, a bud who also had passed over. Even though both were no longer here, they still managed to infiltrate his thoughts. After all, he was a mystic. He was an excellent decipherer/decrypter. Using techniques known only to him, he was able to take any word, turn it on its back so it was no longer on its side and decipher its true meaning. Many times the messages he received were still cryptic, but he figured since his friends were dead, being cryptic was apropos. These messages came in the guise of the TV commercials, newspapers, magazines and sometimes, believe it or not, from *fortunate* cookies.

His favorites were chocolate chip and peanut butter. He made them himself by buying some chocolate chip cookies and dipping them in peanut butter. He followed a ritual with these. He would place a newspaper on the table and eat the cookies after he dipped them in the peanut butter. Crumbs would fall off and land on the newspaper. The peanut butter prevented these crumbs from sliding around and the first spot they landed on was the spot they remained on. After he finished eating, he would take note of the what letters the crumbs had fallen on. Some might say this was a pretty crummy way of getting information. He, however, would say, "You were being jealous and didn't like cookies, let alone peanut butter."

Many true innovators were initially sneered at until the technology was accepted. Look at Newton. Had people believed in gravity before he postulated his theories? Absolutely not. They just believed in applesauce. He often employed another method to obtain his messages by overhearing the conversation of people passing by him on the street. Whether they were on the phone, talking to themselves or speaking to others, it didn't matter. What did matter was their words. He would meticulously jot down these random words and sounds and kept a journal of them. He thought long and hard about what these messages and clues meant. He wasn't able to decipher any of them until one fine day; he realized he was looking at all of this, and everything else for that matter, the wrong way.

Sometimes, what you are looking for is right in front of your own nose. It can even be staring you right in the face. You can be looking right at it and it just goes completely unnoticed. You could be holding it right in your hand and it just doesn't occur to you although you have the answer in your grasp. Well, one day he put his glasses on, upside down. This simple accidental act enabled him to see things completely different. He was able to see things from a new perspective and angle. He was able to see things the way they really were, without having to decipher, decode or decrypt. He called these the Three D's.

He started a new trend in the seventies. The photo above shows him with his new creation. Trendsetting was natural for him. He had visionary finesse. For example, in order not to interfere with the dynamics of his new eyeglass frames, he expertly cut off his mustache and put on a wig. When his friends would inquire, (Yes, the dead ones.) he would say:

> The easiest way to slow down the passing of time and to delay the inertia of immobility was to act young. As everyone knows: If you want to act young, you need to look young. Old people have mustaches and little hair. They are going backward since they are in their second childhood. Everyone knows walking backward takes longer hence it slows down time.

But then he thought back to when he was a child: *I had a mustache and little hair then too?* So now he was confused. *Was my first childhood my second childhood, or was my second childhood my first?* This incongruity greatly troubled him again. He needed to reconcile these apparent disparities.

Bonus Mystery Explained!
"Which came first, the Chicken or the Matzah Ball?"

For him it was an easy answer. Everyone knows chickens don't lay matzah balls. Ostriches do. Matzah balls are far too big to come out of chickens. Ostriches, however, have a unique way of creating matzah balls. They hunt around in the dirt with their head. They make sure their head is completely covered, this way no one can see what they are doing so no one can steal their secrets. (Corporate espionage is rampant amongst birds, that's why they are always peeping so much. The species is filled with whistleblowers.) While buried deep within the sandy bowels of the earth, they search for baby *matzah males,* who just happen to live in the sand. This has never been revealed before to the public, so please keep these secrets safe. They then eat these baby matzah males, who subsequently penetrate their own eggs. Anyone who has ever taken a sex education class knows this; just ask them how all this works. (The author does not have room to get into the mechanics of reproduction here.) These *matzah babies* then grow into full-fledged matzah balls.

If the ostrich is constipated, then, the ball is hard, if they have a loose movement then the ball falls apart, but this is the rarity. Just ask any matzah ball aficionado. There are millions. If the ostrich has eaten just the right proportions of cotton candy and peanut butter, then the matzah balls come out just right! Most people don't know cotton candy and peanut butter are the secret ingredients used in blue ribbon matzah balls. Once the ball is duly formed and hardened then the ostrich takes its head out of the ground.

Now the squirrels can look for their nuts since our ostrich has matzah balls and the squirrels wouldn't be confused when they are looking for their stash. The squirrels are very patient. They practice patience exercises, just watch how they can freeze in midmotion: Just like that! They are waiting for the ostrich to lay their matzah eggs. So, there you have it! Matzah balls without even one chicken in sight.

Some people just can't comprehend the mysteries and complexities of the inner workings of the universe. So now you ask, "What does any of this have to do with chickens?" Well, it is a known fact if you combine matzah and chicken eggs the results is a *matzah bride*, which is the female equivalent of *a matzah male*. So now you almost have the complete picture. What confused everyone was you usually ate the balls in a soup made from chickens. So the dilemma arose as to whether the matzah ball was made first or was it the chicken soup? Hence which came first, the chicken or the matzah ball? But the question of where the fried chicken capital of the USA resided still troubled him. There were two major contenders and he hated open ended issues. He and his magic specs were off to other parts of Virginia and Pennsylvania to find out.

25 THE GREAT ESCAPE – NURSE BITEMEI

Banal Mountains, "Painstilvaniya"—1976
Cool Cat
"Meow, growl, snarl, snap?"

LIFE LESSONS
1 Research facilities can lead to unexpected results.
2 Cheating at Solitaire is a lonely affair.
3 Use your time wisely, you never know when the guy looking over your shoulder may pull the plug.

MYSTIC POWERS
27 **Assimilation:** The ability to cull, collect, absorb, ingest, attract and concoct the animal into the animuscle rectally.

BANAL MOUNTAINS, PAINSTILVANIYA—1976

As a result of his deliberations pondering the recent perplexities and incongruities of discordant prepositions postulated previously, The Lonely Mystic embarked upon doing extensive research on hair loss, or as he put it, *Their Great Escape*. This was the second time in his life he did this. The first occurred when he was younger but wasn't too successful. His definitive ideas then became mellowed with age. This led him to travel to an experimental veterinary research facility high in the Banal Mountains. They often had stellar results by injecting people with animal hormones. When he got there, they changed his diet and gave him a new *Do*. However, the innovative treatments he received had side effects. Of course, he was never informed such would occur.

For a period of twenty-eight days, following the lunar calendar, they injected him with one feline hormone from each of the feline species. He received cat hormones, lion hormones, tiger hormones, leopard hormones, cheetah hormones, hyena hormones and female hormones. Although strict animal rightists' and vegans would uphold that a *female* woman is not a feline. He also had the same suspicions. He wondered why their hormones were included in his regime, so he asked the head nurse. Her name was Nurse Bitemei. He couldn't figure out if she was from *Painstilvaniya* or was a snowbird from *Helstinki,* which wasn't far from there, so he asked her.

She answered, "Where I come from has absolutely nothing to do with your treatments. You ought to mind your own business."

"Dear Bitemei, I don't have a business." He often spoke in the form of a letter. It was good practice, should he ever have anyone to write to.

"My dear, dear man, I'm so sorry to hear that."

She figured without a business he must have sold everything in order to travel to the clinic. Since he paid per feline, she of her own accord decided to inject some of her own hormones into his mix. She had a huge head of hair and weighed three hundred pounds, but she was the sweetest person you would ever find. Her hormones would eventually give him abundant hair growth. But he had other responses that started to develop as the moon grew brighter and brighter.

He became nocturnal. Being a vegetarian, he couldn't figure out why he wanted to eat meat? He kept seeing spots all over the place, including on himself. He was constantly sneaking around laughing hysterically over absolutely nothing and had an uncontrollable desire to cheat at solitaire, which he played often since he was lonely. Quite to his surprise, mystically the cards never moved unless he moved them. *I've been staring at these cards for over an hour and none of them have moved, even slightly?*

His mustache thinned out. Long whiskers appeared instead. He found himself often lying on his back with hands and legs in the air. His stomach started growling, often, or at least he thought it was his stomach. He also began sleeping during the day and prowling around his room sniffing and snarling at night.

He asked Nurse Bitemei, "Are these reactions a result of my treatments?"

"Very strange, indeed."

"Why?"

"Well, because we haven't started the treatments yet. They usually begin on day ten. We are only on day nine. The first nine days of shots are just vitamins." She felt guilty not telling him about her contributions to his well-being, but she liked her job.

He was bewildered; he figured the vitamins must have been loaded with the "V" drug. He had read about it. It was the *Vilda Chiyah* drug. It was guaranteed to bring out the animal in you for at least four hours. He often wondered; *where was the timer person with the stopwatch who actually watched you? If there weren't such a person then after three hours, fifty-nine minutes and fifty-nine seconds who would know to turn off the drug?*

26 LOOSING IT - CREW CUT GUY

Vaseline Springs, Poland—1976
Crew Cut Cutie
"You are what you swallow."

LIFE LESSONS
1 Check your bottled water for animal residues.
2 Tap water may cause hair loss.
3 Be careful what you assume.

MYSTIC POWERS
28 **Assumption:** The ability to think with other parts of one's body at opposite ends and still be able to adduce, deduce, induce, reduce, produce and play Deuces Wild while drinking only tap water.

VASELINE SPRINGS, POLAND—1976

The Lonely Mystic took a quick flight to Vaseline Springs, Poland. He went there to figure out why he was having such an animalistic response to his "Banal Treatments." Upon deplaneing, he was immediately sent back on a return flight because he had forgotten his passport. He had also forgotten his wallet too. In fact, he couldn't pay for anything. He didn't have even a penny on him. All he had ingested for the past twenty-four hours was some bottled water a stewardess had given him. Yes, they were still called *Stewardess'* then. They hadn't changed professions yet. He realized somehow something he was ingesting contained or had come in contact with, animal proteins. He thought long and hard. *Eureka!* He realized *the bottled water I was drinking came from spring water! Everyone knows animals have contact with spring water!* He immediately stopped drinking it and switched back to tap water instead. As a result, his hair fell out and he was able to return to being normal once more. He had uncanny deductive, inductive, reductive, and productive reasoning abilities.

27 THE GYM - THE EXCERSIST

Artemis, Geece—1976
The Excersist
"You are what you eat,
Even if you don't exercise,
So why bother?"

LIFE LESSONS
1 If you are wearing a wig check the label.
2 What's in a name?

MYSTIC POWERS
29 **Excersist:** The ability to exercise regularly and not lose a single, solitary iota of any excess weight, molecule, atom or otherwise. The ability to overcome the depression caused by this cosmic incongruity. By pigging out on nourishing soul foods like pizza, ice cream, chicken soup with the skin, ribs, French fries and of course hot juicy buttered calf's brains.

ARTEMIS, GREECE—1976

After having been polluted by spring water, The Lonely Mystic decided to get all of those pure H_20 molecules out of his body by joining a gym. He did extensive research on the best gyms located in his vicinity. He was living in Artemis, Greece at the time. This wasn't a difficult task because there was only one. Even its name made it a *no-brainer*. He used that particular expression quite a bit, he, however, thought *it was quite redundant because you have to use your brain in order to know, so how could, and why would, someone say a* no-brainer?

The gym he found was unusually named. It was called *The Gym*. He especially liked it because the owners were literate enough to know to call it "The." He visited it during the week, figuring everyone was working during the day. Boy was he surprised. When he was taken for a tour, the place was swamped. People weren't *working;* they were *working out* and *not* at their jobs. He was very impressed with the magnitude of the environment. People were waiting in line, so they could use one of the five machines that were operating. There were fifty machines all told, but forty-five of them were being repaired by an elderly guy with long eyebrows, upside down glasses, a wig and was wearing a peace symbol with a piece of it missing around his neck. The downward protrusion between the inverted "Y" was gone.

The guy who was giving him a tour asked the repairman, "How long is it going to take to fix up all the machines?"

The repairman said: "Forever. What's your hurry, Sunny? I can only do one machine at a time. At my age, time is moving very fast, so I ought to be done in no time at all. And as everyone knows, no time is just as long as forever since forever has all the time in the world."

He was very impressed with the philosophical soliloquy of the repairman and decided to join just on that basis alone. It reminded him of Plato's Treat, the place where Plato would teach his theorems and then take a bath along with other recreational activities. He was told since it was an exclusive club, he would have to wait for an invite. He gathered up his camping gear and pitched a tent outside of the gym. He patiently waited there for someone to invite him in, so he could join.

Finally one day, it took several, the owner noticed him and said to him, "You are here so often, you may as well pay to stand and wait for a machine. Right now you are waiting for a machine for free. As everyone knows, nothing comes of nothing and money comes from money."

The owner of the health club was a shifty guy. Contrary to the motto of the club, which was: *Fit to Be Thin or You're Not In,* he was quite overweight. The club initially refused to accept weight-challenged individuals. They were originally called *fat people*, but the Department of Laborites (DOL), sued the owner for discrimination based upon weight. Of course, and needless to say, the Uncle won, and the owner was forced to allow people who needed to lose some of their good times. As a result, the club skyrocketed from a status symbol to a money making one in no time at all. The publicity of the trial caused the owner to become, what he had thought his very own father was, namely filthy and rich.

As a result of this newfound wealth and notoriety, the owner had hair replacements done. This is usually performed when one is younger and still has some hair. The common procedure for this was taking some hair from the back of the neck and implanting it on top of the head. Since he was severely follicularly challenged (The publisher doesn't want to risk lawsuits here by *bald people*, so they changed the word.) he talked the hair surgeon into getting the hairs from another place.

The surgeon was a board certified *hairylogist* as well as being a proctologist. Being a hairylogist required you to also be a proctologist for several reasons; mainly because if you couldn't utilize the hair on the back of the neck for the replacements, you could always use the ones hiding inside the rectum. The hair, which falls out of your skin winds up everywhere. They even escape on to the bathroom floor and hide in the corners and sometimes; you can even see them in the bathtub or shower. They are very shifty and crafty. This proctologist was used to delving into dark recesses of the other place for one's head. His motto was, "We take your head out of your Jack" (He was foreign.) "and put it back where it belongs."

In the case of our gym club owner, the doctor took some hairs from there and put it on his head; this lead to a whole host of nasty remarks from the club's competitors. Some were: "Hairy ass, ass-backward, you look shitty" and the worst one was, "Why don't you put your head back up where it belongs." Of course, the owner had no idea why any of these remarks were being directed at him since he brought a bunch of his wife's hair to the surgery. He handed it to the doctor and said, "Here use this, I kicked her out of the house hundreds of times and she still kept coming back. Maybe her hair will refuse to leave too!" Of course, the doctor didn't use it because it was red and the man had jet-black hair. It wouldn't have matched, and he didn't want to be sued. He knew people sue so often these days. Since he didn't have malpractice insurance, he didn't want to have his butt dragged into court. If that happened he would have wound up pulling his own hair out trying to pay for the expenses.

The doctor gave the hair to his wife who ran a hairpiece business on the side. It was a match made in Heaven. The doctor did thousands of these operations a year, several each day. Each one only took an hour or so. You would be surprised how many patients brought their own hair with them for their surgery. Human hair is difficult to get for wigs. His wife did a nifty business of exporting the hair to China. They were promptly mixed in with other hair collected from you know where and then imported back into the states as *genuine human hair* hairpieces. This was just another one of the economic schemes that were being used against the good old *US of A*; a nefarious scheme which The Lonely Mystic was fortunate enough to discover and report, but who listens to a boy from The Brooklyn?

The wife of the surgeon was called Ima Whoas. The doctor's name was Ivan Pimp. *No, he didn't wear jewelry and yes, she kept her birth name.* She became (*If you see it coming, raise your left hand.*) Ima Whoas Pimp, the doctor's wife. The club owner was appropriately named Izzy Dreck. He was height challenged as well as weight challenged. Despite his cheating, profiteering, deceptive ways, he was charming and had a sense of humor. You could often hear him introduce himself by saying, "Just call me Dreck for short."

28 THE ESCAPIST - EL SICKO

Athens, Greece—1976
The Vigilante
"Be vigilant at all times.
You never know what is lurking
Under the sheets, on the ground
Or in your faucet!"

LIFE LESSONS
1 Don't expect to find true love on a sweaty bike.
2 If it's wet, it might not be your bodily fluids.
3 Sometimes when dealing with dreck, just wipe your hands clean of it.
4 Terrorism may be crawling around right under your pillow-vigilance!
5 If you want to stop being famous, sue somebody.
6 Ground birds don't fly.

MYSTIC POWERS
30 **Infamy:** The ability to become famous and *in* by not wanting either. It works like positive reinforcement, but only in reverse. You trick fate into doing what you want by not doing it. The more you resist it, the more fame you get. If you ignore it completely, then the whole world knows who you are.

ATHENS, GREECE—1976

Once The Lonely Mystic finally obtained membership to The Gym, he noticed it was no longer there. It had relocated while he was waiting on line. The Gym owner, Mr. Dreck, had moved it because there were only one hundred people in town. He calculated how even if ten percent joined, he would be out of business before he was in. He moved it to Athens, across from the Acropolis. This was a mere bus and train ride away from the original location. Once he finally got there, he noticed all the people were coughing and sneezing. He put on his trusty noise-canceling headphones; plugged them into his rusty MP3 player and continued to get thinner and sicker. He was working out in the gym, but somehow the gym was not working out for him. He had also hoped to meet his destined outside-of-dream-state sweetheart there. No such luck. When he was there, he may as well have been asleep or invisible. No one even looked at him, let alone spoke to him.

One day, while he was wiping off dripping sweat from the handlebars of an exercise machine before he even got on it, it hit him: *All of those machines were drenched in everyone else's sweat, and I was touching it. Even if I owned a hand sanitizer factory, I couldn't keep up with removing all the germs I was being exposed to.* He didn't even think about how the lockers had everyone else's dirt in them and how so many different people also used the showers. *How could I be sure if the water I was showering with wasn't the water the bottled water companies used to fill their bottles with? Or worse, perhaps it was recycled dirty water the other club members were showering with? If that were the case, I would be exposing myself to a potential overgrowth of hair again, which is a chance I wouldn't take.* So, reluctantly and with great chagrin, remiss and deep sorrow, he made the decision, then and there, at that very moment, during that significant instance of the unfolding of the universe that declaratively defined itself, quite demonstratively in front of his face — it *was mandatory* for him to *quit*.

He went up to the owner and said:

> Mr. Dreck, I would shake your hand, but I know it has been in places I can't account for. So, please accept my condolences and regrets about having to inform you this establishment is unfit and unclean for human use. Since I am only a card-carrying alien and not a real one, I will have to withdraw my application to become a permanent resident of this disease infested, germ and increment carrying habitat.

He went on saying, "I am at least glad there were no beds to lie on here, otherwise I am absolutely, unequivocally and irrefutably sure I would have found *bed bodies* here too!"

He knew there was a terrorist invasion of bed bodies all over the city. The terrorists easily brought them in and infected all the mattresses and pillows in the hotels as they slept on them. He knew it was a worldwide plot to undermine the Uncle's financial structure. He had heard people were suing the hotels after they spent a night there claiming the bed bodies came home with them. He couldn't quite figure out how the people were managing to steal the mattresses out of the hotel and then have the nerve to sue afterward, but he figured *it wasn't necessary to figure out all the problems of the world in one night.* He was happy he got out of that sick place at the right time and he no longer had to have a piece of Dreck and his club as a part of his life.

The owner promptly promised to sue him for defamation of character. He knew the owner was a character and was also well known. He thought why would Dreck want to sue me in order to no longer be famous? It was very confusing. He was already quite tired of wiping all the sweat off the handlebars, so he just headed home. He hoped his lethargy, and coldness was only due to exhaustion and not to anything else. He tightened his belt, put on his helmet, and hopped on his very, very large tricycle: One can't be too safe in a big city these days. He navigated between the bed bodies and the ground birds and headed home. The streets were filled with ground birds. He figured if pigeons could be called flying rats, then rats could be called ground birds. That night, he slept well, but often awoke finding himself in a cold sweat. Since his shower wasn't working again, he thought *it must be my body trying to compensate for lack of showering.*

29   THE GENEALOGIST - THE RELATIVES

Pasco County, Florida—1977
The Naked Truth
"Blue blood, blue balls."

LIFE LESSONS

1 Contrary to popular beliefs, genealogy does not cure the blues.
2 Do not sneeze in front of relatives.
3 Rubbing garlic over one's nose or stuffing carrots between one's toes does not cure the common or uncommon cold.
4 Listening to relatives may lead to unexpected and dire consequences.
5 Mom always knows best, just ask her.

MYSTIC POWERS

31 **Nationalism:** The ability to turn true blue in honor of family and country. The inability to return back to normal coupled with cessation of breathing or near death experiences.

PASCO COUNTY, FLORIDA—1977

The Lonely Mystic flew all over the world and visited several doctors trying to get help for the mysterious illness he had somehow contracted at The Gym. He visited acupuncturists, chiropractors, masseurs, M.D.s, and Ph.D.s, to name but a few. He had turned blue. Not black and blue, but a royal shade of blue. This was baffling for all who examined him. He even decided to visit a genealogist. Someone happened to tell him only people of noble birth have blue blood.

He located one at a resort in Pasco County. However, they made him take all his clothes off before they discussed his heritage with him. He could understand them asking him to remove his clothes, but the doctors were all-naked too! He had never seen this level of commitment to the patient before. He felt they were showing empathy for him by coming down to his level. He thought *they were very brave to have their little DR. nametags pinned to their skin; otherwise, one wouldn't be able to tell the patient from the doctor.*

They asked him, "Where is your lineage from and did you ever have royalty in your family?"

He became elated; *Mom always treated me like a prince* he thought. So he said, "Yes! Mom always treated me like a prince!"

The Genealogist thought him deranged, so he told him to get dressed, leave and he should go home to his mother and then ask *her* to cure him.

The Lonely Mystic came from a family of healers and diagnosticians. Although there wasn't a doctor in the house, every one of them knew what was wrong with you. More importantly, they all knew how to cure it. Even when there was nothing wrong with you to begin with or that anything had to be fixed. You would get pop diagnoses by just making the wrong facial gestures.

Once he was almost sent to a psychiatric ward for scratching his nose. His uncle, a high-strung sort of fellow, said, "Are you crazy?" This wasn't the only time for him to be accused of such. He knew first edition comic books would be worth a mint in the future. So, he decided to cash in his entire, extensive, complete nickel coin collection to fund his purchase. His relatives thought otherwise. He got comments like, "What, now you can predict the future!"

Whenever he had an allergic reaction to eating eggs, he would sneeze. This, of course, was promptly interpreted as having a bad cold by all of the senior members of the diagnostic team. They hovered over him, arms folded, pacing back and forth trying to come up with a mutual consensus as to what the proper treatment method would be.

He would hear various prescriptions, such as, "Give him a little hot chicken soup."

"Don't take him to the doctors. They don't know anything."

"Maybe we should take him to the hospital; they don't have any doctors there, only nurses who speak to doctors by phone."

"Let's dress him in lots of layers, so he can sweat it out."

"Don't let him eat if it's a cold we have to starve him."

"Put his head over a hot bowl of chicken soup, cover his head with a towel, but don't let him sip it, but keep stirring."

The most imaginative of the bunch was: "Rub some garlic over his nose and put carrots between his toes," one of his relatives was a closet poet.

The treatments went on and on. Luckily for him, when he was a child, he didn't get sick often. The maladies and ailments didn't start until his second childhood. By then his relatives were retired health care professionals. When they heard he was ill they all had a universal remedy for it: "Don't worry, everything will be all right, just get better fast and you will be fine." He thought *it sounded like good advice!* So one time when he did get very sick, he didn't worry about it and did absolutely nothing to get better. After all, he knew how nature was the best healer, and his relatives were the best diagnosticians that existed.

He almost died as a result of it. That was the last time he listened to *unprofessionals*. When the relatives heard about the mysterious *blues* he was experiencing, they took a conservative approach toward helping him. They all unanimously agreed the best course of action for him was to ask an expert. This was the first time he had ever heard his entire family agree on anything! But there are always firsts.

In unison, as if they were a renowned choir in concert at a distinguished concert hall, which had rehearsed for a half a year, in unison, they all sang, "Ask your Mom, she knows everything!" Now he even had a second opinion with the same conclusion. His path was clear, his mind was at ease and his heart was filled with gladness and good cheer.

30 THE GYNECOLOGIST - SAFE SEX

Trinidad, Colorado—1977
The Listener
"My balls are pink again!"

LIFE LESSONS
1 Genealogy is not a branch of gynecology.
2 Don't tighten your belt too much; it may cost you a trip to Colorado and a $500.00 doctor's bill.

MYSTIC POWERS
32 **Emaculation:** The ability to get screwed under professional supervision for only $500.00, with no risk of STD and be happy about it having happened.

TRINIDAD, COLORADO—1977

The Lonely Mystic still lived with to his mother. He went home and told her what the Genealogist had said. His mother said, "You still look sick. You should visit a different gynecologist." She heard *gynecologist* instead of *genealogist* because her hearing was bad. She had never ever heard the word *genealogist*, so she compensated. She knew he sounded all screwed up inside. She also knew gynecologist's deal with that kind of thing. Mom *always knew best* and always had a girlfriend who new even more than she did. So he asked her to get him the name of a gynecologist. The fact the doctor lived in Colorado was unimportant. *Health had no boundaries.* It could reside anywhere.

He jotted down the name of the doctor and decided to visit her, unannounced. He figured *if I don't call for an appointment, then she couldn't prepare to give me a wrong diagnosis. How could she? She wouldn't even know what was wrong with me yet?*

By the time he arrived there, his color had returned to normal. He traced his ailment to him having tightened his pants belt too tightly. When he met her, he told her about his symptoms and his cure.

She said, "Well, in that case, you are all cured. There is nothing wrong with you and there is nothing more for me to do." She then promptly handed him a bill for $500.00.

He thought for a while and then started to rub his chin and just smiled. He *was* cured. He knew gynecologist's deal with sex. For sure, he had just gotten royally screwed out of $500.00. He thought *it was money well spent! At the very least, a professional did it to me. Mom will be happy. Mom does know best!*

31   THE MESSENGER – DIVINE DIRECTIONS

Bedford-Stuyvesant,
The Brooklyn—1977
The Messenger
"Two lefts and a right,
Or two rights then a left?"

LIFE LESSONS
1 If your dead friends don't speak to you, ask a stranger.
2 Too close for some people are great distances for others.
3 Brooklyn is a place for mystical experiences.
4 Distance didn't have to be measured in miles; it could be measured by intent.

MYSTIC POWERS
33 **Incommunicado:** The ability to be unable to communicate with whom you want to communicate resulting in necessitating communications with someone else who doesn't want to communicate with you either.

BEDFORD-STUYVESANT, BROOKLYN—1977

The Lonely Mystic was elated. He was cured. He was even more elated about him no longer being ill! He felt *I am ready to be more of who I already am. I'm not sure what that is yet? Perhaps I need someone to REfold me so I fit better into my present.* He knew if his present was packed too tightly, there would be no room for the future. Although he knew how to pack well, (He could fit a lot into his knapsack.) he also knew he needed to REstructure parts of himself and his life in order to be able to move on. After all, he had spent many years studying QuantumREotics while he lived in Brooklyn. Of course, all that studying occurred on other levels during the time he was playing with his pink blanky, *The Nah*.

However, now he was beginning to be that other he he needed to be in order to have that he REfold him to become more of who he alREady was, but wasn't yet. *I feel lucky that even with all of the being and becoming going on, I didn't get Quantumly REentangled with my other* mes *to a point where I would be so tied up in knots I wouldn't be able to be REfolded. These folds or patterns as I call them were already here, I just need to REfold them to be that me.* For example, he thought *it was kind of like taking an Auragummi that was a skunk, opening it up, smoothing out the creases and REpaterning it into a giraffe.* He called these pattern-forms Soul Auragummies. The REfolded one he called a Horagummi because they were a choice. Put another way, he thought *the mes that I am, was and will be, are facets of my soul. Folds produce straight lines and form facets. REfoldment was the act of becoming who I already am, but not yet, and yet* also *yet*. He folded the entirety of all these new thoughts snugly into his QuantumREotics knapsack, which read: *You alREady aRe You*. Even to him, it sounded a bit gummy. After all, he hadn't worked all of the kinks and knots out from that pile of jewelry chains under his bed yet. Don't ask, he collected the weirdest of things, and of course, they were gold.

After his healing came health. He had REnewed energy, drive and desire to be that inside someone and was looking forward to being that person. He was busy walking around the street lost in deep thought visualizing *MoREgummies* and QuantumREartix', but since his dead friends, weren't talking to him lately, he stopped the first person passerby. He asked him, "Where are you from?"

The man turned toward him and said, "Crown Heights."

Everything started to make perfect sense to him upon hearing this. He thought *QuantumREotics: How truly serendipitous it was that events could REentangle and REfold themselves around me to integrally manifest connectedness with points that were hitherto before thrown asunder in mayhem and confusion.* (Occasionally his literary gene kicked in unexpectedly, it was a rare occurrence.)

The genealogist had told him he was *royally screwed*. The gynecologist royally screwed him with her bill. He then figured *these events were all connected and set the groundwork for some sort of* cosmic sex *the universe was having with him.*

He knew the highest physical chakra in the body was the *crown chakra*, so this *royal* reference coupled with him having prayed to the heavens on high for some answers convinced him *Crown Heights* was a definitively an indication of him having received a message from *above. I live a blessed life* he thought.

As a result of these cosmic singularities and congruities and much to the chagrin of his mother, he grabbed his knapsack and moved to that very same named neighborhood the very next day. His mom felt it was too, too far, far away. She lived two blocks from where he was moving. He thought *distance didn't have to be measured in miles; it could be measured by intent.* "Is anyone writing this stuff down?" They are pricey, "No?"

32 THE COMMUNITY - RITUALS

Crown Heights, The Brooklyn—1977
The Community
"It's a sign from above!"

LIFE LESSONS

1 If you agree with everything then you won't disagree with anything.
2 Follow your dream, but don't let them get too far ahead of you otherwise, you will get lost and have to ask a stranger for directions and wind up living in The Brooklyn, which might not be too bad considering the rental rates of an apartment in Manhattan.

MYSTIC POWERS

34 **Universalist:** The ability to feel comfortable with all cultures, creeds, and races coupled with the ability to blend in with the crowd making others feel comfortable with you.
35 **Richualism:** You don't have to be rich to practice spirituality. Someone misspelled it originally.

CROWN HEIGHTS, THE BROOKLYN—1977

The Lonely Mystic found an apartment on Crown Street, at the corner of High Road. He thought *I couldn't have found a more fortuitous and propitious location.* To him, it epitomized the essence of the section he had moved to. He felt very comfortable with the diverse mix of cultures that surrounded him. After all, he not only spoke Chinese, he was also fluent in Yiddish. Occasionally, he even threw some English in to round out the mix. These were all concocted up into a hodgepodge of accents, which made him understandable mostly to Grandmother Hitou.

Reciprocally, he had difficulty understanding what his grandmother often said. Consequently, no matter what she did say, he always answered, "Uh huh." He had learned that trick from Zen Ben. He considered himself more spiritual than religious. His experiences early on in Asia molded him into being a free thinker too.

For him, keeping up with prescribed rituals was time-consuming. However, he still spent time with his own daily rituals.

Some of The Lonely Mystics Daily Rituals

1   He made a daily donation to his coin box using the change from his pocket. During the holidays sometimes he would distribute this change to free thinker people on the streets, or to places that would happily change his money for him. Can you imagine they only charged him twenty percent to do so? *What a bargain* he thought.

2   He made it a point to shower twice a day because he had heard cleanliness is next to *Godliness* and *two heads are better than none*. So he did things in twos just like Noah did: Two showers daily, two meals, two pillows, two shoes and he made sure his shirts had two arms and his pants two legs.

3   He emptied his garbage religiously and even changed his bedding every other Tuesday.

"Can you guess which one he is in the picture above?" He had uncanny transformational abilities. He used these to fit in with his environment. His father had taught him to always fit in. Never go against the status quo. His father had wanted him to grow up to be an accountant, a lawyer, or a doctor. He felt bad he had disappointed his father, and he was to become, amongst other things, a naturalist and animal lover instead. Although he felt bad he had never lived his father's dream, he also felt good he was living his own. He knew his father wanted the best for him. His father's dream was the best dream his father could envision for him.

He felt he needed being who he alREady was. QuantumREotics helped him be that *he*. It helped him navigate the Multi-dimensional Time Space Continuum (MTSC) and REfold himself to bring forward the best and highest he he could be and translate that to the pREsent. He was to learn who you aRE is alREady pREsent. It just needs being REfolded, to allow you to REsturcture your yourself.

When he thought about it, he had no idea what the specifics of his dream were. He could tell other people about their dreams and their next quantum steps, but he was taking it day by day. Other than trust, belief, and faith in God, he had no immediate game plan, no long-range plan, no agenda and no goals. He strove to be the best "he" he could be. He lived in the pREsent. As a result, his relatives thought he was crazy and he was wasting his life. He checked his waist often; it was surely not shrinking, so he didn't understand what they were even talking about.

They were right about his life amounting to nothing. He only had a few dollars in the bank. He considered himself special in this respect too because the government was not taxing his savings, the way they did with most people. The interest he got on his five dollars didn't add up to a significant nest egg, even at the 17.65% interest rate he was getting then. Can you imagine at one point in our nation's history banks were paying out more than you make on your average investment portfolio? He often pondered *who lost the interest? Where did it go? Does the finders-keepers rule apply to it? If it did, I definitively would make it a short-term priority to look for the interest the government lost, if I could only remember where it went.*

33   THE MYSTIC – RELIGIOUS EXPERIENCES

Jerusalem, Israel—????
The Mystical Mystic Mystic
"The future is already here,
Only we haven't caught up to it yet,
As we are moving way too slow."

LIFE LESSONS
1 If you are meditating and feel wet, check your faucet for leaks.
2 If you are going to get soaked when you are dressed, wear wash and wear clothing.
3 Pounding sounds aren't necessarily loud heartbeats.
4 Neighbors don't always knock quietly.

MYSTIC POWERS
36 **Accountability:** The ability to be accountable for one's actions, both conscious and unconscious. The power does not refer to one's savings or the number of accountants one has. An umbrella policy, which includes property damage, is a good accompaniment to this power. Old age is not a means of relinquishing this responsibility. Ability is accentuated by wearing cool black hats.

The Lonely Mystic often thought long and hard about the meaning of life. He also thought about what lies beyond the great beyond as well as beyond even that beyond. After all, he had visited China, Nepal, South Korea and a whole host of other countries and continents. He was *a man of the world*, both seen and unseen. During one of his water reveries, he envisioned himself as an aged mystic living in the *Land of the Sand People*. He envisioned all the accouterments of the traditions swirling around him. He saw congregants, tablets, chalices, podiums and a cool black hat.

His personal rituals started swelling up around him and started to swirl, first slowly then they increased in tempo and intensity. Soon there was a whirling, gurgling, swishing, sloshing sound surrounding him. His reveries had started to manifest themselves physically. The waters of the visions actually started penetrating the outer layers of his clothing. He thought the heavens had opened up for him. The wetness of the divine cosmic visions was touching him from their ethereal planes, and he had started to rise. He felt elevated, cleansed and thoroughly sopping wet. He made a mental note to either tame his visions a little bit, or wear a bathing suit before he engaged with them.

It was at that point he opened his eyes and realized his bathtub had overflowed. Now the water was gushing and rushing everywhere. He heard pounding and thought it was his heart beating loudly in his chest, yelling at him, "Stupido! Look what you have done! You weren't even wearing your wash and wear shirt and underwear!" He felt his chest and it was normal. He frantically searched around and heard the pounding was coming from his front door and not his chest. His neighbors were screaming, "The ceiling is falling down!" He firmly turned the water off and dressed. At least he was clean. He apologized, but then they started talking about his horsey again. This he totally didn't understand, he thought: *How could I fit a horse into my small elevator? Horses don't climb ten flights of stairs; nine is their limit and besides, only dogs and bed bodies were the only animals allowed in the building.* So he knew although they might be angry, they were definitely wrong about his pets.

34 SHADES - DE JA VIEWS

Teaneck, New Jersey—1977
Shades and the X-Ray Specs
"Do you see me now?"

LIFE LESSONS

1 Turn your bathtub water off before you finish taking a bath.
2 If you take a chin bath, remove your Nehru jacket first.
3 If your water supply is off, cry.
4 If you don't want Nature to hate you, don't vacuum.
5 Dry Cleaners stole their technology from raindrops.
6 Patent your inventions before someone scrapes them off your tongue.

MYSTIC POWERS

37 **Night Vision:** The uncanny ability to see in the dark even during the day, coupled with the ability to see negative space in a positive manner: Heightened by tongue scrapping and eating brownies in reverse order of course.

The Lonely Mystic suffered deep humiliation and shame regarding his religious experience of the *waters overflowing* that he had shared with his neighbors. He equally felt his experiences were of a personal nature, which left him feeling violated. Somehow his neighbors had crept into his visions and reveries? *How they managed to do so was a mystery to me? Perhaps they heard the bath being run and then they turned their baths on too?* He often heard the sound of a toilet flushing when the neighbor directly underneath him did so. He thought *perhaps the toilet got backed up, went upward and then flooded my bathtub. I distinctly remember turning off the water before I got into it. If I didn't, then I would have gotten really wet, and I only wanted to take a hip bath, not a throat-under-the-chin kind of bath.* He was meticulous about these different types of baths.

He took a hip bath when he was going out on a date. *Hip baths* made you cool, even if the water was hot. That is where the sixties got the expression *I'm hip* from. It was because all the people got into one big bath that reached only up to their *hips*, otherwise, their Nehru jacket collars would have gotten wet and would have shrunk.

He only used the *under-the-chin, up-to-the-neck* baths when he was depressed. He felt that when the water got so high he could be cleansed of his sad thoughts because sadness disappears in water. Just ask anyone who cries. They will tell you that when they are sad but aren't in a bathroom, their eyes compensate and start bathing them immediately. Yes, instant bathwater!

The body is very, very smart and knows how to take excellent care of itself. Everyone knows this because if it were up to them, they would stop breathing, and stop circulating. He had very poor circulation. His circle of friends was minimal, next to none. If his body did the same, then he would have no blood flowing through his veins and would have nothing but emptiness. Everyone knows how *nature abhors a vacuum* and since emptiness creates vacuums, so nature would hate him too. He definitely didn't want another mother; his was quite enough. Having Mother Nature up his rear would be a bit over-the-top for him to handle the busy life he already had. So, either the neighbors' toilet backed up and flowed up, or his entire building was so depressed that there was a flood of tears flowing up to his floor. In any event, he was mortified and humiliated and from then on he would wear dark glasses to cover up his deep humiliation and red eyes.

Of course, by choosing to wear these dark glasses he started another cultural following. Just ask anyone wearing sunglasses at night, "Hey Dude, where did you get the idea to wear shades at night?" You will be surprised by the response. He didn't even take them off when he shut off the lights at night. It was already dark, so by taking off the sunglasses, he thought *would that make the room any brighter? Of course not.*

He would lie awake dreaming of his mystical visions, Auragummies, Horagummies and MoREgummies and managed to the fall asleep while he was awake. This was similar to walking between raindrops so that you don't get wet. It could be pouring cats, dogs or other animals, but he wouldn't get one iota of wetness on him. He had learned that space lies between things. Therefore, if you had many raindrops, which is what happens when it rains, then there is lots of space between all of them. If you mentally consolidate all of that space on one side and put the rain on the other side, then you can walk in the spaces instead of the rain and *voila,* you are *dry clean!* That is where the term *dry cleaning* originally came from in the first place. Someone that knew how to use this very same technique invented it. It is now a documented fact that somehow walking between the drops also cleans your clothes, since theoretically; they are being washed and dried both at the same time.

Dry cleaning has side effects and affects your humor too. As a result of walking between the raindrops, your humor becomes very dry. Think about the countries that have lots of rain and what kind of humor they have. He was often accused of being so dry that he had to walk around with moisturizing lotion on his tongue. He needed to apply it before he spoke or the words would get stuck inside and cause great irritation when he tried to get them to come out. As a result of this, since he didn't have lots of money, he spoke sparingly and didn't crack any jokes whatsoever since jokes took lots of salivae. Just watch the mouth of some comedians. They spit and splatter all over the place when they speak because their humor is very wet. He had to scrape the words off his parched tongue. He developed a special tool to do this with. It was the *tongue scraper*. Someone saw him using it and decided to market it as a sanitary tool and made a mint.

He peripherally invented many, many things besides this one and never reaped the rewards. None-the-less, Heaven sees everything. In Heaven, there is a whole accounting department filled with lawyers to oversee the huge accumulations of brownie points that he has culled. His father would be proud.

35 HEAVENLY BODIES – ASTRONOMY GUY

Pasadena, California—1976
Cosmotician
"Please don't moon me.
It's lonely up there."

LIFE LESSONS
1 Three eyes or five eyes, four eyes is totally wrong.
2 A three-year-old understands cosmic physics.
3 The man in the moon is for real.
4 Roses are red because of their blood.
5 Don't cheat on your honey or you may get mooned.
6 If you not hearing this, get your ears checked.

MYSTIC POWERS
38 **Cosmotician:** The ability to reconcile differences by putting great distances between discordant partners. Being skilled in using plants and other indigenous substances to mask the failure of prior failed reconciliations.

The Lonely Mystic was able to see the moon and stars not only during the night but also during the day. He learned that closing your eyes blocks out the light, but you can still see with your other eye: The one between the two you already have. Blocking out the light not only lets you find the space that exists between the raindrops, but also allows you to be able to see in between the light. Even though the light is there, it is moving so fast you might think darkness has disappeared. Well, it hasn't. It is still lurking there. Just ask any three-year-old if it is dark under their bed. Even though their room is brightly lit by the sun or light bulbs they would tell you, "It isn't only dark under my bed. If you opened and closed the door quick enough, you would see the darkness before it ran away and hid between the light beams."

Yes, light beams have darkness hiding within them and even more so, they travel on darkness. Darkness is the super highway that moves them along. Think about it: *If it was always light, how could you tell if it was going somewhere?* You have to see it move to know it has traveled. That is why daylight travels around the globe. If it didn't move it would be dead, just like the Moon. The Moon doesn't have any light of its own because it threw it away millions of years ago.

OUR SOLAR SYSTEM—MILLIONS OF YEARS AGO

Moon said, "I don't want you anymore because I want to hang out by myself under the bed."

So *Light* said, "Oh yeah, who needs you anyway, I'll go and shine on *Earth*."

Earth, of course, was very, very happy and started spinning around in circles. *Light* liked the game and started to chase her.

Earth sang, "Ring Around the Rosy! *Light*, let your love and light shine on me."

That is where the nursery rhyme *Ring Around the Rosy* came from. *Earth's* nickname is *Rose*. That is her favorite flower too. When *Moon* saw all of this happening, he got very jealous and decided to throw a thorn in Rose's sides. This way she no longer would be all smooth and rounded. When *Rose* wasn't looking because *Light* had swung around to her other side, *Moon* slid down and implanted pieces of its craters all over *Rose's* long green legs. They were made of pointy, hard material scraped from *Moon's* own pock mocks.

Moon had accidentally stayed in the sunlight too long one day. This had caused him to peel. *Too much of a good thing can be bad for you,* he would often think. His skin never grew back and pockmarks decorated him along with a dry, chapped, parched complexion. He hated *Sun* and *Light* ever since for having spoiled his once mirror-like silvery skin: Something he often admired at night by looking upon his reflection off of *Earth's* shimmering skin.

It was then he told *Light*, "Go and take a hike!"

Light was sorry *Moon* had suffered so severely. "Dear *Moon*, please let me comfort and shower you with my beneficence. I promise to be gentler to you."

Moon, of course, although pocked up, still missed seeing his reflection and feeling *Light's* warmth. *Moon* said, "OK, please shine your light on me, too."

"Good, I would love to, but first I need to check with *Rose* and see if she agrees."

Moon resented that *Light* had to ask for permission before he could get warmed up again. He then decided to get even with not only *Light*, but with *Rose* too.

Rose woke up that night by pricking herself in her sleep. She found red blood flowing from her green veins. She looked up at the *Moon* and saw him smile and grin at her. She said, "Man, Oh *Moon*, I see you smiling at me! I see that grin!"

It was then she realized who put a thorn in her side. She got so angry that she threw the blood that had flowed from her up to *Moon*. *Moon* turned *blood red*.

This angered Moon. He held his breath blocking the blood from getting sucked into his pockmarks. The blood then fell from *Moon* back to Rose. It took twenty-eight days for the blood to return to *Rose*, as the distance was great. As it was falling from *Moon*, the blood froze into billions of millions of tiny crystals. It turned snow white as it froze. It fell covering *Rose*. *Moon* had turned blue as a result of having held his breath for so long.

Rose refused to let *Light* shine on *Moon* all the time and finally, they worked out a mediated agreement. It was drafted by *Mercury*, their messenger and communicator. *Rose* agreed to let *Moon* have one full dose of light every twenty-eight days. On that day, *Rose* was busy taking care of her own business dealing with the blood that *Moon* had sent back to her. She would dance around in the forest under *Moon's* light celebrating her victory over him and trying to forget his gift to her.

Light, with the help of *Mercury*, finalized a contract between *Moon* and *Rose*. *Venus* witnessed the event. *Saturn* surrounded all in a golden ring. *Jupiter* placed it on one of his moons for safekeeping and as to *Uranus*, well, she was busy taking care of business. *Venus* tried getting *Moon* and *Rose* to love each other again. This was thwarted by *Mars* talking into *Moon's* pockmarked ears attempting to convince him to go to war.

He kept telling *Moon*, "Don't listen to *Venus*, listen to me."

Moon kept saying, "You and *Venus* see things very differently. I don't know who to listen to."

Mars would answer, "You're a man and men are with *Mars*. *Rose* is a woman and women are with *Venus*. Figure it out. Whose side are you on? You can't trust *Rose*."

Moon had already signed the agreement by then. *Mars* turned red with rage and promised to get even with *Venus* one day. But the cycle had begun.

Rose swore, "I will eventually pull every thorn from my side and send a man to the moon with them."

Moon laughed and said, "If you send a man to the moon then it would be a giant leap for man, but a *Rose* by any other name is still a thorny piece of work."

Rose realized the thorns wouldn't go away, so to compensate for them she spawned other flowers to grow alongside and hide her imperfections. She asked *Rainbow* to help her.

Rainbow agreed and said, "I will send each of my seven daughters to you. They will parent flowers and color them by using a single strand of their hair."

Red had already visited *Rose* earlier. *Rose* had previously asked *Rainbow* to help her. *Red* was very creative and with the help of *Rain* and *Air*, they came up with quite a few other flowers adorning Rose's thorny side.

Orange was perky and decided it would not only create flowers for *Rose* but would also create large gourds that would keep an eye on *Moon* for her. That is why on Halloween, people cut faces into their pumpkins and put a light in them. This way both *Light* and *Orange* can see if *Moon* is up to no good.

Yellow was the lightest of the sisters and Sun's favorite, but don't tell anyone. *Rainbow* tried hard not letting the other sisters know this, but sometimes secrets can't be kept. One day it finally came out, and *Yellow* was demoted to the derogatory term of *being yellow*. It was unfair, but sometimes things happen. To compensate, *Rose* talked to all the insects and told them, *"Yellow* is a sweet, loving color and is my *Honey*." She said, "Please make sure to visit her often." *Bee* was the first to agree and did so every spring saying, "I be there buzz."

Green was Rose's second favorite. *Green* knew this and was a little bit jealous and even somewhat envious. *Rose* wanted *Green* to feel wanted so she made green the most widely spread color to blanket her aside from her sister *Blue*, of course. So she told *Green* to cover all of her in sumptuous and prolific growth using all manner of trees, grasses and vines. *Green* was honored and did so immediately. *Green* and *Red* were best friends as well as sisters and could often be seen together. When *Green* and *Red* joined forces they looked brown. But *Green* was still another thorn in Rose's side. Envy is difficult to tame.

Blue was the calming sister. She would always be all wrapped up in herself while she combed her hair. *Rose* decided she would color her waters using all shades of *Blue*. *Blue* loved the idea and created a never-ending panorama. Because she loved all of her sisters, she even extended herself. She asked *Sky* if he would allow her to adorn him with her's and her sister's colors. But *Sky* was partial to *Blue*. He had always had his eye on her more so than the rest of her sisters. He told her, "Only if you dominate me, will I then surrender." Of course, *Blue* was honored to do so and immediately complied. *Sky* was elated. He just rose up higher and higher. As if he was *floating on air! Sky*, however, didn't want *Rainbow* to rule him, so he planned on introducing his son, *White Cloud* to *Blue*. He wanted *Blue* to marry his son. *Sky* allowed the other sisters to freely decorate him before *Night* came. *Sky* introduced *Blue* to *White Cloud*, and it was white clouds and blue skies from there on in. Their first child was called *Sunset*, their second *Sunrise*, their third, *Noon* and their fourth, *Dusk*. *Dusk* was the most problematic, but that is another story.

Indigo was more withdrawn and mysterious in her ways. She was older than the others, second only to *Violet*, the oldest of the known *Seven Sisters of Rainbow*. *Rainbow* just happened to be the wife of *Sun*. *Indigo* saw all the work her younger sisters had done and decided she would use her charm sparingly and be more ceremonious and subtle. She wanted to plant herself firmly on *Rose's* back and make sure she would keep coming back as a result of this. She did so by creating *Eggplant*, as well as beautiful rare flowers.

Violet, the oldest was even more secretive and subtle than *Indigo*. She told *Rainbow*, *Sky*, and *Rose* because she was the oldest, she didn't need to shine on her sister's parade. She would show herself only at the end of the day, right before *Night* (*Light's* husband) begins to spread his massive cloak. His cloak covered *Rose* up so she wouldn't get cold while *Light* visited other parts of her. *Night* often called on *Violet* to help him ease the transition. In between *Violet* found many opportunities to sprinkle her essence here, there and everywhere.

Rose was pleased with all of the flowers that *Rainbow* and her daughters provided for her. She looked at it as a way of making up for her imperfections. This was how *makeup*, the cosmetic, was conceived of. It was part of the original Cosmic *make-up* that occurred between *Rose* and *Moon*, where flower based substances were used to masks imperfections. Whether they were pockmarks or protrusions.

Moon couldn't quite get over his feelings for *Rose*. He hurled seeds at *Rose* at night. Mushrooms and carnivorous plants grew and tried to eat her up alive. They selfishly sucked the light and waters that *Rose* needed for her and her army of foliage and fauna. All was not lost because *Moon* secretly also loved *Rose*. He resented his hasty decisions and vindictive behavior. He hoped that one day he and *Rose* could come together again. Of course, he didn't let *Mars* know this. He didn't want to get him any angrier than he already was.

Rose didn't know *Moon's* true feelings and said, "*Moon*, you can see my asteroids and thorns, but you had better keep your distance. If not, I will send a few of them in your direction. That would surely wipe the smile I see off of your face."

Moon and *Rose* were originally together as were *Mars* with *Venus*. The solar system was one happy place. All things were just running around in circles spinning happily ever after until *Moon* started to have eyes for *Venus*. *Rose* enlisted *Mars*, a close male friend of hers, to go to war with *Moon*. *Rose* eventually kicked *Moon* so hard, he flew into the skies and had to live alone. *Mars* broke up with *Venus* at the same time and they became worlds onto themselves.

Moon still misses his soulmate and regularly sneaks down to visit *Rose* when she is sleeping. Go into the woods on that twenty-eighth day. The day when *Moon* is filled with *Light* and *Rose* has gone to sleep. You will see him lurking in the shadows, behind every tree, and besides every bush. *Moon's* long dark legs stretch while *Light* races to keep up with them. But *Moon* is a speedy fellow and travels stealthily. As soon as you think you've caught him then swish, away he goes, only to come another day, another month, a new moon.

CROWN HEIGHTS, THE BROOKLYN—1977

While the Lonely Mystic would go for long walks on these moonlit nights in order to try to clear his head, the visions persisted. It was also around that time he started to hear bells. The first time this happened was during a stay at a hotel in Bermuda. He awoke to the sound of bells ringing in the middle of the night. He looked all around his room and there were none to be seen. It wasn't during the holidays, so he was sure there were no reindeer roaming the halls, but it didn't hurt to check anyway. He was sure the bells were coming from the alarm clock next to his bed. He pulled out the plug and went back to sleep. At 6:00 am in the morning, he heard not only bells tingling, but also heard buzzers buzzing. (Unbeknownst to him, the alarm had a backup battery. Of course, such mystical explanations are inconsequential to the life of a lonely mystic.) As the clock wasn't plugged in, he was sure he was listening to the mystical *Music of the Spheres*. Another possibility was he needed to get a hearing aid since he had tinnitus. Since he hadn't visited Nirvana yet and since he was the consummate pragmatist, he opted for envisioning what he would look like when he needed to wear a hearing aid instead.

36 WHAT DID YOU SAY? – CAN YOU HEAR ME?

The Bay Ridge, The Brooklyn—1977
Super Sonarist
"If you hear me know,
Move your lips."

LIFE LESSONS

1 If you can't hear what you are thinking, reprogram your cell phone. The signal may be weak.
2 White noise has all the other colors of noise in it only they are just quiet at that particular moment.
3 Don't tell a used car salesman secrets.
5 If you hear yourself more clearly, then more cell phone towers were recently added in your area.

MYSTIC POWERS

39 **Sonarisism:** The ability to differentiate between different types of sounds and determine to which sound family they belong to. The ability to characterize sound by hearing it internally. The ability to synchronize lip movements to internal word processing without software updates.

The Lonely Mystic saw himself as an elderly man, with a hearing aid in place. At first, he was upset with the image. Then he realized since he spent most of his life talking to himself, it really didn't matter much anyway. After all, he didn't need hearing what he was thinking, "Right?" It was all taking place inside his head. He even went to look in a mirror while he was talking to himself to see if his lips were moving. He watched closely and started to speak.

He was amazed. They were moving. But there was a lag between what was going inside his head and what was coming out from his lips. He figured this delay was due to poor cell tower reception because his phone only displayed one bar in the bathroom. At that moment he decided to switch carriers, even though it would cost him a small fortune! He also realized he could tune into different internal conversations that were simultaneously occurring. At first, what he heard sounded like white noise. He could easily tell the difference between the different types of colored noises. There was white noise, black noise, gray noise, grey noise, and rainbow-colored noise.

Black noise was the easiest to identify. If you listened carefully and didn't hear a thing, then it was either your hearing aid battery was dead, or you were listening to black noise. If you weren't wearing a hearing aid, then it was a clear-cut case of BNS (Black Noise Syndrome). Its identifiable characteristics were simple to discern: Black noise was interwoven within white noise. It was the silence you hear before you hear anything. He spent days trying to decide what came first, black noise or white noise. It posed a similar problem as did the *Chicken and the Matzah Ball* issue. Only this time, Ostrich wasn't involved.

White noise was the sound of the wind, the sound of leaves rustling, the sound of branches dancing, and the sound of birds flying. It was the conglomeration of sound being nurtured in the womb of the universe before it emerged full born and defined. When he tuned in, it was easily recognizable after the first few times. The first time he thought he had heard white noise internally, it was really the radiator in his apartment hissing steam. The second time it was his kettle boiling. And the third time it was his toilet flushing. It wasn't until he put wax into his ears, earmuffs over them and one of his many hats over that, that he confidently felt he actually heard white noise. Until of course he realized he hadn't taken off his earphones and the radio was tuned between stations.

Finally, he had a concise, definitive, foolproof method to verify his white noise experience. He listened carefully. First, the black noise came and then the gray noise soon followed. He knew it was gray noise because it began with a very, very faint, "Yehah!" It then switched to grey noise because he could clearly hear, "Cheerio!" The noise started switching colors with crunching sounds similar to those made by biting into a red apple, followed by the swooshing sounds of a yellow banana, then the crunching sounds of a pumpkin being carved and the bristling of green leaves, succeeded by the sound of the blue jays calling to their mate. After the blue jays, purple, violet and indigo were more difficult to discern. By using the ultrasound hearing he had developed as a child (When he learned to camouflage his parent's constant bickering.) he was able to actually visualize the *colors of noise*. All the noise and colors swirled around him. And then, he heard a distinct and quite familiar *tinkling* sound. It wasn't a strong sound, and it wasn't a weak one. It was a constant and consistent drizzle. He opened his eyes and realized he had forgotten he was in the bathroom taking care of business.

He said his characteristic test phrase to himself in the mirror, "Can you see me know?" He didn't get a response, so he first turned his left ear to the mirror and said it again. *Nope, nothing.* So he turned his right ear to the mirror. *Nope, nothing.* So he turned his middle ear to the mirror. Most people don't know they even have a middle hear. But they do. They have two middle ears. Most people also don't know the expression *four eyes* was originally *four ears*, but someone got their bodily parts confused and switched the part names. After all, his four ears were tested when he said his test phrase, "Of course I can see you now." He once told his *autoaudioligist* (The guy who sold him his used car and also checks the sound of his car's engine.) about his mirror sound checks and the guy sold his test phrase to some phone company for a mint. Of course, the autoaudioligist switched *see me* with something else. Everybody has to throw their own two words into the act.

He now noticed there no longer was any lag between his lip movements and the sounds coming out. He concluded someone must have added a few cell phone towers while he was caught up in his inner reveries. It happens all the time. His thoughts transform the world. "Is that mystical or what?"

37 MUSIC OF THE SPHERES - MUSIC MAN

Poriya Elit, Israel
Ting-A-Ling
"I hear you,
Despite what you are saying."

LIFE LESSONS
1 Some theories sound good until you sound them out.
2 The difference between "news" and "history" is only minutes away.
3 The American eagle wasn't originally bald.
4 Ostrich babies know how to *Hora*.
5 Regardless of what you would like, the ringtone inside your ear can't be downloaded and replaced, even if you switch carriers.

MYSTIC POWERS
40 **Transitionist:** The ability to move through time without getting caught up in history or current events resulting in a remarkable stability amidst the flux and flow of the present during its simultaneous movement into the past and progression into the future. Knowing unequivocally where one is at any time, be it now, yesterday or tomorrow.

The Lonely Mystic realized *hearing issues* were not only *his* issues, but great personages in history also had such difficulties. Of course, one of the more famous ones immediately came to mind. He thought he even looked a little bit like him. Then he became very confused and angry with himself. He realized cell phones didn't even exist at that time in history. So his theory about signal lag inside his head went down the drain. He had wasted the $2,563.00 he had spent to switch carriers in vain! Then he became elated because not only was he having hearing and noise issues, he now started hearing celestial music in one ear; a distinct ringing sound had started.

At first, it was intermittent. Then it turned constant. It sounded just like his cell phone! He was vindicated! As he thought, all of his hearing issues *were* cell phone related. History was wrong again. This wasn't the first time history had been proven wrong. History was wrong about many things. An event being called *history* proved it was *old news*, to begin with. If it was, *new news* it would be called news, not history. Once it became *history,* it was doomed to be misinterpreted and misrepresented.

Did your friend ever tap you on the shoulder and say, "Hey, did you hear the *history* that happened today?" Of course, there is no reason to even wait for your response here since it is an obvious one. He often pondered about *how long ago an event has to have occurred before it was considered as being* history *as opposed to being considered as* news? He decided something that occurred within twenty-three hours, fifty-seven minutes and twenty-four seconds was news. Something that happened longer then that was considered as being history.

He specified that particular duration of time since he knew time was slowing down and the universe was contracting. With that in mind, he figured he was safe using his own formula for historical significance. From personal investigation, he knew the sooner something happened, the more prone the event was for interpretation. Conversely, the longer ago it happened, the less prone it was for interpretation. Most people, of course, would have taken the opposite approach. Recent events always seemed to have different people having different opinions as to what had been said. Especially family members. They often argued over what their relatives had said and meant even if it was written down or recorded.

He often heard his parents argue over what one of them had said. Pop would say, "I didn't say that."

Mom would answer, "Yes, you did, and I heard it."

"I didn't hear it."

"That's because you're deaf."

"I can't hear you."

"See what I mean."

"How can I *see* what you mean when you are talking nonsense?"

"Now you are calling me stupid?"

"I don't have to call you anything because you never listen to me anyway."

"Talking to you is like talking to the wall."

"I'd be better off talking to the wall; at least it doesn't answer me back."

"That is because it is smarter than you and knows you wouldn't understand what it had to say."

He, on the other foot, witnessed the whole conversation and had no idea what either one of them were talking about.

History was like that. Events happen, and then some guy with a chisel and a flat rock wakes up one fine day and decides he is a *historian*. He then proceeds to carve out what several people had to say about the same thing. Someone reading centuries later reinterprets it and the original intent is totally lost. The reinterpretation then becomes the historical record of the event, and everyone believes it. For instance, most people think they know who the first inhabitant of America was. Well, they are wrong!

AMERICA—CENOZOIC ERA

The first inhabitant of America was Eagle. At that time, it wasn't bald, of course. It lost its hair when the second inhabitant of America arrived. The second inhabitant of America was Ostrich, with Chicken following close behind. One day Eagle, sprouting a proud big lock of hair, was drifting around in the ethers when he looked down and saw this rump with two legs on the ground. He swooped down several times and couldn't see a head anywhere. He then swooped down to take a closer look and landed right next to the ostrich. He was so frustrated looking for Ostrich's head that he started pulling out his hair while trying to figure it out! A few of them were still left there. As he looked closer, he started seeing white balls dropping out of Ostrich's rear. It was then he decided that Ostriches' head was up its butt. But something happened that caused him to pull the last few hairs he had left out.

The balls started hatching into baby chickens that joined hands and started dancing in clockwise circles squawking, "Hora, Hora, Hora." As they danced clockwise in circles, they aged. When they reversed direction and danced counter-clockwise, they became chicks again. It was too much for him to behold, so he just flew off into the wild blue yonder ditching feathers as he raced away. That is why the American eagle is bald. That is why chicken is America's favorite poultry. And it is also why the ostrich was never able to see its way to the top of the food chain, it had its head up its…

Whenever his ears rang, he ran for the phone and said, "Halaw?" His grandmother, Hitou, the poet, had taught him that. He thought his ears ringing was due to a custom ringtone he had downloaded called *Ting-a-ling-itus*. But, much to his chagrin, no one ever answered…

38 WRONG NUMBERS – THE ANSWER MAN

The Lower East Side, The Manhattan—1977
Ring-A-Linguist
"You dialed the right number,
But it is wrong!"

LIFE LESSONS
1 Wrong numbers are right numbers gone wrong.
2 Public speaking can also be quite private.
3 Intimate lovers were once strangers.
4 Be careful of the hand you shake, you never know where it has been.

MYSTIC POWERS
41 **Intimatist:** The ability to become intimate with total strangers publicly in a private manner without having to shake their hands first.

THE LOWER EAST SIDE, THE MANHATTAN—1977

The Lonely Mystic (upper left, in the photo) started receiving one phone call after another. Somehow his number had somehow gotten mixed up with an *entertainment* website. When he answered the phone, the other party would begin speaking saying, "Hello Honey, do you have time for me?" At first, he was elated. He thought perhaps his old quest for the *piece* had somehow caught up with him now, but then he realized calls after calls were coming only from men.

Not that he had anything against men, he just preferred women. He was at a loss. He didn't know what to say to all these people who were calling him. In high school, he had had an opportunity for public speaking. He was used to dealing with the populace. He was comfortable with the masses, but here he was being tested. This was different. He had to be one-on-one with strangers. Everyone knows conversations with strangers can be one the most intimate ones you ever have since you have nothing to fear and have nothing to hide. He decided to do his best.

He answered the phone, and said, "How can I help you?"

"Well, first tell me what you can do for me?"

"I have no idea; I don't even know who you are."

"Who I am, is none of your business."

He hung up the phone because the one thing he couldn't tolerate was rudeness. Also, ever since he was a child, he was taught never to talk to strangers. Later on, in life, he realized this was the primary reason he was still single: When he first met someone he might have had a relationship with, initially, they were strangers. Since they were strangers, he wouldn't have entered into a conversation with them even if such had had the possibility of leading to friendship. This single thought kept him lonely all these years.

If wasn't until he eventually met someone who began the conversation with "Hi, I know we are going to become great friends," that he was able to enter the relationship of his life. They began as friends. She was the one destined for him. From the very first moment, that soulmate was never a stranger to him. She gave him a big hug right from the start. Strangers don't do that. They usually shake hands.

He was greatly disturbed by handshaking. *How do I know where that hand was a moment or an hour ago? Perhaps the person was a picker, or worse! How do I know they had washed their hands recently? Perhaps the bathroom's water faucet was broken?* He didn't want to pick up any souvenirs from people he didn't know. He got around shaking hands by telling people who offered their hands to him by saying, "Sorry, I'm not a palm reader, but I can recommend one to you if you like." People would just chuckle and put their dirty hands back into their pockets where they belonged in the first place. Of course, he felt very comfortable talking to his best friends, the dead ones, and Irving and Shirley. He also didn't consider people who he met in the local tub to be strangers. *How could they be?* They were in the same place as him. If they were strangers, they would be in some strange place. "Right?"

39 CAN YOU SEE ME NOW? – SERIOUS DUDE

Osaka, Japan
Serious Dude, the Wholeagraphist
"Don't get stuck on me."

LIFE LESSONS
1 Looks can be deceiving to the looker, especially if the "looke" is trained in Wholeagraphy.
2 If you are what you eat and you art what you are, then all of us defecate masterpieces.
3 If "non" is a combination of "no" and "on" then this explains why saying, "No" can be a turn on.
4 Save your paper straw sleeves you never know when you might need to let one rip.

MYSTIC POWERS
42 **Wholeagraphy:** The ability to project aspects of your being as a whole on yourself causing you to believe you are someone other than who you are until you realize although before you weren't you, now you are who you were to begin with. This ability is often accompanied by the desire to change your appearance on a daily basis with different outfits and accouterments.

The Lonely Mystic decided to muster up his most serious face. As you have and will see, he has many faces. In mystic parlance, the technique for appearing different to others is called *masking*. With a master of this technique, as he was, one could call up prior or future lives and wholeagraphically project their image upon oneself. It will most probably not be until quite later in the chronicles of his life for him to reveal what he looks like in this life. By not doing so now, his intent isn't to keep the reader in suspense. Far-be-it for him to want to do so. But rather, he isn't photogenic and he has yet to find a true and accurate representation of what he looks like; both inside and out. Meanwhile, the reader is being introduced to the myriad masked selves' he has and will be and is getting glimpses of his multi-dimensional being. Of course, his imagination is also considered as a part of his being and following suit, not all images are actually physical representations of him. But as the sage once said, and that sage being, of course, none other than the late great Zen Ben Kohan: "You Art What You Are." *So who's to say what is or isn't?*

The distinction between fiction and nonfiction is held in the hands of two "n"s and an "o." Now "non" is "no" backward and forward. This means any which way you look at the word it is confusing, to begin with. Matter of fact, the person who invented the word *nonfiction* stole it from the word *fiction*. Fiction came first. If fiction came first, it must have been true. Everyone knows religious works came before other works and no one is going to take the position they are untrue, *are they?* "Are you?" So, if they are true, then to call them nonfiction would be putting the apple before the cart. Everyone knows, horses like their apples in their mouth and not in their carts. If they were in their carts, how could they eat them?

So now that we straightened that out, he visited his magic bathroom mirror again. He checked his cell phone for bars and tested his perceptions once more by saying, "Can you see me now?" He always expected the mirror to answer back, "Yes." But it never did. With his cell phone propped close to his ear, he waited for the ringing to begin again. He waited, and waited, and waited, and waited. Nothing. No calls. No ringing. Nothing.

He had heard if you wait long enough, all things return to the same place. He decided to try that. Five minutes later, he figured he had given it his best shot. He looked at his phone. "No power." His battery had run down. He quickly plugged it in. For some mystical reason, the ringing in his ear and from the phone had ceased.

He began thinking about all the other things in his life that once worked and then stopped or had occurred and then ceased. He became sad over having lost his baby teeth. He loved his baby teeth. After all, they were with him since he was a baby. Then he cried about losing the peach fuzz on his face and the day he lost his innocence. He had bought some at the local *innocence* store. He preferred the sticks to the cones. It was a personal preference. He had purchased them with some of the pennies in his penny collection and walked out of the store with them in a paper bag. At that time, the convenience grocery stores didn't introduce plastic bags to the states yet. Up until then, everyone stilled used paper bags. Well, his paper bag was missing one corner on the bottom because the clerks had a spitball fight with it the night before.

Spitball was the mother of paintball. Spitball was a Zen discipline. It was the offshoot of the ancient art of *Origumyou*. Origumyou was a technique where you put gum on your opponent's shoe. Doing so caused him to pause as he tried extricating himself from your devious tricky, sticky mess. During his moment of hesitation and disoriented distraction, you would then slam him with a nice juicy wet spitball. This was delivered through the bowels of your trusty malted milk straw. They were the fat ones. No regular soda straws for the trained spitball enthusiast, only *malted milkers* were the preferred method of delivery and assault.

Of course, the stalked *Origummer* was devastated by the attack and often resulted to religious outbursts and physiological exclamations of retaliation and hostility. The trained *Spitballist* was well prepared for these retaliations and recited holy ritualistic mantras to divert the psychic energies being directed toward them as a result of the hostile's poor gamesmanship. Although the mantra has been kept secret for countless numbers of years, he obtained permission from the *Mantraistist* (The master who decides the fate of mantras and it is revealed here, for you now, for the very first time.) to use as you so choose. Be forewarned it is truly potent and powerful, so please use it sparingly or your assailant will be reduced to tears.

Of course, it is debatable as to whether the tears thus produced are tears of laughter or tears of fear. The fine line delineation of the inherent stimulant nature of the tear ducts is yet to be determined. Current consensus is: If the assailant is crying and at the same time producing belly laughs then he wasn't adversely affected by the mantra. Consequently, if the reverse occurred, the practitioner would have to resort to *Plan B*, which is *run like all*...well, you know. Here is the mantra. Please guard it and keep it safe.

"Chuahhhhhhhhhhhhhhhh." It has to be pronounced with a vibrating throaty sound.

Of course, it is a translation of an ancient and archaic language so some of it has been lost in the transliteration. As he walked out of the store the sticks of innocence fell out of the bag. He never realized it until he got back home and wanted to light up. He got really upset.

After he had lost his innocence, he also lost his car. He didn't really lose it, but the police thought he did. He remembered parking it in front of his house one night. When he woke up the next morning, he noticed it was gone. When he reported it to the police the next day, they told him to let them know if he ever found it again. Needless to say, he figured *the person who stole his baby teeth, his peach fuzz and his innocence also took his car.* He hoped one day all of these, as well as his other prized possessions, the ones that were in the trunk of his beloved misplaced car, would eventually be found. If you happen to see an electric blue 1967 coupe parked somewhere, immediately call the police and tell them it was stolen. This way they will return it to him.

While he was caught up in his reveries, he remembered all the ringing from the prior day. He was glad it had ceased. He started wondering again, *why are so many men calling me?* He thought *was the universe was trying to send me a message? Perhaps it was bad hairma?* He remembered an incident of *hairma* that had occurred earlier on in his life. Hairma was different from *swarma*. It was a close cousin and related, but not quite the same. Swarma was the general way of things. Hairma, well, that only affected you above the neck follicles.

His mother always complained of her *bad her daze*. He also had a *bad her daze* with Mom once.

40 BAD HAIRMA - UNSURE GUY

Usacka, The Former USSR
Do D Dude
Master of Movements
"Are there any side effects?"

LIFE LESSONS
1 Some medical procedures have minor side effects.
2 A man of few words often says very little.
3 Not everything that gets advertised is good for your health even if they tell you it is.
4 Before you go to the bathroom, ask yourself: "Do I really have to go or is someone making me leave?"

MYSTIC POWERS
43 **Celluhairity:** The ability to regenerate cells without thinking about doing so. Often accompanied by sadness over the departed cells having left in order for the new ones to replace them. The mourning process varies, but with 3% of the population it may linger forever and manifest various other symptoms. Consult your medical help professional if you are experiencing, severe uncontrollable fits of laughter and profuse and excessive tear duct emanations prompted by reading this.

CANARSIE, THE BROOKLYN—1971

The Lonely Mystic recollected an incident that happened when he first started losing his hair: An incident that occurred prior to his Banal treatments in Painstilvaniya. His mom had recommended him to a specialist. He reluctantly went to the doctor, who examined him and said, "If you would be willing to let yourself be injected with female hormones, then you could eventually grow all of your hair back once more."

"Would there be any *side effects*?" He shuddered at the sound of the word.

"Only one."

The Lonely Mystic became elated. "What?" He was a man of few words.

"You will become more *feminine*."

This was not the sexual preference he preferred. Not that there was anything wrong with it, but he preferred to stay persuaded as he already was. Not that he had much opportunity to persuade the opposite sex to come his way anyway.

The side effects of the drugs instantly reminded him of some of the ads he saw on TV. He was amazed how someone would even think of taking some of those medications. Up front you were told by taking them you may increase your risk for heart disease, cancer, limbs falling off, loss of sight, becoming accident prone, bone loss, organ failure and most importantly, the drug only works on a percentage of the population. He thought *who in their right mind would take a chance on them being that percentage of the population who might be helped by the drug when such a high percentage of the population could suffer the side effects if they take the drug?* He was convinced the ads were hypnotic in nature. *They must have been filled with subliminal advertising for another product, which had nothing to do with the drug that was being advertised.*

    He noticed frequently after one of those commercials, he had to make use of the facilities. He was convinced those commercials had a subliminal message put there by some toilet paper manufacturers to induce you to take a dump. He was no fool. No one was going to kick the business out of him unless he wanted it to leave. From then on, when the commercials came on, he left for the bathroom: He went the exact moment they started and never waited until they ended. He was his own man, made up his own mind and ran according to his own schedule.

    He couldn't even pronounce the names of the drugs that were being advertised. *What did those companies think of when they named their drugs? Did they figure only people with Dumb-'N-Dumber (DND) degrees would purchase and remember their names?* Well, he didn't have a Dumb-'N-Dumber degree, and for sure he couldn't remember the names, let alone want to use any unnatural substances. He was a *naturalist*. For him, only things that grew and were harvested were going to be used as medical remedies. Substances that were manufactured in a psycholatron were not considered as being *natural*. No one was going to run rings around him. He thanked the doctor and promptly headed back home.

    Although he wasn't letting anyone stick pins into his butt, he decided to take the information home to his parents, this way as a family; they could come to a decision together. He wanted additional input in the rare circumstance he was viewing the information incorrectly. He had an open mind ever since he fell off his bicycle and landed on his chin, the injury never healed completely.

    Upon his return home, his Mom, who only spoke broken English then, asked him what the doctor had said. He informed her verbatim of the doctor's prognosis. She became elated. At the time, she understood *gay* to mean *happy*; she as yet had had no knowledge of the words other meaning. So she told her son, "Great, you will become gay, I will become gay and your father will become gay! Oh, we will all be so happy!" Grandmother Hitou and Grandfather Zen Ben, who were also present, started to applaud! Zen Ben blew smoke rings in the air. This was his signature *mystical* act. His grandmother circled his grandfather as he blew rings. He was quite happy eating the jelly rings his mother had taken out of the fridge. They were always there as treats for a celebration. And if the event called for a real *hurrah*, Mom broke out the chocolate covered donuts that were also in the fridge.

His mother had a way with words. Idiomatic expressions were common to those indigenous to a country. For immigrants, they were perhaps the hardest things to learn. As a project for his fourth grade English class, he compiled a listing of her favorite idioms.

For her *Heads up, tails down* was the way dogs walked in a dog show.

Open-and-shut was her refrigerator rule. Of course, she never used the name of the type of product she was speaking about like the *refrigerator*; she always used the maker of the product she was describing.

But the most entertaining element of her conversational abilities was the ingenious way she juxtaposed several idioms on top of one another and melded them any which way; sideways, up or down.

Chip on the shoulder became *if you have a chip on your shoulder, then wash it immediately, since chocolate stains.*

She was always full of good advice whether you wanted to hear it or not. *A drop in the bucket* was what she used when someone died. Of course, you know what she meant.

A penny saved is a penny earned somehow got mixed up with *penny wise, pound foolish*. They both became *if you're not wise, then you are foolish and you will only earn pennies.*

Be careful, if you bite off more than you can chew, you may bite off your tongue was another favorite.

She didn't speak French, so she often said, "Excuse my Polish."

A bird in the hand is worth two in the bush became, *if you have a bird in your hand, then cook your goose.*

A *French kiss* became *hit and miss*, she figured the two people couldn't' find each other's lips and had to use their tongues to guide them.

Funny Farm became the name for her bungalow colony since it was a farm and she had lots of fun there. She was bad at remembering names. Just like her son.

She mixed up *get over it* with *get on with it* quite often.

A leopard doesn't have stripes, replaced *a leopard can't change his spots.*

She often described her poker-playing husband as a *go for a smoke man* instead of *go for broke*.

A dime a dozen was always confusing to her because she was excellent at math and knew a dozen was twelve and a dime was ten.

Go out of the way became *get out; I'll do it my way.*

Go the extra mile became *go out in style.*

Great minds think alike became, *eight minds think better than none.*

She inherited her idiomatic interpretations from her Zen father and poetic mom.

Creative spelling ran rampant in his family. There wasn't a word she couldn't spell creatively in her own manner or an expression she couldn't interpret. On a lucky day, you might find he even spelled a word or used a hermetic expression correctly.

41 WHAT A BOD! – THE VISIBLE MAN

Okeechobee Foreverglades, Florida
BaH D, The Visible Man
"I see right through you!"

LIFE LESSONS
1 Check your cereal for female hormones.
2 Simon Says was invented by a *Saydhis*.
3 Before you meet yourself halfway, get directions first.
4 If your T-Shirt is too big, shrink it before it becomes a P-Shirt.
5 Check your bathroom mirror often and make sure it is you. If it isn't then put on your sunglasses so whoever is in there won't be able recognize you.

MYSTIC POWERS
44 **Hypergliseemenu:** The ability to overcome addictions by gliding past them. The ability to see yourself and others simultaneously even when not looking. The ability to see sweets on a menu and not eat them.

Of course, The Lonely Mystic decided not to inject himself with any hormones, this time. He was very careful of what he pumped into his vessel. Only the finest ingredients would go into making him, the *him* that he was. No more *soda pop* for him. Well, he couldn't even always stick to his own plan. He thought he had gotten over that addiction when he was younger. He had to check himself into a halfway house for sugar addicts. Their treatments were quite easy, although the cost of enrollment was quite high. Once he got in, they told him the secret to overcoming his sugar addiction was to use the *Halfway Method* of curing your cravings.

During orientation, he asked them, "What is your secret to curing my addiction?"

They told him, "You can buy absolutely anything you are attracted to and want."

He became jubilant but was a bit confused as to how that would help him. "How would that help my addiction? That is how I'm currently dealing with it."

They responded, "The trick is even though you buy anything you want to eat, you have to meet it halfway, afterward."

He knew he was bad with directions and started to have an anxiety attack right there on the spot. He pulled out the bottle of soda pop he always kept in his back pocket.

They grabbed it from him and told him, "Meet it half way!"

He thought he had enrolled in an insane asylum instead of a sugar addiction cure facility. He said, "OK. What does that mean?"

They said, "By buying into your addiction you did your part of meeting it halfway, now do the other part and don't destroy the good you just did. Don't follow through."

This was a tough one for him because he was good at everything he did. He never did things half-ashed. It was always the *Full Disclosure* for him. So now they were asking him to *give up the goose* and *Buy But Not Try?* He finally understood what that logo on the *P-shirt* they had given him meant. He called it a P-Shirt because they only had the XXX-Large size. It was way too big for him. Then when he went to the bathroom... Well, you get the picture. The back of the P-shirt had another logo. It read, "Just because you buy, you don't have to try. Free Session, low introductory price." He thought *these cryptic, mystic sayings were more difficult to comprehend than the tenets of the Polyanderists I had encountered in Asia years ago.* He was no fool. He took the P-Shirt off and put it on backward-facing forward. Now no one was going to put anything over on him.

As soon as he did, a policeman came over and handed him a summons for pandering. The policeman said, "*Male* prostitutes are not as common as the other kind, but still, you are advertising your services in public. That clearly is a public offense. You ought to be ashamed of putting yourself up for sale and offering samples to boot." He ripped the P-shirt off his back and walked home semi-naked.

Because of the strong sun, he caught a wicked sunburn on his back. It was the middle of August. When he walked by the swamp near his home, a mosquito bit him. It was at that very moment he decided not to inject himself with those hormones. He had always disliked being bit by mosquitoes and needles reminded him of that. He thought *who in their right mind would volunteer to get mosquitoes bites on a regular basis? The itching alone would drive me crazy!* He opted for wigs instead. *With wigs, I could be a different me whenever I wanted to be. With real hair, I was limited to only one type of haircut at a time.* After this realization, he shaved his head completely and went totally bald. Once again he started a new trend that reached as far east as the monks in Asia. He had always had the capability of influencing the present, the future, and the past, but not necessarily in that order.

He attributed his visionary abilities to the sunglasses he liked to wear. The glasses had a special mirror finish. He figured *people would want to come over to me and make friends since they could see themselves in the mirrors.* Everyone knows people like to see their own reflections. *It's not like there is a picture of someone else over your bathroom sink.* "Right?" *No. It's an image of you.* He could tell people weren't looking at him when they spoke to him. When he asked them, "Why?" They would say, "Because we can't see you anyway." He thought about it, and it made lots of sense. So he decided to have a pair of sunglasses with special "see-through" mirrors made. This way he could see-through whoever approached him. He had a heightened sense of perception, and this would accentuate it. *With these special specs, I could see-through anyone who wasn't transparent. If they wanted to see me, well, they could always ask to borrow my sunglasses.* "Right?"

42 SALON – THE MECHANICS OF GENEALOGY

Wall Street, New York City, NY—1974
Wall Street Dude and his Gene Pool
"Don't screw with me,
Or I'll throw you into my gene pool."

LIFE LESSONS
1 A permanent resident never leaves their home.
2 If words come out of your mouth by themselves, switch cell phone carriers.
3 Make sure your gene pool is clean, or your future descendants will have to clean it for you.
4 Always carry a spare screw. You never know when you may have a screw loose.
5 Don't cut your hair too short or it may never grow back.
5 Only let your Optometrist look deeply into your eyes or they may see you lost your shirt.

MYSTIC POWERS
45 **Aquaniscience:** The ability to swim around in your own pool, keep it clean and replace any loose screws that may pop out unexpectedly. Accompanied by the ability to see into windows and resist buying what is there. It's usually hereditary.

WALL STREET, NEW YORK CITY, NEW YORK—1974

After having shaved his head, The Lonely Mystic did the next logical thing; he decided to open up a Hair Salon. But finding the perfect location for it was a tough one. Still living in New York City for the moment, he figured the city would be a prime location for his new financial venture. He didn't consider himself a permanent resident of New York City. He often flew to other states and countries. He knew permanent residents reside there permanently. They never ever leave even once. The meaning of *permanence* was a vivid member of his knowledge base. Remember, he was a philosopher, a mystic, and primarily a linguist. He was an expert at moving his tongue and making sounds, although at times they weren't in sync with his internal thought process'. He knew this to be a common minor affliction. He had often heard people say, "How did that come out of my mouth?" He would go over to them and ask them who their cell phone provider was. Much to his chagrin, he was never able to track down this malady to a specific company. He thought *perhaps it was a genetic defect?*

From his visit with the genealogist, he knew certain people had certain predilections to certain things as a result of one or perhaps even more of their ancestors not having cleaned their pool. He was happy to know one of his ancestors was rich enough to have owned a pool. But when the Genealogist said, "It was a common gene pool," that feeling went away. He now figured his ancestors never cleaned the *Mikva*. Of course, you know a Mikva is a communal pool where people communally pool together. It was quite possible all the poolers pooled and never had cleaned up after having pooled themselves.

He then asked the Genealogist, "How could a dirty ancestor who never cleaned up after themselves possibly have an effect on me?"

The Genealogist answered, "That you are even asking this very question is proof enough there is a screw loose somewhere in your gene pool."

Now that *really* concerned him. He had heard about how a dam had burst open and how a guy with his first name stuck his weenie in there to plug it up. The guy had yelled so loudly about there being a hole in the wall, a whole country, *Hollarland* was named after him. He was afraid one of his ancestors saw a loose screw had fallen out in the Mikva. Then they found the hole and courageously put their weenie in there plugging it up. All that water, for sure, would have altered the genetic structure of his *communal pool*. Everyone knows what water does to your skin. This definitely explained why even at the young age of only ninety-five, Grandma Hitou's face looked so shriveled up.

But the upside to this (There was always an upside otherwise they couldn't say there was a downside.) was, a courageous gene was floating around somewhere in that pool. But even more importantly, there was ingenuity, self-sacrifice, dedication to humanity, and an endurance swimmer, swimming around somewhere in there too. He was proud to be swimming in such a historical and *tsunamic* body of screwed up genes. He wondered if that loose screw was ever handed down from generation to generation. He made a mental note to ask his parents if they ever received a screw that might have been an heirloom.

But this then brought up other questions because now he didn't know if the screw was loose from his father's side or his mother's side. He thought deeply and realized it must be from his father's side because of several reasons:

One, his mother can't swim.

Two, only his father had the weenie.

Three, if his father's ancestors didn't reproduce he would never have been born because men need to reproduce, whereas women just give birth on their own.

Four, his mother always asked his father, "Do you have a screw loose up there?" His father would respond, "Go screw it yourself."

He wondered *where is up there? When I was a child, my home didn't have an attic? Was she referring to Heaven? Is Heaven made up of loose screws?*

His mother would answer back, "Why not, I do everything by myself anyway." His mother was excellent at fixing things. His father always kept hundreds of screws in the garage. They were all sizes and shapes. He thought *was that a sign?*

He once asked his father, who was an excellent mechanic, "Pop, why do you have so many screws lying around?"

His father would smile and say, "Son, you never know when you lose a screw and have to replace it. It could fall out if it was loose."

When he remembered these words, it was like an epiphany to him. He was right! It was from his father's side. What cinched it was he remembered his mother had once told his father to buy a pool and put it up in their backyard. When his father did so and when it was almost completely assembled, it was then they discovered *one screw was missing*. His pop told him to hold up the pool while he went to the garage to search for its replacement.

His father must have forgotten because it took Pop three hours to come back. Meanwhile, he was inside the pool, which was now filled with water because there was a freak thunderstorm and torrential rains. When his father eventually came back with his mother at his side, they both asked him, (in unison) "What happened?"

He responded, "Pop, I lost a screw and had to hold up the walls. Even my weenie is shriveled up from all the cold water." He shivered and shuddered.

His mom quickly retorted to Pop, "It looks like losing a screw runs in your family; your son must have caught it from you."

He now knew genetics was hereditary and history repeats itself no matter how hard you try to hold it up. He swore to himself never to visit Hollarland or to screw around again, especially in a pool. He did notice when he went swimming in a communal pool he emerged with knowledge and abilities he hadn't had before. Somehow the waters triggered ancestral and genetic remembrances. Later on, his father's mechanical skills got translated into him becoming an excellent Quantum Mechanic. He was able to fix things in the quantum world similar to how Mom and

Pop were able to fix things in the physical one. The apple didn't fall too far from the tree. (It's always about an apple. "Isn't it?") He even thought of opening up a repair shop called. *Invisible Mechanics*: *We quantumly fix the things you can't see, but you know when they are repaired.* Heredity is a potent force.

His thoughts swam back to his sunglasses store. After careful deliberation and extensive research, he decided the perfect place for a salon would be on Wall Street. He thought *people were always concerned with ups and downs and ins and outs there. I know people would welcome the opportunity to come into my shop, have me shave their heads and then put a wig on them too!* His reasoning was as follows: *Since everyone I know has lost their shirt in the market, they wouldn't want to spend money on a haircut. They were used to walking around naked because they were penniless. Shaving their heads would match the rest of their outfits. Being penniless, they couldn't afford haircuts, so shaving their heads would also save them money. They only needed doing it once because everyone knows: If you shave your head, your hair never grows back.* His mom had told him that when he was young. Even then he had wanted to do it. He was always ahead of his time. But most importantly, wearing a wig would allow them to go around incognito. This was a necessity for them. All the people who were after them because of having had their life savings destroyed, wouldn't be able to recognize them with one on.

He also opened a sunglasses store right next to the salon. *They could always come to the sunglasses store to buy sunglasses so no one would be able to look deeply into their eyes.* He knew *eyes were windows to the soul*. He logically figured *if you put shades over the windows, then people wouldn't know who you are, or for that matter, what amount of money you had lost.* He was not only fashionable but was also a really deep thinker too!

43 SUNGLASSES – ICMEUCUWECUS

The Internet, Anywhere, USA
ICMEUCUWECUS Dude
"Even if you run away from me,
I will still be here."

LIFE LESSONS
1 Walking is fast becoming an obsolete means of locomotion.
2 No matter how fast you run, you still have to walk home.
3 Dead animals make interesting souvenirs.
4 Be careful about whom you send $10,000.00 checks to.
5 Just because it says it's real doesn't mean it is.
6 The good thing about not having any money is no one can steal any more from you.
7 There is no official *Post Office Lottery*.

MYSTIC POWERS
46 **Locomotion:** The ability to withstand the rampant craziness about running in place or in the streets half-naked. Accompanied by an innate sense not to wrap oneself in a foil blanket on a cold day and think it will keep you warm. Also the ability not to go *loco* when hailing a cab and they don't stop.

The Lonely Mystic knew people would need to take taxis to get to his sunglasses store. Taxis were the best way to get there, since not too many people walked to shops anymore. People preferred the Zen approach: Either they ran or they were conveyed in some manner. The *Middle Way*, that of walking was fast becoming an obsolete discipline. Scooters, bicycles, mopeds, uni-pods, and omni-pods were replacing the once ancient and time-honored means to have an opportunity to commune with nature while traveling. Now, people communed with their phones instead.

The preferred way of walking was *The Sound of Walking and Going Nowhere Fast*. This was also known as, *The Way of the Walker*. It was a form of meditation that had simultaneously swept the country and boosted the economy. Hundreds of thousands of meditation machines were sold and installed in homes and gyms. *The Way of the Walker* consisted of two state of the art devices, namely a track machine and a listening device. The adherent religiously put the listening devices into his or her ears and then mounted a treadmill. He called adherents of this discipline, *Mill People*. They then proceeded to go nowhere fast or slowly. Their speed was dependent upon their degree of attainment coupled with their ability to do nothing while shedding the excess *swarma* they had accumulated. Of course, our current society called it *fat*.

Some adherents were so fanatic about their devotions they ran from their homes daily; running away from their issues. After several miles of escape, they would decide to return. This became so rampant several movements under various banners started. Annually people congregated and ran away in unison. The fastest of the bunch was awarded foil blankets and medallions. After the annual devotions ended, everyone took taxis back to their homes, since they were exhausted from their great escape run.

Seeing the future, The Lonely Mystic enrolled in a mail order school to procure a Taxidermist license for his store. This way he could call a cab for his clientele after they purchased sunglasses from him. In a brilliant marketing ploy, he figured he could also sell the same customer the dead animals, which were lying on the road of their run, as a souvenir. Of course, he would have to stuff them first. Stuffed *flying rats* and *ground birds* would make excellent additions to any *Way of the Walker* home.

He was an excellent buyer, a skill he learned in Asia. He roamed the streets of the city buying sunglasses from the street vendors and displayed them proudly in his store. When there weren't any customers in either of his two shops, he studied taxidermy online.

Being multi-dimensional and ambidextrous, he was able to juggle being in both stores at the same time. But he started having concerns about the longevity of his stores. After being opened for one month, he began to wonder why no one was frequenting his establishments. However, he was quite excited, since he had just received his taxidermy diploma from the online school. Upon enrollment, they instructed him to mail them all of his personal information along with a check for $10,000.00. Upon completion of the course, they would promptly mail him a diploma. With high hopes and sustained excitement, he mailed them the money and his information.

He expected lots of supplies to start arriving at his doorstep because he noticed his credit card was racking up charges. From the total of the charges, he thought an arsenal of supplies would arrive. He didn't mind reaching the

$25,000.00 limit his card had because he knew taxidermy would eventually pay for itself in the long run. He knew only wealthy people had animals hanging from their walls. The poor ones had animal parts hanging from their mirrors in the car. He himself had a genuine, authentic and real *Made in China* rabbit's foot dangling from his mirror.

The supplies of course never came. When he tried contacting the *mail order school*, he found them to be *out of order*. He eventually contacted the authorities about his experience, and they told him to be more prudent as to whom he gave his information to in the future. He felt better about his experience after he heard that advice. At least now he could rest assured his future wouldn't hold the same ramifications for him as did his past, He already paid for his taxidermy license and therefore there wouldn't be any need to give anyone else his personal information. He learned from his mistakes, no matter how costly they were.

The very same day he received an *official letter* from the US postal service. It stated they were holding a package for him. They needed to verify all his bank accounts, credit cards, birth date and social security number before they told him where to retrieve the package. He had won the *Official Post Office Lottery!* He always had thought he would win the lottery. He knew the winners were notified by mail, so he had hopes this was going to be that long sought after notice. He eagerly sent all the required information to the address requesting it. It wasn't until all his accounts were wiped clean he realized he had never even entered the lottery. The letter and package couldn't have been from them. He would have taken the train down to the local post office to ask them, but every single penny he ever had had been wiped out. He was finally able to breathe clearly and freely without any pressure to pay any of his outstanding bills, for a very simple reason: Namely, he was broke.

44 TAXIDERMIST - UNFORESEEN EVENTS

Midtown, Manhattan
The Taxidermist
"If you are all stuffed up,
I can sell you."

LIFE LESSONS

1 Don't talk to strangers carrying loaded guns.
2 Don't accept gifts from people you don't know.
3 Banks don't allow loaded guns at teller windows.
4 If you are going to withdraw some money from a bank, make sure it is yours, to begin with.
5 In NYC, you need a degree in order to know how to hail a cab or how to navigate around Broadway if you are driving.
6 When you are under a tree and hear laughter, it must be squirrels. If there are no squirrels up there, then you are short an acorn.

MYSTIC POWERS

47 **Depositionist:** The ability to position yourself in the right place at the right time. To know how to navigate in trying times with or without college training. To know when to get out of a moving vehicle. To know when to line up your ducks, whether they are dead or alive.

MIDTOWN MANHATTAN

The Lonely Mystic borrowed some money from Mom to set up his taxidermist shop right next to his salon and sunglasses store. He then applied for a gun license. As soon as he walked out of the licensing office, someone came up to him. They stuck a gun in his back and whispered, "Give me all of your money."

He responded, "I've just been ripped off, they drained all my accounts and left me penniless."

The robber had pity on him and gave him his gun. The robber figured The Lonely Mystic needed it more than he did. Besides, the robber had another one tucked in under his belt. The robber said, "Here. Why don't you go *deposit* this in the bank? There's lots of extra cash in there."

Since he had a gun license, he was legally allowed to carry a gun. He thought *how propitious the universe was for providing for me so expeditiously.*

He didn't know what to do with the gun. He walked into the bank and figured he would put it into his safety deposit box for safekeeping. He had always read guns should be kept under lock and key when they aren't being used. The teller saw the gun and immediately put all her money into her own shopping bag for him. While the teller was stuffing her bag, he was daydreaming and looking around at the cameras in the bank. He smiled and made faces so the security company technicians would have a good laugh and be unbored. He always thought about the average Joe and how he could make their life more of a fun-filled one.

He figured somehow the bank had heard about his mail-order fiasco. He hoped she was busy putting some of the gifts banks give out into a shopping bag for him. Being the respectful person that he was, he would never rush the teller. *Perhaps she was sorting her dirty laundry under the counter.* He did notice she was profusely perspiring. *Maybe she had a bad cold?* He knew banks give customers gifts all the time. Since he was a long-term customer of the bank, his account had now been open for thirteen days; he figured he was due for a gift, even though all of his funds were stolen. Thirteen may have been unlucky for some people, but not for him. He pointed the gun at her and asked her, "What free gift am I going to get today?" He couldn't wait to open it. He asked her, "Where can I unload my gun for safe deposit?"

She whimpered out, "Please don't unload it at me; we don't allow guns in the bank." She handed him her shopping bag.

He was disappointed.

She fainted.

He started leaving the bank with his bag. The guard at the door saw he was a hunter because he was wearing his gun tucked into his belt and had a big hat on. He asked the guard, "Kind sir, can you please get the door for me. This bag is quite heavy, and I have both my hands occupied." Since the teller had fainted before she was able to hit the alarm button, no one knew he was walking out of the bank with stolen cash.

The guard, a two-time war veteran (The Bronx Gangrene Wars and The Brooklyn Used Car Wars.) was more than happy to be of assistance to our hero. He opened the door gladly and said, "Have a nice day. Thanks for banking with us!"

He was so happy he had met a nice lady and a nice man. It was the small things in life that made a difference to him. Now if he only had some cash, he would be able to afford a taxi and a real diploma. Everyone knows you really need a diploma to find a cab in New York City. At the time, he didn't know he had a bag filled with money. However, he was to find out soon enough.

Taxidermy taught him never to wave for a cab that had its light on. Those cabs are empty and broken, otherwise, the light would be off and the cab full. However, he was at a loss since the full ones also never stopped. He knew he should have enrolled in an Ivy Leaf campus or college instead of a rinky-dink mail-order university. There he would have gotten his degree. He ought to have known better, but it was his first mail-order purchase and the ad in the tabloid distinctly said: "We are an approved business." They listed a whole host of testimonials from people like Dave, Susan, Betty, Paul, and Noah. He thought *I knew all of these people from The Gym.*

He showered with those three guys and got rejected by the two women. He figured *if they had endorsed the site, then they could be trusted since they weren't exactly strangers to me.* He did wonder *why didn't the ad mention their last names? But then again, I didn't know their last names also. Maybe they didn't have any? If they did, then both the tabloid and I would have known them.* "Right?"

A taxi came right up to him. As soon as he got in, he heard hoards of police sirens in the distance. He said to himself, "Sounds like there was a robbery. I hope they catch the thief!"

The cabbie turned to him and said, "Brother, *we must get outs of here in a fast.* Otherwise, we will be *struck* in traffic forever."

He didn't recognize the *cabbie, why is he calling me brother? I'm sure he isn't at all related to me?* He told him, "Step on it." The cabbie tore *asinus* out of there.

The guard from the bank ran out and started firing random shots into the air. The guard was quite old and was lucky he hadn't shot himself. The bullets went straight up and hit some flying ducks who were minding their own business. The cabbie just happened to drive right underneath three of them. The ducks landed on the hood of his cab.

The Lonely Mystic yelled, "Stop. We have to save the ducks!"

The cabbie stopped dead in his tracks. He said, "They are already saved. They are dead."

"No. I have to save them. I can make them immortal!"

Now the cabbie was getting worried. He asked him, "Are you some kind of *Animal Salvationist?*"

The Lonely Mystic didn't know it, but he got into the cab of a nuclear physicist who had graduated from *Harvhood University*. This Ph.D. was out of work because squirrels had gotten into the nuclear reactor he was in charge of and had eaten up all the wiring. The ARLFTPONDTA, (Animal Rights League for Prevention of Nuclear Damage to Animals) filed petitions against the physicist for cruelty and failure to secure a nuclear facility so squirrels couldn't hide their nuts in the reactor. Of course, this was the first case of a nutty reactor in the USA. No one had ever heard of atomic nut butter before. Nonetheless, the physicist was a scapegoat and was promptly fired on Ground Hog's Day.

He was barred from working at any nuclear facility again and was thereafter known as *A Corny Guy*. Of course, the physicist thought everyone else was short an acorn and he had gotten a bum rap. Now the only other thing he was equipped to do was drive a cab in the city. You not only needed a degree to hail a cab there, but you also needed one to know how to drive around Broadway after all the pedestrian mall changes had been made.

The cabbie had a real thing for animals, but being the intelligent man he was, he moved passed his hatred for them and stopped the cab. This allowed The Lonely Mystic to get out and collect the three ducks that were now on the hood of the car. No sooner had The Lonely Mystic gotten out of the car and collected the ducks, when a huge truck rear-ended the cab. The cab had swerved not to hit a stray dog, which just happened to be crossing the street, looking for a fire hydrant.

The truck hit the cab, and the cab went spinning around and around and landed in the window of a pet store. The glass window in the pet store broke and a cage was ripped open. All of a sudden you could see dozens of animals fleeing from the pet shop. There were birds, gerbils, hamsters, dogs, cats, Shetland ponies, rabbits, a baby alligator and one ostrich holding some matzah balls? The cabbie managed to get out of the cab. If one listened very closely, (He was mumbling.) one could hear him say, "It's my fault for going against my own better judgment. I should have known better. You never ever stop dead for a dead duck."

The cabbie shouldn't have looked up because there on the branch of the tree directly above him were a family of squirrels laughing their nuts off. He was quite unlucky that day, so he did look up. But sometimes in life, we do things that shouldn't have been done. We realize it only after it's done. By then, however, they can't be undone. He recognized them immediately. Done, done, and done. Again. They were the very same ones that undid him at the reactor! Swarma can be a cruel mistress sometimes. She can also be a cruel mister, but if that was the case *she* would be a *he*. If, however, that was so, then it would be called *swarpa*, not *swarma*. Since it wasn't, rest assured it's a mistress and our do-good cabbie has just been screwed, again. The Lonely Mystic started walking...

45 FOREIGN TONGUES – THE I-DIOT

Midtown, Manhattan
The Man
"I don't look like a sausage,
Do I?"

LIFE LESSONS
1 The French have a way with words.
2 Will someone gently tell him it is not a sausage?
3 Grocery shopping bags also can be used to carry small fortunes.
4 If you are going out, check your local weather report. It might be raining other animals besides cats and dogs.

MYSTIC POWERS
48 **Odoriforist:** The ability to smell out good or bad situations regardless of confusing aromas and ancillary smells that might be confusing the issues. Often combined with:
49 **Digitterity:** The ability to count with fingers sight unseen.

WALL STREET-NEW YORK

The Lonely Mystic was used to tall tales and long hikes. One day he decided to walk to Wall Street from The Bronx. He was always curious why all the other boroughs, cities, towns and countries were all misspelled or mispronounced. He never wanted to be called a donkey again so he made sure when he spoke about them, he made the necessary corrections. He also corrected people when they mispronounced these locations. For him, his stores were located in *The* Manhattan, and he grew up in *The* Brooklyn. People must have liked it when he corrected them because they burst out laughing hysterically. Why they kept referring to some kind of new electrical device called "what an..." when they heard him doing so was a mystery to him.

They kept saying, "What an '*i-Diot*.'" He thought *Diot* sounded French. Somehow he felt a connection to the French people. This was something, which he attributed to a past life experience. He thought *why are they calling me a piece of meat? I remembered having diot once, or was it in another life?* Sometimes not only the days got mixed up, sometimes so did the lives.

He looked into the bag the teller had given him. He was quite stunned by what he saw. Actually, he looked in and up at least fifteen times. It's not like he expected the contents to change during those numerous looks, but that he couldn't comprehend what he saw. The shock prompted the spasmodic responses. He had expected a bag filled with groceries, toiletries or other give-a-ways. He imagined that was what homeless people were given. Not that he was homeless today, he wasn't. What he saw inside there was quite surprising and disturbing at the same time.

The bag was filled with stacks of money. There were bunches and bunches of bills wrapped with paper bands. He stealthily maneuvered his hand in there and must have counted at least fifty stalks of assorted denominations of bills. He now had a major problem. In the past, he spent money as fast as it came in. This way he wouldn't have to deal with planning and savings. It was a simple and easy financial philosophy that had worked for him his entire lifetime. He called it, "Easy in, Easy Out." No fuss, no bother, and no concern. But now, he had more cash on hand then he had ever had during his entire lifetime. He didn't' know how or what to do with it all. He did know he had adequate money to get on the train instead of walking and he surely wasn't going to take a taxi. With the way his day was going, it might rain ducks again.

46 RELATIVES - THE COMMUTER

Underground, Hudson River
Incogmento Man
"If no one sees you,
Are you really there anyway?"

LIFE LESSONS
1 Wear red when you are out in public.
2 They call them "rose" colored glasses for a reason.
3 Make sure your barber doesn't have a hearing problem, or you might wind up looking like a bunch of flowers.
4 Beware of relatives asking for dimes, it may just be a prelude for taking you for all that you have.

MYSTIC POWERS
50 **Redirectorist:** The ability to redirect attention by using color. The word was originally invented by the "Uncle" and clearly indicates the subterfuge of the red spectrum. The ability to see through blocked spectral ranges and steer clear of prying eyes. In rare instances, it is coupled with the ability to look cute in the color too.

The Lonely Mystic didn't want to be recognized when he traveled on the subway. He felt traveling incognito, especially when you are holding a bag of *free groceries* was wise. He didn't want the *Uncle* to know what he had in there. From watching all of those TV shows and movies he knew public places had hidden cameras everywhere. If for any reason whatsoever the Uncle had wanted to track you, he could easily have done so. But unbeknownst to most people, the Uncle's cameras were color blind. Put more succinctly, they had a blind spot. They couldn't see red.

The reason for this dates back to the sixties. Yes, many of you reading this weren't around then. In the sixties red was anti-American. Red was the color of the enemy. It was a visceral trigger that prompted a whole host of verbal, physical and emotional responses. The Uncle and his teams spent fortunes fine-tuning surveillance equipment not to be red sensitive. This way, unwanted responses from the members of the armed forces, which were using this technology, wouldn't be triggered. Military uniforms were turned green. Ribbons became black. Medals were any color, but not red. The *red badge of courage* was never awarded anymore.

Following suit, future surveillance equipment removed red from the spectrum. This was no small feat. Much to the chagrin of *Red*, the color was downplayed in the *Eye of the Pyramid* land. This caused much suffering for *Rose*. Needless to say, one of the primary colors of love, was being covered up. New breeds' of roses with other colors were created in the *psycholatron* in order to mask the conspiracy to remove *Red's r*ed roses from *Rose*. *Rainbow's* other daughters tried hard to find ways to help ease the pain of *Rose's* and *Red's* loss. In order to accomplish this, a plan was hatched to make flowers more accessible to the general public. Up until then, flowers were mainly obtainable via designated flower stores and had to be delivered by vans and trucks. *Rainbow* had her own ways to inspire. She looked into a colorful future: Years later, technology would develop to allow *Red* once again be the front-runner as the color of love. *Rose* could then celebrate again. They all felt much better.

However, the Uncle on the pyramid was unaware of any of this and was busy coming up with a pseudo red color called *infrared*. It was called *infra* because it referred to a portion of the color spectrum that precedes red and yet contained some variants of it, in it. The Uncle and his team felt comfortable including this in their surveillance. Those of the opposite spectrum ironically capitalized on this defect by always dressing in red when they wanted to mask their identities and whereabouts.

Much to the Uncle's surprise, Red Square wasn't detected, or even known about until in the seventies there was a massive power failure in Harlem. All of the Uncle's detection equipment went down. One of the Uncle's planes happened to be flying over Red Square during the blackout. The pilot was looking down instead of watching his monitors when he noticed a whole area of the city previously unseen. He quickly reported his findings to the higher-ups. To avoid being fired by their higher-ups, they kept his report hidden for decades.

Most historians, when asked why the Union fell would say, "I don't have a freakin' clue." But those of us that are privy to the red cover-up know the real reason: It was because the Uncle and his team got lost when they entered the red part of the city. They had been wandering around for too long. Out of sheer frustration, they yelled, "I give up!" The Union's leader and troops who were in the building directly above them heard the cry. All turned to each other and said, "The Uncle gives up. If he doesn't care anymore, why should we?" They all clicked potato whiskey glasses, got plastered and ordered *Humpty Dumpty's European Wall* to come tumbling down the next morning.

The *red gap* in surveillance still continues. The higher-ups didn't want to alert the attention of their higher, higher-ups. They would have been held accountable for decades of surveillance gaps that resulted because of this. This was also the reason why there were so many different branches of the Uncle's organization.

He found out about all of this one night at a barbershop in The Brooklyn. The barber had mistakenly thought he wanted his hair dyed instead of shortened. He had longer hair then. There were about eight or nine hairs on top and a ponytail that stretched far down his back. The barber dyed them all red. The barbershop was in Brighton Beach, The Brooklyn.

When he opened his eyes and said, "What have you done to me? I look like a red man!"

The barber said, "Not really, red men have a red mustache and a red beard. Yours are still brown."

He retorted, "Why did you do this to me?"

The barber used to be a used car salesman in Bay Ridge, The Brooklyn. He quickly concocted the whole red story in a flash. Our hero, bought into it *hook, line and stinker*. From then on, he always kept a red wig in his bag in case he wanted to go undetected from the Uncle's prying eyes.

As he had just walked out of a bank with a bag filled with money, he thought it prudent to pull out the red wig and a commuter hat. He also pasted on a mustache. He was a master of disguise and always carried props in his trusty knapsack that would enable him to travel unobserved at a moment's notice. Sometimes, he didn't even recognize himself: Using his trusty magic mirror, he just stared at whoever was staring back at him. He was at a loss for words at those times and swore the bars on his cell phone went up to five when he didn't need them.

A man on the train came over to him and asked for some money, "Brother, can you spare a dime?" He was elated. Someone had recognized him and even more so, that someone thought they were related to him! He checked the big bag he was carrying. All he could see were hundreds of hundred-dollar bills. He pulled out a bunch and then asked, "Would you take a hundred instead?" The man grabbed the bag and quickly raced out of the car, nearly trampling all of the people standing around him. He was left standing there with a bunch of hundreds in his hand and a dumbfounded look on his face. His hat was tilted too. He wasn't sure if his mustache was also coming loose. He felt vaguely OK about it since the man was *family*. From early on in life, he knew family showed up when you came into money. He was somewhat expecting a relative to show up sometime soon, but not as quickly as he actually did. He felt the family member was quite rude. His newfound *brother* hadn't even said, "Goodbye," let alone thanked him for all of the cash he left with. He thought *what about the hug I didn't get either?* All the people on the train must have spoken French also because all he could hear was, "What an i-Diot." He could also swear he also heard someone mentioning his horsey again, but he may have just been imagining it.

47 RUSH HOUR – A OK

The Brooklyn Bridge, The East River
The Lumanist
"Just because you can't see it,
Doesn't mean it isn't there."

LIFE LESSONS
1 Sometimes Tuesday falls on a Monday.
2 Even strangers can be after your money when it's in transit.
3 There is always a brighter side even though it may be eclipsed at the moment.
4 If you don't want to get wet, carry an umbrella.

MYSTIC POWERS
51 **Illuminary:** The ability to see the bright side of dark circumstances. The ability to lighten up when you are feeling down and dirty. The ability to find humor in tragedy, beneficence in hardship and wisdom in chaos. The ability to shine brightly as a beacon of hope and resiliency, despite circumstances indicating the opposite.

NEW YORK CITY SUBWAY SYSTEM—RUSH HOUR

The Lonely Mystic had boarded a Monday rush-hour train. It was especially crowded. Each day of the workweek had its own rhythm and intensity.

Friday was his favorite day because it was like pulling into the hanger from a very long flight.

Thursday was next in line because it was always his lucky day. It wasn't other days weren't lucky, but his selective dysexlic memory recalled Thursdays as being the anniversary day for many of his memorably good events.

Wednesday was a day he liked because it was the solidarity day. When he finally made it to Wednesday, as he put it, then things were, "A-OK." He had made it through the start of the week, and now it was at its middle. It was only a push and shove until the week moved to his favorite days.

Tuesday was the odd day of the bunch. It was the day of unexpected happenings. Tuesday was not here, nor there. It was a day unto itself. It had no relationship to the end or the beginning. It was like the middle child. It didn't know how to define itself. It could say, "I'm the day next to the first day or the day next to the middle day." It had no identity of its own other than as an in-between day. It was the saddest day of the bunch.

Monday had the most pressure on its shoulders. It carried the most responsibility because it had to support all of the other days. It was the first person on the Totem Pole, the first tag teamer, the first of the first. All eyes were on Monday. No one bothered about Tuesday. Wednesday was preoccupied. Thursday was too busy doing everything, which needed to be finished up, because no one wanted to do it on Friday.

He boarded the train on a Monday morning. It was packed tighter than wet sneakers around thick, wool, scratchy socks. The Lonely Mystic could never understand why they called it *Rush Hour*. No one was able to move around in there. *How were they rushing?* It was another one of those cosmic mysteries he kept note of in his *Journal of Mystic Quandaries, Quagmires and Enigmas*.

The people had stopped speaking French by then. He was left alone to retreat deep into his inner depths. His eyes must have begun to tear because the man next to him offered him an umbrella. As he took it, the guy grabbed the rest of the bills he still had left in his hand. He thought *how rude was that?* The man wasn't even a relative.

So there he was with an umbrella in hand and penniless. He looked at the brighter side of the experience: He had begun the week without money. Now he was in the same position as he was in when the day started. So, in reality, nothing was lost and nothing was gained. He was excellent with math, philosophy, and self-deception. He further continued, *I was enriched by the entire experience because now I know all about how to transport my funds in a public, fast-moving economic environment: Don't let any of my relatives know what's in the bag. From then on in, mum was the word. And most significant of all, if it rained, now I wouldn't get wet.* He had to sit down and figure out what his next move was going to be. More importantly, he had to remember which stop to get off at. That was a toughie.

48 BEAUTIFUL DREAMER – UMBRELLA MAN

The Manhattan Bridge, The East River
The Exacerbator
"Are you sure I am Heterohomographonymphic?"

LIFE LESSONS
1 Don't weigh yourself while you are waiting, you might get upset.
2 Speak to your body carefully; it may do something you didn't intend for it to do.
3 Have your eyes checked if you have REM.
4 Some women have PMS, but all men have PSNS.
5 If your girlfriend likes to swim, she may be a nymph.
6 Dinosaurs may still exist.

MYSTIC POWERS
52 **Exacerbation:** The ability to take staff in hand and overcome hereditary limitations whether they occur when on one's back or on one's toes. To be able to rise high above commonplace needs and retreat into deep dreams and visions of times gone by, times to come, or just plain hallucinations.

The Lonely Mystic propped up by his new umbrella sat there with head-on-hand. The stress of the robberies stimulated both his fat producing as well as his hair producing glands. Within a few minutes, he put on at least fifty pounds and grew a long beard. Such was his transformational and hereditary endowments. Some people gained weight from overeating; he lost weight from overeating. His metabolism worked triple and quadruple time when he ate and wound up losing instead of gaining. Under stress, the exact opposite occurred, he gained weight and hair. Of course, he could always drink some bottled water to lose the hair, but the weight was a different story. It was all tied into the *Spellink B's*.

You see *weight* and *wait* sound the same since they are *homonymphs*. Whenever he had to wait, he put on weight. Somehow his genes interpreted waiting as putting on weight. Perhaps it was some eccentric fluke of nature or some glitch in the endocrine system, but it wasn't farfetched. The body didn't need to be told how to take care of itself. It also understood commands, but one needed to be careful of the words that gave a confused command to the body. *Wait* and *weight* were but only one combination of these.

He had to tell all four of his friends never to say, "Hi" to him as a greeting.

Of course, it was difficult telling the dead ones. He could speak to them, but he wouldn't be sure if they were listening. He would mention it to Irving and Shirley, should he happen to ever see them again. Someone in a grocery store once said, "Hi" to him by accident; they thought he was someone else. Of course, he was always himself and not someone he didn't know, but the person didn't know that. His body got so confused when it heard, "Hi" it started to grow taller and intoxicated, both at the same time! This also caused him to experience vertigo and motion sickness because he was allergic to heights and rapid movements.

During sleep, when REM (Rapid Eye Movements) occurred, he would have puked all over his bed sheets if he weren't asleep. One could only imagine the cacophony of events, which would occur, if he happened to be waiting for something and at the same time someone said the magic words: Taller, heavier, higher, and heaving all simultaneously. It was tough being a mystic.

When he went to a shamanic healer for treatments, the healer told him he was "*Heterohomographonymphic.*" It was a rare Eastern European affliction. It affected the neurons in the brain stem, which sent out mixed messages to the receptors of the nervous system. It was exacerbated in the vertical position when the sympathetic nervous system was in control.

When he was lying down and the parasympathetic nervous system was in control, he was less prone to these types of outbursts. But the position of *lying* down had its own issues with the *enteric* nervous system. Just the mere mention of the word *lie* would cause him to have sympathicotoniaic symptoms of vascular spasms and goosebumps in addition to lacrimation, defecation, and urination. He called it the male version of PMS (Premenstrual Syndrome) or the PSNS (Parasympathetic Nervous System), which was a child of the ANS (Autonomic Nervous System) and a sibling of ENS (Enteric Nervous System). When the shaman had finished with his diagnosis, he had to assemble all the words together in his head so he could understand them. This was his way of owning the message. Here is what he was able to understand:

I had the male version of PMS called PSNS. It caused me to mix up words, which sound alike and have different meanings, with words that are spelled alike and have different meanings. This was hereditary. I was also a Hetero-Homo-Nymph that had to urinate and defecate right after I lied down. If I decided to exacerbate when I was lying down, I would cry about it and the get goosebumps. I understood the Hetero-Homo part, after all, all people are homo-sapiens and if they are into the opposite sex they are heterosexual. The nymph part briefly confused me until I remembered my teens and how I always seemed to hook up with the girls who liked to swim. I knew nymphs were from the sea so now it was all crystal clear to me.

The gentle rocking back and forth while leaning on his umbrella brought back warm memories of him riding his donkey in China. As he sat there, his hat fell off, touching his feet. People saw it and started to put money and coins into it. He must have looked quite despondent. He then started to dream. Gradually the sounds of the people talking and the train rushing started to fade out and he found himself in another time and another place.

The first thing he noticed was the beautiful woman lying on the ground right in front of him. He thought she was the most beautiful woman he had ever seen. He also noticed she must have been robbed too because she was missing some of her clothes. *Strange* he thought *because it was winter and she was dressed for summer.* He began to look around and saw birds, a dog, some people climbing a mountain and even some dinosaurs.

He said, "What's your name?"

She replied, "I am The Lonely Mistress. I have no name. I just am. Just like you!"

He thought *I must have been talking to myself again! She didn't look like me, although her breasts were about the size of mine. I am very confused.*

49 DINOSAUR – THE LONELY MISTRESS

LIFE LESSONS
1 Are there realms beyond the present reality?
2 Can a dream be real?
3 Can you dream dreams of dreaming dreams?
4 Where did that thought just come from?

MYSTIC POWERS
53 **Aspiritor:** The ability to move to places not traveled to before by means not often used in ways that defy common perception.

Spirit-Soul World, Unobstructed, The Now
Quizator
"Are you for real,
Or am I just not here?"

SPIRIT-SOUL WORLD, UNOBSTRUCTED — THE NOW

The Lonely Mistress continued speaking with The Lonely Mystic for a very long time. One could even write another book about all that was spoken.
She said:

> Your confusion is a good thing because it allows you to straighten up things that were mixed up inside. The mountain you see is a *soul place* and the people on it are you but from different lifetimes. When you aren't *alive* you live on that mountain in the world you are in now, a world of spirits and souls. The animals you see used to live on Earth, but now they live in Spirit-Soul World too. It is unobstructed.

She went on and on about all kinds of things.
He felt his head getting bigger and bigger and his body getting smaller and

smaller. Then she took him by the hand. She was dressed in different clothes by then. He figured *she had finished her sunbathing.*

She said, "I'm taking you to another one of your lives."

He looked at her and asked, "Have I died and is this Heaven?"

"No, it is just a dream. Dreams are the reality when you are dreaming and just dreams when you are not. Do you remember where you were when you started to dream?"

"I don't remember."

"Perhaps that's the dream?"

He didn't know what to say. He was so confused and at the same time, he felt so full of new thoughts and images he had never thought of or seen before. *Where were they coming from?*

50 ANGEL RAYS – A GLIMPSE OF HEAVEN

Angelic Realms, All That Is
The Intermediary
"Was I just touched by an angel?"

LIFE LESSONS
1 Angels do exist.

MYSTIC POWERS
54 **Hiearchistic:** The ability to commune with realms higher than common consciousness. Expanded consciousness awareness of other planes of existence and the ability to interact with them.

ANGELIC REALMS, ALL THAT IS—ETERNITY

Within an instance, The Lonely Mystic heard a choir of angels singing. When he turned, he saw a tree with four spheres. The markings on them looked unfamiliar. The tree was coming out of a mountain. In front of him stood a female holding a golden rod that radiated and pulsated seven rays of beautiful rainbow colors. Near her stood someone who appeared ill. On line, someone else was waiting to approach closer. All around them angels were dancing in the air. To the right of all of this, there appeared a face. He was only able to catch a glimpse of this face for an instance. It was even shorter than a split second. It then disappeared into the mist forming above the waters at the foot of the mountain. One of the angels had a sword. Another was holding a cornucopia basket, and a third was dropping seeds onto the land. The angel with the multicolor rod motioned for him to approach. He was speechless. He started to walk, but his legs became weightless as he glided toward her. He looked behind him and questioned how he was able to do so, but because of the mist he couldn't see anything. He wondered *what happened to The Lonely Mistress?*

The angel touched his forehead with her staff. A multicolor pulsating light filled with vibrations surrounded him. They started at the top of his skull, then raced down throughout his entire body and ended at his toes. It felt like something he had never experienced before. The closest he could come to describing it was the time he went for an acupuncture treatment. As the needles were put in, he felt currents running down his legs and into his toes. The angel must have then touched his head to the staff again, or at least he thought so.

When he opened his eyes, he had bumped into the handle of the umbrella. The train had stopped and it was time for him to de-train and go back to his stores. He remembered the visions in vivid detail. He didn't know what to think or say, even to himself.

51 ONLY THE PLUMBING – NEW BEGINNINGS

Down & Out, The Dumps—1974
The Plumbing
"If I gave you a nickel,
Can I buy your company
For five cents on the dollar?"

WALL STREET,
NEW YORK CITY—1974

LIFE LESSONS

1 When all is lost, at least you can still flush the toilet.
2 If you have a feather in your hat, check it. There might be some money in there too.
3 You don't need to have a financial degree to be able to move money around.
4 If you watch carefully, and if you don't spend it first, you can watch your money shrink.
5 Dust masks can also block out thoughts.
6 People transported their money in stagecoaches because the dollar was much bigger then.

MYSTIC POWERS

55 **Numismatician:** The ability to calculate the value of money by direct observation. Coupled with:
56 **Notaphilyiac:** One who knows the worth of coins by counting them, over and over so they have more of them each time.

The Lonely Mystic walked into the first of his Wall Street shops. He looked around to see if there were any customers. He was quite disappointed. He was also very surprised by what he found. Except for the plumbing and the sign that read, "Be right back" everything in the store was gone. He had left the doors open figuring customers would wait for him to return. He quickly ran into the other two shops, but it was too late. They too were empty. As he scratched his head money started falling out from under his hat. He realized he had picked it up from the floor of the train after he was snoozing and put it on his head. It did feel strange on, but recent visions were preoccupying him so he had ignored all of the things rolling around on his head.

As a result of the robberies, all three shops had to be closed. He only had sufficient money left to pay for a simple meal. As he was walking out of the sunglasses store, he saw a feather lying in one of its corners. When he went closer, his heart skipped a beat of joy. It was one of his favorite hats. They had missed it. He thought *at least I still had my favorite red feather hat.* As a result of his reading, he always tried finding the positive in all that occurred. While he was waiting on line at the local grocery store, he had read about the power of positive thinking from one of the tabloids.

He found lots of information in those tabloids. One time he read a particular article that stated, "If you mail a check for $1,000.00 to the address listed below, you will positively double your money in ten days or you get your money back." He loved positive guarantees. They were heartwarming and inspiring. If he had had $1,000.00 in his checking account, for sure he would have mailed it to the outfit listed. He knew it was some kind of university because the name ended with the letter "U." The first part of the name was *WECON*. He knew they were very big because they even had a PO Box. They must have been very busy too because there wasn't any phone number listed. It also must have been a public company because not even one name was listed in the article.

That particular tabloid issue was a remarkably educational one. There were loads of positive thinking articles in there. One was on *Mind Control*. It taught you how to move objects around by using only your mind. One of the exercises was to place a feather on an empty table. Next, you would put your face down really low over it. Then you would breathe deeply and visualize the feather was to move. The first time he tried it, he was amazed because it really worked. As soon as he bent over and breathed deeply thinking, the feather was going to move. It did! The power of positive thinking!

The next exercise given used positive thinking to call the last person previously dialed on your cell phone. All you had to do was think hard about that person and then press and hold down the send key. *Voila!* You reached the last person you spoke to by just thinking about doing it!

The article was filled with psychic discovery techniques too. For example, you could tell who was calling you by looking at either their picture coming up on your phone or their phone number, if you remembered it. There was an exercise that predicted when a month would end. You just needed to look at a calendar, circle the current day and count forward to the end of the month. The number of days you counted predicted how many days would occur before the month ended. There were money mastering exercises too. For example, if you wanted to know how much money, in bills, you had in your wallet or pocket; you divided up the bills into the denominations they belonged to, counted the number of bills in that group, multiplied that number by the group's designation and totaled the results. *Voila!* You were an instant accountant. No need to go to business school. You learned how to manage your money using the power of positive thinking! You positively had known you could do it before you did it and did it positively! Since he only had three one-dollar bills in his pocket, this money management skill was easy for him. However, he did get a little confused since three times one is equal to three. He didn't understand *why did three one-dollar bills only come to three cents? If three one-dollar bills amount to three cents, then what did three pennies amount to?*

From his physics class, he knew two of the same bodies couldn't occupy the same space at the same time. Yet here he was having a situation which defied the laws of physics, let alone the entire financial structure of the Uncle's country. He decided the best way to deal with it was to get rid of the pennies. *They couldn't possibly amount to any significant value. But when I thought about it further, I realized copper was worth a lot more than paper? Silver was worth a lot more than copper too! How could paper money be worth anything at all for that matter? It was just a bunch of colored ink on some kind of rag.* He searched through the entire tabloid looking for answers to his financial panic. There was nothing there at all about the value of paper money.

He did find an interesting article about money and how it became worthless if you held onto it. It stated every year the value of money decreases unless you utilize it for investments that increase its value. He decided then, *that was why the dollar was said to be shrinking. If the value of my money decreased every year, then at one time in the future the three dollars I now have in my right hand would vanish completely into thin air, right under my nose.* This he wanted to see for himself because he really wasn't completely sure if he should believe everything he had read in the tabloids, as you shouldn't be. "Should you?"

You, however, can believe everything you read herein because editors have approved it. Everyone knows editors are the strictest authorities there are for the written word, and if they let this book get published, then for sure it's perfect just the way it is. No grammatical errors, spelling errors, or inaccuracies of any kind are contained within these pages. Even the concepts have been field tested by a diverse cross-section of various peoples, who were selected from random locations. They were then sequestered in a remote part of some undisclosed section of The Brooklyn where The Field used to live before it ran away to LA. Now back to our tabloid...

When he returned home, he took his three one-dollar bills out and placed them on his desk. First, he was going to use his recently developed power of positive thought feather technique ability. He bent closely over the three bills and started to breathe through his nose. *Low and behold,* the bills moved. He scared himself. He decided if they moved, he might be unable to see them shrinking. He ran over to his supply cabinet and got two of those white masks. The ones you put over your nose and mouth to prevent infection or the inhaling of toxic fumes. He figured *if it prevented infection or toxins, then it might block thoughts that move objects.* He never understood how they could prevent either. If the openings on it were sufficiently large to allow air to move freely through it, then it was big enough to allow molecules of germs or toxins to move through too. You would think, "Right?" But who was he to argue with technology? He placed one on the top of his head, securing it around his ears. This one was going to block his thoughts. He placed the other one over his mouth and nose to block his words, in the event he spoke his thoughts out loud. He was prone to do so on occasion. He did, however, notice the masks somehow blocked his positive thinking since the bills didn't move when he bent over the three bills. He was now all set to watch his money shrink. He was prepared, "Are you?"

At the local library, he looked up the rate at which the dollar was shrinking each year. He learned in the past decade; the dollar shrank twenty percent and in the last two decades a total of thirty percent. He also learned since the Uncle had been managing the dollar back at the beginning of the century, the dollar has shrunk by about ninety-five percent. He got his ruler out and put it on the table. Remember, he was excellent at math. He measured the bill to be exactly four inches long. With a twenty percent decline in the dollar, the dollar would have to have been five inches long ten years ago, seven and a half inches long twenty years ago and about *twenty-three inches* long at the beginning of the century. He then realized the dollar was shrinking for a good reason; namely, people couldn't handle such large bills. There just wasn't enough room in your wallet for the size it currently was.

He knew that because people never used bills anymore, they always used plastic. Plastic wasn't shrinking unless you put a heat gun to it. But who was stupid enough to put a hair drier over your credit card? He couldn't fathom people carrying a *twenty-three-inch dollar bill* to the general store in the 1900s. But he realized they traveled in covered wagons that were pulled by horses then. There was plenty of room in the wagon to hold stashes of such large bills. He remembered all of the cowboy movies he saw about how robbers were always holding up stagecoaches. People needed the wagons to move their large bills around. Now that he understood the mechanics of high finance, he was prepared to witness the *ever-shrinking dollar.*

He took out his trusty magnifying glass and trusty magnet. With a mask over his head and his mouth and with his ruler in his other hand, he was prepared to wait. Using his money magnet, he tested the bills to see if they were real. He knew money attracts money since rich people only get richer. So he figured money was magnetic. If he held his magnet over it then the bill, if genuine should get lifted up. If it didn't get picked up, he would have to tear them up because they were counterfeit. You can't imagine how many counterfeit bills he found this way. He ripped up a small fortune of bills since he started using this technique. Of course, as soon as he started waiting, he started gaining and his hair started growing. Soon the hair covered all of the bills, and he couldn't scrutinize them anymore. He gave up on the project within minutes and decided the easiest way to avoid having your money shrink in value was to do what everyone else does, spend it. This way you never saw it decrease. Everyone knows, *out of sight, out of mind*, even *with* mind control.

It had been an exciting day filled with dramatic events. He had to rush home because he had responsibilities waiting. He liked walking across *The Brooklyn Bridge* because they got the name right. Instead of taking a train or a taxi, he walked all the way home. It took him quite a while, but he wanted to save the little money he still had jingling around in his pockets. He wasn't quite sure how he was going to get some more, but somehow, in some way, he knew someone would provide him with something.

52 DOG GONE IT – MAN'S BEST FRIEND

The Streets of Manhattan, The New York
Animaal and His Pack
"Of course you can pet me."

LIFE LESSONS
1 Who needs a gym when you can live in a ten-story walk up?
2 Why only walk one dog when you can walk a whole pack at the same time?
3 One day color photography will be invented, as well as 3D and wholeography.
4 Look before you walk into a crowded elevator, there may be something in there that gives you a lasting impression.

MYSTIC POWERS
57 **Animalism:** The ability to love animals deeply. The ability to care for animals and attend to their needs. The ability to receive love and protection from animals.

SOHO, NEW YORK CITY—1974

When The Lonely Mystic got closer to his apartment, he could hear his best friends calling him. Since he liked walking up steps, he picked the highest walk-up he could find when he was looking for a place to live. Ten floors were just a *mere yawn* for him. He climbed each one of them like an athlete would. He was warmly greeted by all of his loves. Each and every one of them. He enjoyed walking a huge pack of dogs daily. They were all exceptionally well trained. One day, he fell down an open and loosely covered manhole. Luckily the dogs' sensed danger. In unison, and as one huge pulling machine, they managed to lift him to safety. As a result of this incident, he did lose one of his many hats. That is why he isn't wearing one in this photo. His fake mustache had just happened to fall off too. Most probably it fell down the manhole. Among other descriptives; he is a transmorphing, bi-locating illusionist, so don't be surprised if you don't recognize him from one photo to the next.

He absolutely adores black and white photography; which is the reason why these pictures aren't in color. A color version will be in the works, once color photography gets invented. He read that would occur after 3D and wholeography (Where the whole person can be captured by the camera.) get invented. At present, the photographer is only able to capture parts of a person. You might see him from the waist up, or perhaps a headshot. He was looking forward to being able to see a picture of all of him.

This particular night, he quickly walked his pack. Upon their return, he let them run up the stairs. Many times he would huddle all of them, along with himself, into the elevator. Yes, even though his building had an elevator, at times, he still chose to walk up the ten flights of stairs. He wasn't one to give into sloth and inactivity. The hardships he had endured during his many travels at an early age prepared him for the vicissitudes of life he had yet to encounter. Fortitude, determination, and buoyancy were just some of his developed qualities. All of which kept him from becoming jaded by the *flings and sparrows of an enormous portion* of stuff that happened to be sold to him. It was truly a sight to behold.

One time, however, the mailman accidentally walked into the elevator without looking. You can only imagine what happened when eleven dogs met a mailman in a crowded space. It gave a new meaning to *Impress Mail*, the new next day delivery service. It definitely left its mark. He hoped the dogs had left a good impression. One would hate for the mailman to complain to the building's management about the quality of his work.

53 IVY LEAF SCHOOL – THE GRADUATE

Pebblestream U, Stone Ridge, NY
Mr. Collegiate's Epicurean Delights
"If you can't spell it, or eat it,
Then wear it on your head."

LIFE LESSONS
1 Who says desserts can't be appetizers?
2 Is angel hair pasta really an angelic food?
3 Sometimes you have to screw up to get what you want.
4 If being online gets you down, then get off it.
5 French hats are named after their houses.
6 Some hats are named after animals, sports and desserts.

MYSTIC POWERS
58 **Epicurious:** The ability to cook and search for knowledge simultaneously while wearing specialty head coverings and being linguistically capable of eating assorted foods while being properly dressed for the occasion.

    The Lonely Mystic rushed up to his apartment and prepared a healthy meal for himself. Of course, he did so only after feeding the dogs. He loved eating healthy food. He spared no expense at obtaining only the finest ingredients to cook with. For him, to down a bowl of ice cream topped with peanut gutter was number one on his scale of what was best for you. It was seconded only by black forest cake, topped with maple syrup, a squirt of whipped cream, and finished off with tart cherries on top. This was just the appetizer. The main meal consisted of a huge bowl of angel hair pasta (He preferred divine foods, being the mystical, mystic mystic that he was.) smothered in onions and peppers and drowning in marinara sauce. For dessert, he loved a light snack of *crepe suzettes* filled with assorted fruits, covered in chocolate and glazed with sherbet and pine nuts.

    He was the consummate gourmet health food chef. He had a whole index card repository of recipes containing his favorite inspired creations. Many people often ask him for his recipes; perhaps one day he will put something together to oblige them. One can't keep a demanding public waiting. He secretly wanted to be a chef, but cooking was outlawed by his upbringing.

Pop would tell Mom, "Food, you think this is food? This isn't food; this is..." And then he would finish it with, "You can't cook! Nobody in this family knows how to cook! We are eating out, right now!"

He could never understand why Mom was never upset by these outbursts. She secretly started to smile after each one, as if she had accomplished what she had set out to do. One time, she even threw a wink at him. It was then he decided to cook clandestinely. He buried his passion deep within himself. He even hid away a small burner in his room and cooked meals for himself and the Boychickle while Pop was snoring. This way Pop wouldn't smell the food being cooked. One ominous night Pop caught wind of some of it and asked him, "What is that?" He answered, "Oh, that must be me digesting Mom's *excellent* cooking!" Pop would laugh and would let the whole matter pass by.

Mom asked him to teach her how to cook. He did so with pleasure. Of course, at the time, he only knew how to make charred vegetables. He took some cooking classes also, so strong was his need to feed himself healthily and deliciously. He was not only blessed with an ability to cook, he was also blessed with the ability to eat whatever he wanted without gaining a single pound. Actually, he always gained his weight in multiples of three pounds at a time. Somehow, in some way, something caused him to gain weight overnight. He knew it wasn't the food because as you can see, his diet was healthy and non-fattening. But when he got on the scale in the morning, he weighed more than when he got on the scale the morning before. He figured he ate in his sleep. He often dreamed of eating when he was asleep. He had a sneaky suspicion the dream food had a lot more calories in it than regular food. Everyone knows things you crave in your dreams are far worse for you than things you actually eat.

The reason, however, he was in such a rush right now was because he had to attend night class. Most people don't know it, but he was attending an Ivy Leaf College in luxurious downtown The Brooklyn. The fences were filled with ivy. He thought that is where the expression *going green* came from. More importantly, since he was a child he had always wanted to attend this caliber of a college. He felt shaken by his mail-order fiasco. Being accepted by this school renewed his faith in his ability to express himself, as he wished. He decided to major in Haberdashery and Linguistics to better himself and learn more about his handicap, *dysexlia*. This way he could both design hats, and know how to name them properly.

He still wears this school sweater today. Right from the start of the class, he already had some favorite hats. Even though he had always loved them, he now knew how to spell them correctly. His favorite hat of all hats was the *French Chateau*. For him, it encompassed all hats into one. In truth, a Frenchman who taught his class called every hat there was *a chateau*. That was how much the Frenchman loved it too. He was a bit confused because when he asked Louie, "What exactly did that chateau look like?" Louie started pointing to the buildings outside of the window. The rest of the class must have been confused too because they were all pointing to him and laughing while they made snorting donkey sounds.

His second favorite hat was the *Porkupie* hat. It was an unusual hat named after two animals, namely the porcupine and the pig. It was usually worn in the rain, so it was short and had bumps in the middle because the raindrops always weighed it down. Sometimes, if it had a *boo-boo*, it would have a band. He also loved the sports type of hats. His favorite sports hat was the *Bowler*. He always wore it when he hit the *pins*. The hat he wore when he read the paper was a *Newsboy Cap*. He also wore a *Fez* hat when he ate his favorite candy, a *Beanie* when he had franks and beans, a *Sugar Loaf*, when he had dessert and *Somehairo*, when he had Mexican. That one allowed his hair to get into his food.

He loved his first day in class and couldn't wait to go back for seconds and thirds, for reasons that weren't so obvious at first.

54 LIVE WIRE – MR. SELTZER

Autumn, the Four Seasons
The Socialite
"If you think about it,
Someone falling all over himself or herself,
Just isn't physically possible."

LIFE LESSONS
1 Sometimes love has obstacles by the name of Sven.
2 Club Soda is the king of social drinks. That's why it got its name.
3 Avoid drinks with violent names like *Tokillher*.
4 Next time you trip, immediately look behind you for aliens.
5 Autumn is a very sad season.

MYSTIC POWERS
59 **Photophotisisis:** The ability to see a photo and know about the subjects being photographed.
60 **Sonosteroistic:** The ability to hear things within in stereo or mono depending upon which channel is operative at the moment. Also works for the past and future.
61 **Dexteriosity:** The ability to raise oneself back up to the same, or even better position one was in before one fell.

Although The Lonely Mystic wouldn't admit it, the real reason he was in such a hurry as he didn't want to miss the cheerleader's after-class practice. He was in love with Matilda. So was Sven. No matter what he tried to do to get Matilda interested in him, Sven always seemed to be doing something better than him. He thought it was because Sven had better music than he did. So it was at that moment The Lonely Mystic decided to become a rock guitar star, again. "It's always because of the women isn't it?" He figured if he could learn to play better than he already did, then he could record some tapes and woo his Matilda away from Sven.

Now he had a plan, but before he was able to do this, he had to visit the local watering hole after school. He was addicted to club soda. He became addicted to it because one of his hairy girlfriends had told him it was a social drink. She said, "If it wasn't, why on Earth would they call it *club soda*? It's not like it hits you on the head with a bang like *Tokillher*, the Mexican alcoholic beverage of choice." He was always afraid of that drink. He thought *it was too violent and suggestive*. He was very suggestible and avoided anything vaguely post *nymphotic*. No one was going to *Svengali* him. His eyebrows were close enough.

He also avoided a *Slow Gin Fuse* because he knew the DHS (Department of Homeland Security has been around for decades, but only recently had tipped their hat.) was watching all alcoholic beverages since they were manufactured overseas. Otherwise, why would there be a tax on them? Who in their right mind would put a tax on products manufactured in the United States of America? Didn't they know God had an eye on everyone, even if they didn't live on a pyramid? Not to mention a Slow Gin Fuse referred to a bomb and the mere mention of a bomb caused everyone to vacate the premises. Imagine someone at the bar yelling at the *bizarre tender,* "Hey Buddy, make me a Slow Gin Fuse." Soon to be followed by everyone starting to scream, "A bomb, a bomb head for the toilets." It was safe in the toilets because they could always stick their heads into the bowls like our ostrich friend.

For him, the only safe drink was The *Manhattan Iced Tea*. He would always order it *decalf and virgin*. He didn't want to stay awake after hours. But his beverage of choice was always the same; he was a die heart club soda aficionado. He could actually taste the distance between the bubbles and feel the dimension of their size when he sipped a glass of some. His olfactory sense was so highly developed it enabled him to be able to discern the purity of the CO_2 bubbles. He could tell if he was drinking CO_2, CO_3, or CO_4. Of course, just plain old CO was a big NO-NO. It had no aroma and knocked you out permanently. This he avoided, as should everyone.

Sometimes the bubbles and fizz would go to his head, and he would become light headed. He had an easy fix for this. He would just ask the bizarre tender to dim the lights. His *photophobia* would then instantly dissipate. Photophobia also caused him to blink whenever a flash photo was taken. He had to have his eyes penciled and painted in on all family photographs. Even his driving license had to be altered.

He was an *acrophobiac* too. Whenever he saw women or men wearing heels or platform shoes he would become afraid for them. Since they were precariously balanced on heights. He was also *sonophobic* and smelled things that weren't there yet. But most importantly, he was *dextraphobic*, which was the ability to trip over things, which also weren't there yet. This happened a lot, and not only to him. Haven't you ever noticed people tripping on the street when there was nothing there to trip them? All of them would turn around and look for the *nothing* they just tripped on, knowing full well nothing was there. He thought *this mysterious tripping was an epidemic of enormous proportions. It was being covered up by the TIA, which stood for The Invisible Aliens.*

He knew aliens were here in abundance, and figured *from time to time they stuck their heads up from the ground. How else could they see what was happening?* Their protruding heads caused people to trip. But when people looked back to see what had happened, they were gone. TIA knew to pull their heads back into the ground like a reverse ostrich. Continuing along, he was also *imaginaphobic*, which was the ability to react to things, which he thought had occurred, but actually had not occurred yet, or ever would.

His abilities were not limited to these alone and were well above and beyond the norm. His was a repertoire which was quite overwhelming and intimidating to the average Ivy Leafer. Of course, he never could understand why the school didn't close down in the fall to mourn all the leaves that had died during transformation. He thought such death should be commemorated. Their springtime reincarnation shouldn't have precluded the school from honoring their memory. Can you imagine, instead of burying the leaves or cremating them, the school just stuffed them into brown paper bags and dumped them like garbage. How insensitive and disrespectful was that? "Right?"

He wasn't worried because he knew Mother Nature kept her eye on these things. He was positive she sent the winter snows to the school grounds just to punish the school officials for their gross neglect. Their snow-shoveling costs skyrocketed. He felt he needed a stiff shot of seltzer to help him mourn these feelings.

Tonight he especially felt vulnerable. As a result, he thought *why not flavor the seltzer with something potent like a splash of spamberry or the yellow and green,* lend-me-a dime. His long-lost relative, the guy who robbed him on the train must have liked that flavor, too. Now he was off to the local *Tub*. You know the communal watering hole.

55 BEST FRIENDS – IRVING & SHIRLEY

The Tub, the Washington Heights
Mr. Singularity
"Time is relative,
Subjective and is sometimes even late."

LIFE LESSONS
1 Childbirth can affect how you tell time.
2 Genetics can determine your body's structure.
3 Technology may be difficult to keep up with if you are a slow runner.
4 Filing an insurance claim can bring unexpected problems.
5 True friendships can develop in a matter of minutes.
6 The precision of the universe is not dependent upon a person's mathematical prowess.
7 Mystical events occur all around us, whether we notice them or not.

MYSTIC POWERS
62 **Overcompensatus:** The ability to overcome genetic defects by altering one's genetic structure to be able to fit into one's jeans after they have shrunk. To be able to stuff cell phones and other technology into the pockets of one's tight-fitting jeans without having to file insurance claims for breakage.

WASHINGTON HEIGHTS, NEW YORK—1974

The Lonely Mystic arrived at the Tub a quarter to ten, or perhaps it was ten to nine. He could never tell the difference. Because of his dysexlia, he had a tough time telling the difference between the shorter and the longer hand of a clock. This was a genetic defect that was caused by the elevation of his ancestral birthplace. He had heard stories about how his mother's, father's, father was born on a hill. In truth and not an often discussed fact, it was a difficult birth. His mother's, father's, mother was lying on an incline with her head pointing downhill. The bed was placed this way to improve the malady of poor circulation. If the blood rushes to your face then the heart has plenty of blood to pump. If she would have been lying in the opposite direction, all the blood would have rushed to her feet. Everyone knows the shortest distance between two points is a straight line. (If you, the reader connect these just made two points, you will get it straight, and not from a horse's mouth.) His relative's birth on the inclined bed was such a difficult birth, the midwife accidentally pushed the bed on an angle. This caused the baby to be born crooked. It came out slightly off-kilter and off-center. This instantly precipitated genetic patterning to occur. It is a known theory that all that occurs at birth affects the electromagnetic neurons and force fields surrounding a newborn child. That is why children are born in hospitals. Their parents want them to become doctors. If they were born in pubs, they would become bizarre tenders.

This accidental act eventually manifested itself in various known and yet-to-be-known positive and negative effects for that side of the family. For example, instead of being ambidextrous like most children are, the male members of the family were either lefties or righties. The female members of the family weren't either; they just ordered their husbands around to do everything for them by just pointing a single finger. Another example was the male members of the family never wore long pants. Their tailors were unable to hem both legs the same length since one leg was always longer than the other. To avoid the tailors charging extra for the longer leg, they wore shorts. However, this really didn't take care of the issue. People would look at their bare skin, even in the winter and question, "How come one knee is covered while the other one isn't?" The female members of the family didn't have this affliction since they were the ones who always wore the pants.

One time, when one of the males got up enough nerve to ask his wife, "Why can you wear the pants and I have to wear shorts?"

She retorted, "Don't you get short with me!"

The malady also prevented him from being able to tell which of his hands was longer. He knew one was longer because every time he reached over to touch the other one the one reaching was always on top. But when he did the same thing with the other hand, he got confused because he figured they both were the same. The clock created similar problems. He solved that one by buying a digital clock. This, however, also confused him because it took too long to count all the little lights. Besides, they never added to the right time when he did so. Although he loved technology, with its issues, he could never catch up to it.

Technology had a mind and a timetable of its own. He was convinced it was out to send him to the poor house. As soon as he bought a new phone, that very instant when he had it in his grasp; the absolutely definitive moment he turned it on in the phone store, it immediately became obsolete and was discontinued. In order for him to replace it if it broke, and it almost always broke the day his warranty ended, he would have to pay for insurance on it. The insurance cost him more than the phone itself. One time his phone broke and he called the insurance company. It took him two weeks to get through. Finally, when he did get through, they told him he needed to file a police report before they would reimburse him.

"Why?"

"To get a replacement you will need to get booked and obtain a police report number."

He went down to the local police department. This was the first time he had ever done so. He was so distraught and frustrated about not being able to use his cell phone, for two weeks he hadn't shaved or bathed.

When he walked into the police station, the desk sergeant asked, "What can I do for you?"

"I want a new cell phone."

"The phone store is around the corner, why are you asking me?"

"I'm not brain dead; I know where the phone store is."

"Then if you know where the store is, why are you here wasting my time with directions and technology issues?"

"Because you need to book me and give me a number."

The sergeant was now really annoyed and said, "OK buddy. You want a number, I'll give you a number!" He called over the policeman standing right next to him and said, "Book him!"

Before he knew it, he was handcuffed and dragged into a room where he had a picture of him taken while he held up a sign with a number on it. He was ecstatic he was finally going to be able to replace his cell phone. They then put him into another room, which was filled with other men. He heard one of them refer to it as a *cell*. He pondered *perhaps they give you a new cell phone in the cell?* One of them came over to him and said, "What you in for?"

He answered, "I have no idea. This is my first time. I hope it's quick so I can get out of here and get a new cell."

The guy looked at him and said, "i-Diot! First, you tell me you are here for the first time. Then you tell me 'you hope it's quick so you can get out.' Then you tell me 'you want to get a new cell.' Are you nuts? This is the only cell here. It is the waiting room until you are either released or get sent to the *Island*."

He was happy because he hadn't been to The Island for a very long time. He could use a vacation after all the trouble he was having with his cell. He told the guy, "I don't mind either waiting or going to *The Island*." He thought *at least the man was wise enough to call it* The *Island.*

The guy said. "You definitely have a screw loose somewhere!"

"Where? Can you see it? Did you see where it came from? Can you see if it fell out? How big is it? What color is it? Is it wet? Does it look Scandinavian?" He felt *maybe the man was a closet genealogist or even a hardware manufacturer. Perhaps he knew his distant relatives?* So many thoughts raced through his fertile mind. Then he asked him if he could borrow his cell phone.

"I'll lend it to you if you give me twenty bucks."

Of course, he didn't have twenty bucks; he just had a few bucks. He took one out and said, "This is all I have on me. Do you have any change?"

The guy laughed, yanked the bill out of his hand and walked away.

He yelled, "Thief!"

Everyone in the cell turned around and said, "Yah, what's' up man, you rang, yooo dude, you callin' me?"

The officer escorted him out of the holding cell into a room with a table. He was told to sit down and was offered some water and a mug. He asked, "Did this water come from a bottle or is it tap water? Can I have a paper cup? I definitely don't want anyone else's germs."

"Use your hands!"

"Of course I'll use my hands, but I need a cup to put into my hands!"

The officer took the pitcher and poured it over his head and told him, "Now you don't need a cup or your hands."

The interrogator came in and asked him, "Do you know why you are here?"

"Of course I do."

"OK then, why are you here?"

"Because the insurance company told me I should come here, get booked, get a number and give it to them so they could pay me. Only then could I get a new cell."

"Who is your cell provider?"

He told him. The interrogator started laughing and said, "That outfit is a joke, get yourself a real phone from a real company and get out of here now!"

He said, "OK, but what was the number you gave me so I can use it?"

The policeman literally grabbed him by his shorts and threw him out. He definitely needed a stiff glass of club tonight.

That night he hung out with two of his best friends. The woman was Shirley. He knew her for about two hours. The man was Irving. He felt like he knew him for a lifetime. It was actually only five minutes. But who was counting? *Counting did no good anyway. Whether you counted or not, time still ticked.* He heard it, for sure. *Do I really think if I stopped counting all those sheep before I went to bed they would stop jumping over the fence? Or cows would stop jumping over the moon? Or Humpty Dumpty would have no fall? No sir, clocks would still tick, the national debt would still increase and your unpaid parking tickets would still be accruing interest.* It really made him wonder *why do they even bother teaching math in elementary school?* He thought *if everyone got amnesia one day and forgot how to add, would the national debt still increase and interest still continue to increase? In a way,* he thought *this was similar to trees falling in the forest and no one being there to clear them out of the path.* He wondered *did they really still fall? And more importantly, did the path need to be cleared if there was no one there in the first place? Would they still have to pay the gardener? Would he even know to show up in the first place? Who would call him if there was no one there?*

He pondered these deep perplexities and philosophical quandaries as he slowly drank his club soda. He didn't want its bubbles to enter his brain. He had heard bubbles in the blood were not a good thing. He liked living on the edge and in the heart of danger, so he defiantly drank the fizz. Unlike The Shirley or The Irving, (He called them that out of respect.) he didn't drink the stuff that was good for you. Shirley liked twenty-year-old scotch. He thought *if something has lasted for twenty years how bad could it be?* Irving drank vodka. He also knew *if something could survive in the freezing winters of Siberia, it too was good for you.*

He was a daring rock star to be, and would only drink what would put hair on his chest and palms. After all, *a hairy palm loses no picks*. His all-time favorite was *the early worm gets stuck in the mud because it isn't fully wet or fully dry and since worms are not really awake so early in the morning, they get confused and don't know in which direction to crawl. So, they get stuck.* He was truly his mother's child, although he had a sneaky suspicion, *Pop may have had something to do with it too.*

He had an expression for everything and could quote foreign sayings too. He was happy with his best friends, after all, he was *The Lonely Mystic* and knew these people didn't know *anything* about him. "Isn't that mystical or what?"

56 EYE TO EYE - NIGHT AT THE OPERA

The Opera House, the Olde Quarter
Mr. Supplemental
"I like everything well done,
Or is it done well?"

LIFE LESSONS
1 Cold Seltzer can cause brain freeze if you don't allow the bubbles to escape through your nose.
2 Bad dates can ruin your beard and goats.
3 Like attracts like, so beware of catching colds from cold foods. They hang out there.
4 String your own beans, it's easy.
5 Eat rich foods well because poor eating isn't healthy.
6 Everyone needs to worship something.

MYSTIC POWERS
63 **Obviosity:** The ability to see the obvious. Such as the ability to stay healthy by not eating fruits purchased in a vegan health food store, since worms weren't allowed.

After finishing his seltzer, The Lonely Mystic said goodbye to his best friends Cynthia and Bob. He never drank more than one club: no brain freeze for him. Besides, he was so bad with names. He surely didn't need any to get frozen in his brain. He had heard things you eat or drink, as well as what you do or don't inhale could cause many maladies. He made it a point never to inhale second or even third-hand smoke. Whenever someone offered him a cigarette, he would refuse. He knew if someone gave it to you then you were getting it second-hand and that was very dangerous to your health.

At the supermarket, he always checked the dates. He had heard *outdated* dates could get you very sick. As a result, he also checked figs and other fruits and veggies at the store too. No bad dates were getting his goatee. He only bought apples from vegetarian food stores. If you bought them elsewhere, you might wind up with worms in them. Vegan stores wouldn't allow any meat onto their premises. No fowl smelling foods for him. As a result, he avoided chickens and ducks. He avoided all spicy foods because he had heard hot food can burn your tongue and hurt your digestive organs. He also avoided cold foods because he knew *like attracts like* and colds hung out in cold foods. He usually had good luck, because he didn't eat foods with pits. He especially stayed away from prunes because he didn't want to wind up in their house. He could never understand, *why would people pay all that money to buy string beans? They could string their own with some beans, a needle, and some thread.* He never drank coffee. He didn't need developing respiratory issues.

His financial planning was based on agriculture: He let his dough rise, his eggs up and no pork bellies for him now or in any future. He made sure he had and used his daily portions of precious metals. He took silver with him every morning; he made sure mercury wasn't rising in his thermometer; he checked the zinc in his car batteries and put pennies under his pillow before he went to sleep. You can never get enough copper.

He also checked the planets daily, and even though one of them referred to a part of your anatomy, he still checked his religiously. A yet to be told fact was he made sure to exercise it at least twice, if not three times. He knew prune juice was the champion of knockouts. If you didn't want to be *down and in the dumps,* then you needed to get one step ahead of them. He followed conventional wisdom and the common advice for the masses and made sure he had eight full portions of water daily. He used shot glasses so the water could be absorbed as fast as a speeding bullet. According to him, supplements were a necessity for good health. So he had fun, exercised, cleaned his hands and ate well.

Whatever he ate, even if it wasn't good for him, he ate it well. Poor eating habits always got you into trouble, and that was something he didn't need. He slurped up and finished the very last bubble in his glass of club and headed out to a concert, becoming a rock star guitarist required constant study.

THE OPERA HOUSE,
THE OLDE QUARTER OF RANDALL'S ISLAND

During the concert (lower left, he is wearing a wig so he wouldn't be recognized, notice the fake eyebrows) he went all-gaga over the performer. He couldn't believe he was able to actually look into her soul windows. He figured *this was a* face to face *with a Diva.* Divas were representatives of the divine world residing here on Earth. *Her name – Diva, was derived from it, otherwise, where would she have the audacity to name herself after some spiritual being?*

All the other people around him were staring at a former pro player who happened to be walking out to visit the men's room. He wasn't going to let himself get distracted and focused on divinity. It was then and there he had an epiphany about why people worship performers: It was because of the spelling.

His grade school teacher, Ms. Hyposapienitzky (She shortened it to Ms. Hypo when she went on stage.) had always taught him to worship foreign words. One of her favorite foreign words was *i-Diot*. She was actually the very first person he remembers who spoke French to him. He was a little confused as to what this evening's performance was about. He thought *the performers were obviously either all immigrants or all aliens. They didn't know a single word of English. And each one kept yelling louder than the other albeit to music. I don't get it? And what were all those costumes about? Don't they know no one dresses' like that anymore?* He felt really comfortable in his college sweater. He couldn't wait to get home and practice. From then on in, he decided to also dress up when he played guitar.

57   Mr. Fashion - Guitar Man

Another Dimension, an Alternate Universe
Mr. Metalico
"Heavy metals
Can be listened to, worn
Or even eaten."

LIFE LESSONS
1 Looks can either be revealing or deceiving depending upon whether you see what you are looking at or not.
2 The value of your body fluctuates with the price of the metals commodity market.
3 You may not be where you think you are.
4 Check your glasses; they may have been dipped in roses.

MYSTIC POWERS
64 **Damensia:** The ability to simultaneously exist in multiple dimensions without evening knowing that you are. No recollection of parallel lives being lived simultaneously and frequent bouts of memory loss in the present reality. Repetition of thoughts without remembrances of having said them already. Repetition of thoughts without remembrances of having said them already. Repetition of thoughts without remembrances of having said them already.

SOHO, NEW YORK—1974

Unbeknownst to most, The Lonely Mystic is really a musician and composer masquerading as an artist and writer. One day, feelings of being run down and tired prompted him to go and see the doctor. He had been diagnosed with a metal deficiency from early on in life: His iron levels were too low. To compensate for this, he put rings all over his body. He did extensive research on the subject. People had ingested hammers, nails, saws, and all sorts of metallic objects in order to combat this. What he didn't know was the nurse in the doctor's office had been up all night partying and had somehow mixed up his charts with a certain Mr. Toitendreaht, a ninety-five-year-old man. In actuality, his iron and precious metals levels were so strong he could attract magnets if they were in his immediate vicinity. None-the-less he was officially branded for life as being non-metallic. As a result, some kind of metal could always be found on him.

Of course, over the years, this varied. At first, it was jewelry, then watches, then pens and then official stock certificates for the metal holdings he had acquired. But when the market crashed, he opted for various bodily piercings to remind him of his stupidity for having purchased penny stocks. His reasoning was simple: *If they are already worth a penny, they can only go up.* Of course, he was wrong.

That night, he wasn't dwelling on his gains or losses, his ups or downs, or his ins or outs. That night, and from then on in, his operatic experience inspired him to dress in more distinctive and colorful outfits all the time. He always liked to dress for the occasion, either publicly or privately. However, privately he felt he was underdressing or more aptly put, undressing more than he was dressing.

For example, when he took a bath, everything came off. When he had to go to the bathroom, he pulled down his pants. When he came in, he took off his shoes. When he went to sleep, he took out his teeth. Somehow he realized he was taking off more than he ever put on. He attributed his recent weight loss to this. In the photo above, he proudly displays his guitars, his multicolor plaid vest he now wears daily (even under his regular clothes) and most importantly, his nose ring, chin ring, and two nasal studs. These enable him to hold together all of his multi-dimensional talents. He looks at them as the studs that conjoin the cosmic glue he stepped in that time he fell down the manhole during his fateful dog walk. He had heard when people step into a *certain* organic substance, it is said to bring them luck. Well, he must have stepped into a huge pile of *nothing* when he fell down the manhole cover. *Can you imagine what that brought me? Yes, you guessed it, a whole lot of nothing.* He would have been better off stepping into it because at least then he would have had something. But little did he know there were magnificent forces at work then and now well beyond the comprehension of mere mortal minds; even mystical ones.

In actuality, when he fell down the manhole cover, he came back through another parallel world. He was sure of this. When people saw him after that occurrence, he was constantly being told, "Hey man, you are so, so, totally out of it." Another one was, "You don't look like you belong here!" In truth, no one in his neighborhood dressed as flamboyantly as he did after visiting the Opera. He wasn't quite sure if he did or didn't enter an alternate reality then, but he decided to meditate on the possibility. Although he was fond of different types of eyeglasses, he did remove them when he meditated. He wouldn't want to color the experience with a rose.

58 OUT OF THIS WORLD - HEAD START

Somewhere Else, The Real
The Meditator
"I am who?"

LIFE LESSONS
1 Meditation is an opportunity to spend quality time with you, alone.
2 Being ironic may be related to metal deficiencies or surpluses.
3 Levitation has been linked to mercury.

MYSTIC POWERS
65 **Mediator:** The ability to become who you originally were, but were too busy to recognize it because you were very busy trying to find yourself, although you had never lost who you were, which is what you discovered when you meditate. An act of self-rediscovery. The ability to overcome the illusion that you aren't you, but are someone else. Once you find out that you are you, then that someone else that you were is no longer there. In a sense, you integrate who you were to become with who you already are when you thought you weren't you. You mediate.

The Lonely Mystic meditates daily. Sometimes he even does it every day of the week and on weekends too. For him, it's an opportunity to visit with his *very own lonesome*. He is always so busy, opening shops, meeting people, visiting banks and discovering new openings. He rarely has time to be alone. Actually, he thinks it very ironic. Most of the time he isn't alone, and yet, he still feels very lonely. *This irony may have something to do with the iron pills I take.* He read in one of the definitive tabloids at the supermarket if you ingest an excess of iron as part of your diet, then strange things start happening. Since he liked living on the edge, he increased his iron intake and *voila!* Irony started happening all over the place.

For example, take the time he closed his eyes during a deep meditation and could not figure out *why in this world or the next, everything had turned pitch black*. Yes, you too think *how ironic*, but it actually happened. He couldn't see a thing! *Zilch, nothing. Total irony*. He thought *this reaction wasn't limited to just ironic circumstances.* For example, when he put on the pink gold ring his father had left him before he passed on, at that exact moment, a golden delicious apple fell on his head when he was apple picking in the orchard. Amazing, "Right?" Or after wearing the copper *arthurandidas* healing bracelets he had ordered from the tabloids, he immediately noticed police (also previously known as "Coppers") were attracted to him as if he was wearing *cop magnets*. But one of the most mystical experiences he had ever had was when he made mercury levitate.

All he had to do was either hold the thermometer or even more mysteriously, put it into his mouth and it would start to rise. Magic! *Presto, Gizmo, Digito, Whamo!* "Who else in the known world do you know who could do this?"

59 TAKE ME TO YOUR LEADER - THE ALIEN

Tabloid City, Inner Damensia
The Space Cadet
"Don't micro-manage me,
Or I'll have you shipped out!"

LIFE LESSONS

1 You don't have to marry a woman in order to appreciate her beauty.
2 If you are in the dark, then turn on the light, within you or outside of you.
3 Some aliens masquerade as taxidermists in their taxis.
4 Aliens use microwaves and speak in foreign tongues.
5 Words without order are like talking to relatives. No matter what you say they pick the words they like or don't like and confront you for having said something completely different.

MYSTIC POWERS

66 **Alienamongus:** The ability to spot aliens no matter who they masquerade themselves out to be. The ability to find wisdom and beauty even though it is in plain view, unseen or hidden.

THE EQUATOR—THE CARBONIFEROUS PERIOD

The Lonely Mystic closed his eyes. He rolled his eyeballs around and around. *Perhaps this will help me find the light the supermarket tabloids always talked about.* It didn't. This was not the only thing he got out of the tabloids. He found you could get a wealth of other really useful information out of them. (We, however, know it was *damensia* at work!) He found his visits to the supermarket therapeutic in so many ways. For example, he was able to see all of the beautiful women he would never meet and always regret never having said, "Hello" to. He could find all the out of date produce and help the store get rid of it. Somehow he wound up taking them home and discovering that fact right there and then. Amazing, "Right?" Yep, straight to the recycling bin. Nothing ever went into the garbage. He had to pay for garbage removal, while recycling was free. He was such a shrewd businessman. So what if it cost him to purchase the outdated produce. He was recycling and preventing others from eating foods that were past their expiration date. He looked at this as community service.

As for that mystical light he had heard so much about, he sat there for a very, very long time waiting for it to appear. Of course, he did this in the dark; otherwise, it would be cheating, "Right?"

Then he started thinking about the other stories the tabloids were often speaking about. Next to people coming back from the dead, there were stories about people meeting aliens. This reminded him of the time he had met an alien too. Namely, the taxi driver who took him to his first vasectomy. He had three because the first two were practice.

This particular driver had a major impact on his life. When he asked him where he was from, the driver said, "I'm an alien. I can't tell you because if I did, they would deport me." It was then The Lonely Mystic knew space beings were watching not only him but were spying on taxidermists all around us too! Now he had to be *very* careful because he didn't want to be *deported* also.

THE ZONE—1974

In a mediation, he saw a sphere spinning in rotational orbits. On it was a humanoid shaped being. There was strange writing on the platform. He couldn't quite make it out. Although he was fluent in several languages, he still wasn't able to decipher it. *It must be foreign* he thought. It read as follows:

ĤÃl Gǫulz,
   Ɛl Anðth,
      Menñ Kåhli Nõn,

The rest was garbled.

He was excellent at subtractive reasoning. He could reduce any complexity to its elementary basics without extensive effort or even any type of reasoning at all. He induced the inscriptions on the cylindrical platform were instruction for operating the huge microwave that appeared to be resting on the rotating structure. His thinking was thus:

How else would anyone know how to operate the microwave if it wasn't staring them right in the bottom of their feet? He knew deep knowledge came from the soul. He also knew the soul resided on the bottom of the foot. Therefore, *soul knowledge could even travel through sneakers. It could be assimilated by the transients who were traveling around the sphere. I know they were transients because they weren't going anywhere since there was no way off the sphere. This made me wonder, what were they going to cook in the microwave? But, more importantly, how did they plan on getting all the way up there?*

His queries were premature. The ship hovering above began to evacuate the transients and move them up to the microwave. This enabled him to have an *antipathy* because he finally understood what *premature evacuation* meant. He thought *this must be a desirable occurrence because there were dozens and dozens of beings waiting to get into the micro.* He did wonder *why didn't anyone ever came out?* He then thought *perhaps it wasn't really a microwave at all. Perhaps it was a trans-matter mutator*, which was one of those machines, that alter whatever gets put into them. This was kind-a-like talking to someone who takes all the words you say to them only to then scramble them up into something you never said. Then they give you an argument for having said stuff that never came out of your mouth in the first place. But then again, they did come out of your mouth; only they didn't come out of your mouth in that order. So they were right and wrong, but also not necessarily in that order.

After coming to this conclusion he realized *order was necessary for accurate communications*. Therefore, he decided to alphabetize his sentences and put the words in their proper place. *Otherwise, who would understand me?* This caused even more confusion. Doing so, he too didn't understand himself. So from then on, he decided, *I will just keep my thoughts to myself. This way I will know what I am saying and won't get mixed up.* See, every problem has a simple solution, "Right?"

60 ANCIENT DANCER – DRESSED IN DRAG

An Island, Any One, You Pick It
Shirley, the Exotic Dancer
"Don't you use that ring tone with me!"

THE QUEENS,
NEW YORK CITY—1974

LIFE LESSONS
1 Space is easier to move than time.
2 If you aren't aware of events occurring, then you may be time traveling or going through dimensional rifts.
3 Nano-bots cause more havoc then bed bugs.
4 Pitch black can become pitcher black and pitched black as well as strike-out black.
5 Some women prefer "Mink Farms" to jewelry gifts.
6 Sometimes it's better not to do it at all than to start and stop.
7 At times, your back goes out while the rest of you just wants to stay home and watch TV.

MYSTIC POWERS
67 **Trancepotatoed:** The ability to be in the right place, at the right time. Coupled with the inability to sometimes be aware of events occurring because being in the right place at the right time necessitated one to be trancepotatoed to other times or places which weren't present. Sometimes also referred to as being coach potatoed.

The Lonely Mystic allowed himself to drift deeper and deeper into his meditation. This was actually happening since he was sinking lower and lower into his seat cushion. At this rate, he would be about the height of a coin in one hundred years or so. He decided to tone it down a notch. He went deeper without moving space. He could move space or time. Space was easier than time. Moving space meant throwing out the garbage or shifting the dining room chairs. Moving time was harder. Those frisky little knobs on the watch had to be grasped by nails. His were prone to breaking off. As soon as he grew a good one, he would chip it or it would break off. Of course, this always happened when he wasn't looking. He never actually remembered breaking or chipping the nail. One moment it was whole and the next moment it was, *Whamoo!* Chipped or broken.

If it had a deep defective, he would have to pull out the emergency nail rescue facilities. He had a whole kit prepared. First, there was the itsy-bitsy tube of glue that was super-intelligent. He knew for sure there were nail nano-bots immersed in the fluid. He put just the smallest amount of a drop on the nail and somehow, in some way, the liquid *slid* and *glid*. It found the crack and mended it miraculously; instantly without fuss or bother; without pomp or circumstance and without cheer or jeer. *Voila!* Instant *fix-a-rama*! But sometimes that mysterious force, which caused damage, took chunks of the nail off too. *Can you imagine that? How could I lose a whole chunk of a nail and not even know it happened? There were sinister forces at work here.*

That was when he first realized he was time traveling, shape-shifting, dimensional rifting and singularity exploring as well. It was all due to incidents with his nails. Most astounding of all: They grew when he *wasn't* looking. He could spend hours looking at them and nothing. But when he woke up at night, without even having taken a peek at them, *Bango!* They had grown. He was sure it was the MAA (Metal Association of America) who were responsible for it.

He knew the MAA hired people who had been convicted by the *Etiquette Police* for nail-biting. They then forced them to go door to door at night spreading invisible nail polish growth hormones. These undetectable hormones had tiny decadent nano-bots that were programmed to do major damage to your nails. Then, to facilitate their nefarious plans, nail salons were opened up. They used special nail polish and clandestinely introduced these nano-bots into your pocketbook during your *treatments*. When you placed your bag down at home, they crawled out and made their way onto your nails in the form of rhinestones or decorative flowers. Women were extremely paranoid about this happening but didn't want to tell anyone. Instead, they just kept buying more and more bags thinking their bags were the problem. The SAA (Shoe Association of America) was going bankrupt because of the demand for new shoes to match these new bags. Shoes cost considerably more than bags because they have heels. Heels require cows and cows cost astronomically more than the metal hinges on bags. The CAA (Cow Association of America) was up to their knees because the BAA (Bull Association of America) couldn't keep up with all the cows that needed to be populated in order to keep up with all the shoes that had to be manufactured as a result of all the bags that were being sold. So the SAA, the CAA, the BAA and the HAA (Handbag Association of America) called a conference to investigate what was *sandbagging* their economy.

After extensive research, they were able to determine the MAA was responsible for all of their troubles. They came to this conclusion because most of their nails were broken when people tried to open the latch on their bag or pull a tongue through their buckle. They then knew some invidious, insidious, sinister force was breaking their nails: A force, which was unseen and unknown to them. Luckily for them, our hero, The Lonely Mystic was out walking his dogs the day of the conference. When he passed by the hotel, in unison, the pack ran in and started sniffing all the shoes and bags in the conference room. Although he was out of breath, he was running not too far behind them. Everyone was up in arms about what was happening.

Finally, he was able to collect the pack and the speaker on the podium asked him, "What just happened?"

He answered; "It appears my dogs are telling me you have tiny nail nano-bots hiding in your bags and nail polish."

Everyone in the room feverishly took out their bags and dumped the contents on to the table. They started looking for nail nano-bots. Luckily for them, the theme of the conference was *Black Night, taking your colors to another wavelength*. The room was filled with black lights and under the blue-purplish glow, everyone could see the itsy-bitsy little buggers scurrying around on the table. They were trying to infiltrate the napkin and cutlery industry.

Soon the entire room was swatting the bots with their shoes. Heels were flying everywhere. Grown women were atop tables stomping and cursing. Plates were shattering, forks were flying and the air was filled with both exhilaration and derision, simultaneously. The press got wind of it the next day and the MAA was brought down to its knees by the BAA, the CAA, SAA and the PAA (Pressed Association of America). He theorized that a few days after the *MAA* was brought down, metal prices sunk to an all-time low and gold hit thirty-five dollars an ounce again. *Wall Street most probably planned the whole conspiracy. These stocks went sky-high because all of the inside traders had known about the events beforehand.* He was lucky. During the entire ruckus, he didn't break even one nail!

Meanwhile, he knew he was getting deeper into his meditation. He could tell because the pitch black was getting darker and darker. Further, he knew this was occurring because light travels very rapidly. Since it was dark, everything was slowing down. As everyone knows when you slow down you sink into a comfortable spot on the couch and get ready to relax. His reasoning was honed like *a fine tooth cat* and was impeccable. He was so relaxed he actually started seeing something.

At first, it frightened him, but then he realized it was him. He could tell because no one else has a belly button shaped like a nose. He even had eyes tattooed on his belly, so it would look like a face. "Cool," you say. So here he was face to face with himself dressed up exactly like his last blind date had looked when he picked her up at her house.

He had a sneaky suspicion it was going to be a strange date when he asked her, "Where do you live?"

She answered, "Riker's Island."

Immediately he knew she was ignorant. First, she didn't say *The* Riker's Island and second, everyone knows *no man is an island. Why would I want to meet her there?* He agreed to meet her in The Manhattan instead and gave her the benefit of a doubt.

She showed up wearing all kinds of things hanging from all kinds of places on her. He could swear (Although he never does. He avoids anything legal and everyone knows you only swear in front of a justice of the peace right before you get married.) she had marriage on her mind. The marriage license, which just happened to be protruding from her handbag didn't give him any clues at all. He had not even met the woman yet, let alone was he ready to propose. Besides, if he gave her a ring, she would most probably throw it back. She didn't need him to give her a ring. She already had quite a bit of them on her body. With the price of gold being what it was, $2,000.00 an ounce, he wasn't about to spend his hard earned cash on buying her one.

He just imagined saying, "Hi Shirley, I want to propose to you with this ring."

She would have answered, "What? Are you serious? I already have enough of them hanging from my body. Does it look like I need a ring? Take me to a *mink farm* instead."

He was very confused, so he asked, "What is a mink farm?" He thought *maybe it was a place where farmers raised minks?* Since he didn't know of such a place, he waited absentmindedly for her response. By then he already knew it was over before it had even begun.

Shirley said, "If you expect me to marry you, then you had better have a mink coat waiting to be draped over my shoulders when I emerge from the ritual conversion baths—*The Minkva*." She wasn't Jewish, he was. She knew she would have to convert before he married her.

It was then he realized *Shirley must be one of the* alien transient microwave lost souls. *Otherwise, how could she have so much knowledge about all of the intimate details that were going on deep inside the caverns and crevices of his head? It's not like she was in there.* "Was it?" She had struck a familiar *chord on his palm.* His palms responded to chords, "Remember?" He kept his pick there. Please try keeping up. "Is this moving too fast for you?"

He didn't know what to say. Shirley wasn't his type anyway. He preferred blondes and she was bald. Not that there is anything wrong with baldheaded women, he wasn't prejudiced. But, since he was bald he figured if they both were in the bathroom at the same time and happened to look in the mirror, he would get very confused and not know who he was looking at. Because of that confusion, he might shave her mustache off instead of his. He knows that could really get someone upset. One time he tried shaving his girlfriend's armpits and she nearly belted him one.

Hair is a tricky thing to deal with. He decided to avoid the whole issue and cancel the date. It was then he realized how wonderful meditation was. It avoided potential discomfort and potential humiliation. He didn't have to endure any of that now. Now, he just had to figure out *who was this Shirley? He had never ever heard of or seen her before.* He then opened his eyes.

He felt a sharp pain in his lower right back side. The lotus position had caused his back to go out on him. He knew he shouldn't have put his right foot over his left ear while he put his left foot over the top of his head. As soon as he did, he heard a loud crunch. He knew he would have to find an *Adjuster* really *quicko*.

61 THE ADJUSTMENT – IDO EVERYTHINK

Out of It, Inner Sanctum
The Contortionist
"Please, bend me to your will,
Will you?"

LIFE LESSONS
1 Potatoes, like salt, are measured in grains.
2 Next to dogs, your couch is your second best friend.
3 Try giving your pain away. But be forewarned most people will not accept it.
4 Beware of letting aliens into your kitchen when they say "Be right back!"

MYSTIC POWERS
68 **Momentitus:** The ability to momentarily alleviate pain by convincing oneself it happened in the past. The ability to be oneself even when one can't be oneself. The ability to alter one's posture and still be able to think. Accompanied by a strong conviction that one day, although one's back left, it will return.

SOHO, NEW YORK CITY—1974

The Lonely Mystic just loved sitting and waiting because potatoes were his favorite grain. He knew they were grains because he had always put salt on them. Everyone knew you put salt on grains otherwise they wouldn't have said, "A grain of salt." "Right?" Of course, his couch was his favorite place in the whole world. He even wrote a poem for it.

Ode to My Couch
You fit my butt so well.
It almost feels like you were tailor-made!
You are always there for me when I need you.
You are season sensitive.
You allow me to fall in and spring up.

Loosely put, you are good at hiding my clumsiness.
'Cause, when I'm eating and drop something,
You provide instant cover-ups.
My imperfections somehow disappear
Into the *crooks and crannies*,
Of your inclined recessed crevices.
You, my trusty couch,
Are service free.
Being dark, you never have to be cleaned.
Being textured, you never have to be polished.
Being plump, you never have to be straightened.
Being old, you never had to be replaced.
I love you! My trusty old couch!

Every time he reads it, it brings tears to his eyes, as it does to yours too, "Right?"

You don't replace your elders. But more importantly, its main purpose in his or its life was always without hesitation, without a moment's reticence, without the need for rhyme or reason, to be there for him. Always. It was there when he slept. It was there when he ate. It was there when he watched. It was there when he meditated. It was there when he fooled around. (OK, so it was out to lunch when he fooled around since he really didn't.) It was always there. For him, sitting and waiting on his couch was the solution for all of his problems.

He had often heard Mom yell at Pop, saying, "All you do is sit around and wait! Do you really think by doing nothing that something good is going to come of it?"

Pop would always answer the same way, "Ov cause it vill."

Mom would then yell at him again saying, "Nothing comes of nothing and no good comes unless you turn the page and plant good seeds. Money doesn't grow from trees unless you put nuts into your acorns and use your sweat to moisten them."

"Shua, shua I'm gona go don to da forest and pluck da money from da squiels whos eating dhem sweaty nuts. I'll be righta bek. Don't go avay. Don't hold ur breathe."

Pop spoke perfect English. He, however, spoke with a Polish East New York *dial-a-tech*. Later on, he lost it, the accent that is and he spoke quite eloquently. Of course, the first time Pop went *don to da forest to pluck da money*, his *back went out on him*. From then on, it became a genetic trait. Being that The Lonely Mystic had already been born at the time didn't stop heredity and genetics from doing their thing since *Heredity* was a close cousin to *Swarma*. Of course, Heredity and Swarma both came from his father's side, although he had never met them. Heredity was his uncle's daughter, and Swarma was his aunt's daughter.

When Pop's back went out on him, Pop would take his belt and tie it, tightly around his waist. This caused him to turn blue. "Sound familiar?" The Lonely Mystic now knows he came from royal birth although he hadn't previously realized it. One time he asked Pop, "Pop, can I have the belt?" So Pop took it to him. Of course those days you could get love pats from your parents without the NG (National Guard) and HS (Homeland Security) being summoned to your house to arrest your parents. He looked at his marks as an ancient form of tattooing: You would bear the marks for several days. You were lucky if it occurred in the winter. It was quite difficult to explain them in the summer. Although The Lonely Mystic was creative and often attributed the red bars to having fallen asleep under the Venetian blinds on a bright sunny day.

He desperately needed having his back fixed. Being trained in the mystic farts of pain tolerance, avoidance, and non-acceptance enabled him to walk down the ten flights of steps in excruciating pain. He just made up his mind the pain was someone else's. He felt bad for that person and started to cry. *How terrible it must be for that other person to have to walk down ten flights of stairs with such a backache!* It was then because of his compassion he first stepped out of his body and was standing next to himself. Now both of them were walking down the stairs. He had bi-located. He wasn't feeling any pain whatsoever, but the other *he* must have been hurting big time because he was sweating salty acorns.

Once they both reached the front door, they became one and he sat himself down on the stoop well prepared to wait for his solace to arrive. *Lo and behold*, a person with a *We Fixa You Upa* sign on his car appeared, as if by magic. Amazing, "Right?"

He came up to him and said, "Bud-e, Iz you got andythink wronga?"

The man sounded like another alien to him. He motioned for him to come closer and asked, "Are you an alien too?"

The man's eyes lit up and said, "Yez, me tooz! Bat dona tela dhem."

The Lonely Mystic looked around for the Space Police who deported people, but the coast was clear. So he asked the man, "What's your name?"

He answered, "My name iz *Ido Erythnik*."

It sounded very foreign to him, but he had lived in Tibet and even Asia and was used to speaking in foreign tongues. His last girlfriend taught him how to even kiss in foreign tongues.

She said, "Lonely Mystic, stick your tongue into my mouth." She was foreign and never used *The*.

He said, "What?"

She then started saying things in languages and use words he had never heard before. She looked upset when he said to her, "Why are you doing that? If you want to know how I taste, then just ask me. I would have told you I taste everything before I eat it."

She then took that evasive tongue and stuck it right out at him, and left. He thought *she must have some kind of tongueitus. Boy am I glad I didn't go tit-e-tit with her!*

Ido asked, "Hey youza, what youza needed to be fixad?"

"My back."

"I canz does itz, I havaz alz the paintz thatz I nedaz in myzaz trucka. I be rights backa."

That was all The Lonely Mystic had to hear. Ido had clearly stated he could right his back! He was ecstatic. Ido, however, came back with a crew of people. The Lonely Mystic started getting worried. *Perhaps his back was worse off than he had imagined it to be?* Those sweaty acorns started sweating even more.

Ido explained, "Thiz iza meinz Momz and Popaz. Theyz directaz me whenza Ia workaz. Thenz I havez ahz coupleaz peoplez thatza watchaz meaz. I ama zah profeshionalz, so Iahz needaz a audianenza."

All six of them then proceeded to walk up to his apartment. Ido asked him to lie down on the kitchen table. Ido's assistant helped him up. The reason for this was he had pointed to his back when Ido asked him where he wanted to begin. So The Lonely Mystic started to bend over when his back went into a spasm, his eyeglasses fell off and his teeth fell out. Now he couldn't see, or talk as well as also not be able to move a muscle. He was a captive audience while Ido was in ecstasy! Ido took out a roller and started to paint the back of his red college sweater. The Lonely Mystic started to cry tears of sadness about his sweater being ruined. Ido thought they were tears of joy, so he pressed even harder, loving to get positive feedback. Then, as he pressed, they all heard a loud "pop!"

Everyone applauded! The Lonely Mystic stood straight up, put his glasses in his mouth and his teeth into his left eye; sometimes he got confused. He started to talk to Ido but was looking at Ido's mother instead. He tried saying, "How much do I owe you?" Ido's father slapped him in the face thinking he was propositioning Ido's mother. Meanwhile, Ido's mother was starting to fantasize about running away with him.

Ido said, "Mizta Mista, pleeza payzme forza paintz." The Lonely Mystic thought *he is asking me for my pants. That's strange*? He was used to under-dressing at social occasions since he was a card-toting nudist. Although where to put his card when totally naked always confused him. He took off his pants. The mother fainted. She had never seen a bellybutton looking like a nose before. The father pulled her out of the apartment, and Ido grabbed the bills that had fallen out of his pants when he had taken them off. The other three people truly loved the performance and were applauding and yelling, "Pravoz, Pravoz." The Lonely Mystic tried pulling his pants back up, but they dropped down. As he bent down to pick them up, his back went out on him again. The three people started applauding once more since they thought he was taking a bow and imitating the sound champagne made when it was opened.

Even though he was in pain again, he was happy it had been such an eventful day and night. He was ready to take his dogs out one more time before he *hit the sack*. Yes, he liked boxing a bit before he turned in for the night. He had constant dreams of being a pugilist. Boxing was only one of his many, many hobbies. It was second only to *spellink* and Irish *lexicons*. He had a fascination with them. He had made up his mind to one day to try and find that *pot at the end of the bowties* and when he finally did, he promised never to inhale.

62 THE HITCH HIKER – DESTINY CALLS

On The Road, US Highway One
The Hitch Hiker
"My way, or the highway.
What if they are the same?"

LIFE LESSONS
1 Sometimes living in a holy place is exactly what it sounds like.
2 Honor and respect your feelings, they may lead you to your destiny.
3 If you are going to travel on fruit and nuts, you might as well pick an exotic location.
4 Beware of French-sounding neighbors in the middle of the night.

MYSTIC POWERS
69 **Fidgititus:** The ability to come to rest by moving somewhere else. The ability to go away and return back to oneself. Finding oneself by getting rid of who you were and then becoming who you are. Traveling to exotic locations without ever having left your house. The ability to use your thumb as a GPS device to guide you to your intended destinations. Often resulting in cost-free travel and unusual adventures.

As The Lonely Mystic laid on his bed staring up at the stars (Yes, he had a hole in the roof, proving the commonly held notion there are distinct advantages to living in a top floor apartment, even if it is ten flights up.) he started having feelings of wanting to *hit the road* again. Over his lifetime those repetitive feelings persistently cropped up every now and then. His back was now back to where it was before it backed out on him.

One fine morning in 1971, he just packed up a bag of dried figs; some mixed nuts and hitched to Mexico. He thought about how he could easily give his dogs to his friends, Shirley and Irving. With all the money he saved on the subway last night, he could most probably finance an exotic trip to the jungles of Africa, or perhaps the beaches of South Jersey. Perhaps he would visit the Arctic Circle or the South of France. The more he thought about it, the more he started leaning toward *evaporating*. He leaned so significantly, he fell out of bed. Upon hearing the noise of him falling the dogs started barking quite loudly. Before you knew it, the entire building was wide-awake right smack in the middle of the night. It was then he heard pounding at his door. He was dubious about opening it, but someone with a French accent started calling him. He wondered how these people know all of my nicknames. Perhaps it was a common expression? But the pounding got louder and the French started becoming garbled, so he opened the door.

63 FRENCHIE – THE GENDARME

Rue De La Seine, Paris
Frenchie
"Please keep your nose,
Out of my business."

PARIS, FRANCE
IN YOUR DREAMS

LIFE LESSONS
1 Sometimes you can be cold and not be sick.
2 Visiting France doesn't always have to be a plane ride away.
3 How come trees only grow in The Brooklyn and not in The Bronx or The Queens?
4 Some noses are musical.
5 Not all strangers will give you the full attention you require or the answers you would expect.
6 What is the guy behind the gendarme doing?

MYSTIC POWERS
70 **Olafactorius:** The ability to play tunes with your nose. The ability to keep other people's noses out of your business whether they are aware of it or not. The ability to discern the subtle differences of indiscernible conglomerates with the agility of a butter knife cutting through a block of ice. The ability to don disguises and pull the wool over everyone's eyes so they can't see your true features because wool itches and they are distracted.

    The Lonely Mystic was struck on the head as the door forcibly swung open. It hit him so hard he fell down and was knocked out.
    The next thing he knew was seeing himself as a gendarme in Paris. He had always wanted to visit Paris. This now seemed like an inexpensive way to get there. He was so happy. Besides, he didn't even have to endure the grueling six-hour plane ride. He hated plane rides because you couldn't smoke on them, anymore. Although he didn't smoke, he felt it was unfair to penalize the cigarette industry, by not letting people burn up their money in smoke while on a plane. He loved the smell of burning paper. To him, that was a close second to smelling burning logs in a fireplace. It was difficult to tell them apart. Since both came from trees they both seemed the same. He couldn't understand why people would say, "Why are you

spending all that money, it doesn't grow on trees?" He figured *it was the same people who forgot to call The Brooklyn, The Brooklyn.* Everyone knows trees grew in The Brooklyn, and not in The Bronx or The Queens. "Right?"

He loved the tights and the little skirt the gendarmes wore. He loved the French fries, the croissants and onion soup. And he loved sweet crepes. But most of all, he loved the perfumes. He had a highly developed olfactory organ. In actuality, some people even compared it to a musical instrument. Someone once told him it sounded like a trombone when he blew it. Someone else compared it to the size of his house.

Another person asked him, "Why don't you get it fixed?"

He answered, "Why should I? It isn't broken?"

Once a complete stranger approached him and asked, "Would you like me to break your nose for you so you would have an excuse to get it fixed?"

"I don't need an excuse."

"Then what is stopping you? Let me do it now; it is an affront to public decency."

He had no idea what the man was talking about. So he stopped the first woman on the street and asked her, "Miss, does this affront your decency?"

She answered him, "Mr., are you accusing me of being indecent? Besides, please keep your nose out of my business."

He didn't remember doing any business with her. She didn't look like *any* of his dogs, although there was a slight resemblance to his tiny baby *snoozer* and *pigtose*. He apologized to her and asked the next person he saw, she was a younger woman.

"Miss, do you feel my nose is publicly indecent?"

"First of all, I'm not a *Miss* and second, yes I do feel so. It is large enough for you to put it in plastic and use it to…"

Well, he just can't repeat what she said here since this is a children's book. One mothers read to their twenty-six-year-old boys who got kicked out of school. For reasons they did inhale and are still living at home since they can't find a job or a girlfriend.

Big mistake. He didn't give up here. He stopped an elderly woman using a walker. He said, "Dear Mrs., do you think there is something wrong with my nose?"

She said,

> First of all, I'm not a *Mrs., I'm a Miss*. My marital status is absolutely none of your business. But, since I'm a considerate,

compassionate and loving person, I'll respond to your question. I'd ask you to come closer to me to better hear what you are saying, but I'm afraid you might stab me with it. It is that huge. Turn your head sideways and ask me again.

He said, "Dear Miss, do you think there is something wrong with my nose?" She said,

> Why are you again referring to me being single? I told you it wasn't any of your business. Here I am being nice enough to speak with you, a complete stranger, and you totally disregard what I expressly asked you not to do. But, since I'm the nice person that I am, I will respond to your question anyway: No not at all. It reminds me of the National Debt. It is so big there aren't enough numbers to calculate its size.

He said, "Dear Elderly Lady, I'm not in debt, so I'm not part of that problem. You never answered my question?"
She said,

> Now you are being totally inappropriate and referring to how old I am. Didn't anyone ever teach you it isn't polite to refer to an old person's age, especially a woman? Why don't you just refer to me as I really am, which is a beautiful, vibrant, stunning, gorgeous and young looking lady? I hate being called a *woman* since it is so impersonal. But since I'm a nice person, I will respond to you as soon as I turn my hearing aid up, ask me again.

"Dear beautiful, vibrant, stunningly gorgeous and young looking lady, do you think there is something wrong with my nose?"

"You must be pointing to your knee; a nose is slightly smaller than that. Are you telling me you have your foot up your Jack, and it's coming out between your eyes?" She then spoke French and hobbled away.

He gave up. It was at that point he figured it was time to take off the rubber nose and glasses he had on. His eyeglasses had broken earlier, and these were the only other pair he had lying around. He had wondered *why didn't my vision improve when I put them on and why wasn't I able to smell things?* But then he chalked it up to one of the arms of the plastic glasses being bent. As everyone knows, "When something goes crooked it misses its mark."

It was then he felt water splash on his face. He began smacking his lips looking for those French bubbles when he opened his eyes and looked up.

64 ODD LOT – THE NEIGHBORS

The Threshold, Inn Between
The Neighbors
"Please keep it down a little."

SOHO,
NEW YORK CITY—1974

LIFE LESSONS

1 Energy is like a water hose. Be careful where you aim it.
2 Don't plan on staying at rest for too long a time or you just might grow roots.
3 Silence may be golden, but only for a few moments otherwise, it may turn to lead. Kinda' like reverse alchemy.
4 Plan next year early, before the holiday rush starts.
5 Beware bamboo armed bicyclists who grin.
6 Playing ball is not a solo sport.
7 Empty fields can be filled with unseen players.
8 Altered realities beget altered realities.
9 Contrary to popular opinion, not all neighbors are friendly.

MYSTIC POWERS

71 **Tailoristicus:** The ability to alter the fabric of time mentally and hope it will hem its way into the folds of reality without being cut off before it is seamed. Being able to visualize alternate realities without lending energy for their creation until the right time, place and person is present to wear the mystical garment so it can be seen by others.

The Lonely Mystic had taken a nasty fall after the door hit him on the noggin. He had only slightly opened it. The parties on the other side of it were the cause of the wallop that had sent him reeling. This wasn't the first time he was the recipient of overzealous energy being directed toward him unintentionally. Unintentional or not, energy once released has an aim and purpose. That is why people are cautioned to be careful of what they wish or ask for. They just may get it.

Recently and to varying degrees, the public has become aware of the laws that govern energy. But this isn't a new revelation. It is really an offshoot of laws, which were discovered, in *Physics 101*. Namely, *a body in motion stays in motion and a body at rest stays at rest.* This wasn't the first time he ran across this law. It affects everything. Which is why it is so difficult to get off your couch after you have watched your favorite TV show or sports game. Your body was at rest and wants to stay at rest. But your mouth was in motion and wants to stay in motion, which is why you can't stop eating while you are at rest. If you kept, your mouth shut, then it would be difficult for you to get it going again. You know that intuitively. Thus, you stuff your face over and over: Basic physics. "Right?"

Your partner knows that too. He or she doesn't stop talking to you especially during the most critical and crucial moments of the show. If they stopped talking, they would also have difficulty coming up with something to say. Most of the time they are just talking and it is easy to talk and really say nothing. But to talk and say something after a moment of silence, now that is a very difficult thing to do. Moments of silence are inspirational and devotional. *Who wants to stay silent for a moment, especially during a game or drama?* Nature always has its own agenda. Before the advent of the TV recorder, it would always call at the least appropriate moment.

For example, isn't visiting the bathroom the first thing you want to do when greeting the first new day of the rest of your life? Of course not. You would want to open the window and smell the roses, or go out on the balcony and look at the sky, or go for a brisk walk. No, you do what you have to do, squeeze and squish foul tasting stuff in your mouth. Then you drown yourself in water. You wash away all the things you did during the night you have no clue about having done but know you did.

The last week in December was reserved for energy planning. It is reserved for making wish lists, want lists, to-do lists, and change lists. The universe works overtime in December trying to accommodate everything everyone has decided to do all at once. Can you imagine how busy the caretakers of the universe are during this time? They are trying to balance everyone's needs, wants and wishes with what is supposed to happen anyway? Do yourself a favor. Plan early. Like on Thanksgiving weekend, when the universe is busy dealing with the death of all the exiting turkeys. At least then, it can hear you clearly, and you won't be a small fish in a big pond.

The first time he received misdirected energy was when he was a child. He was riding his bicycle to a friend's house and a guy on a bike came by swinging. He struck him on the back with a bamboo pole for absolutely no reason.

For no reason? That was a troubling thought for him. *No reason for whom? For me? Obviously, the guy on the bike who hit me had a reason to do it; he had a big smile on his face afterward. The guy must have singled me out for a reason. He* must have selected me for a reason. And he must have aimed at me for a reason. Otherwise, the universe was governed by chaos. If events happened randomly, then random events could cause random destruction. There had to be a reason for me having been struck. Perhaps it was swarmic payback of some kind?

One thing was clear to him; he needed being more aware of his environment. So the next time he took a bike ride, he made sure he looked both ways in addition to looking front and back. Then, for no apparent reason at all, he took a nosedive off his bike and landed on his chin. No helmet of course. No one wore them then. No need to get into details. Whatever was giving him the experience of getting acquainted with circumstances, not under his control, gave him another one as a child in a neighboring schoolyard.

He was having a wonderful time playing ball with himself, even as a child he played with himself. It was exhilarating. He would throw the ball up and slightly forward. Of course, he wasn't there yet, but he then raced against time and space to arrive at the intended destination for its descent. At that early age, he wasn't able to bend time and space yet, so he never got there before the ball landed. He was able to retrieve it moments later. Since he was playing alone, he was able to act as if he had just caught it directly. In reality, he was only a few moments behind. But much to his chagrin, he learned a few moments late could affect many things. Just as he arrived where the ball had landed, a guy pulled him up by his collar and belted him in the stomach several times. The guy yelled, "Hey, you are interrupting my ball game."

He looked around and saw no one on the field other than this guy, his baseball mitt, and a pink rubber ball. He could hardly breathe. He tried catching his breath. When he finally did, he made a big mistake. He said, "What ball game?"

A moment later he realized he should never have opened his mouth and questioned the guy. The guy took his pink rubber ball and threw it directly at you know where. This *pitcher* must have eventually landed a job with the majors because it landed exactly where he wanted it to land. He was now in excruciating pain: both in his stomach and lower down. As he hobbled away he saw tampering with the metaphysics of the universe was a tricky proposition, to say the least. He realized he had opened up the realm of infinite possibilities by wishing and imagining events, which weren't possible, in his present reality. By imagining he could race against time and space and catch the ball he had thrown must have allowed the sadistic pitcher to do his thing. Somehow he had opened up the possibility for someone else to imagine pitching to himself and batting a ball. Then taking it one step farther, even fielding and catching it: That someone else being the *considerate* fellow who had beaten him up. Had he not imagined his own universe, he was sure the fellow couldn't have entered the time warp he had created and would never have accosted him.

He had developed a profound understanding of universe dynamism and mechanics, which was extraordinary at so early an age, from that painful experience. He was now used to taking a fall. So when the three people from down the hall helped him up and put his hat back on his head for him, he wasn't surprised. He was lucky to have such good friends. He was about to thank them when he remembered he had forgotten their names. He was so bad with names. He even forgot his own name. That is why he called himself The Lonely Mystic. He also repeated himself, as we already know, "Yes?" He figured *if it was good and important to say once, then saying it again was all the better.* "Right?"

The three fellows were an odd lot, to say the least. They all wore glasses and all spoke in unison. It was like being surrounded by 2.1 surround sound including the bass speaker. The tall man with the pointed hat was just that. He had a very deep voice. The small one with tiny glasses and a flower on his belt had a high-pitched voice. The middle one was the most talkative one of the bunch. He communicated using sign language. The Lonely Mystic knew he was mute because the man would always say to him, "Mum's the word." He would then hold his index finger over his lips and then point it at him while motioning to cut his throat with his finger. The man was also very religious. Every other word out of his mouth referred to God and some another place, lower down. The fellow used the expression quite frequently. The short fellow kept shrieking,"Keep your dogs on a leash and keep them still." He never understood *what the purpose of putting the dogs on a leash was if your intention was keeping them still? If you wanted them to be still, you would put them on a bed, not on a leash.* He figured *the little guy was confused; perhaps his belt was too tight also?* After all, he had turned blue once because of this very same thing.

The tall one was the strangest of the bunch. He kept picking up the little guy and holding him right in front of The Lonely Mystic's nose. It wasn't like he couldn't hear them. He figured the tall man had an inferiority complex. Somehow lifting the little guy made him feel big. The Lonely Mystic was a profound analyst of human nature. He could size someone up right away.

For example, he knew immediately the tall guy was about 5'9", the short guy 4'8" and the medium guy 5'3". He was great with math and long distances.

This odd lot of fellows had obviously made their point because the dogs had quieted down. The Lonely Mystic ushered his new friends out the door while promising to get to know them better at another time and he went to sleep. Finally.

65   MAN OF MANY HATS - MR. WARDROBE

Closetville, Studio, USA
Mr. Wardrobe
"My shoes have soul!"

LIFE LESSONS
1 There is diversity in one and multiplicity in singularity.
2 Dogs tear poorly designed shoes and clothes to shreds.
3 Dry cleaning shrinks people as well as clothing and apartments.

MYSTIC POWERS
72 **Envoirnmentalist:** The ability to convince oneself one's living environment is larger than it really is by subdividing it into other spaces normally occupied by rooms bigger than the entire space being subdivided. The ability to utilize existing space and enlarge, shift, bend and reorganize it into something much bigger and better than it originally was. The ability to increase space by moving around in circles within it and thereby exponentially expanding it by elongating it with time. Using time to alter the fabric of space by removing all of the crumbs on one's mattress and picking up clothes that may have been lying around.

Upon awakening, The Lonely Mystic entered his walk-in-closet. He selected something from his huge wardrobe. Of course, his walk-in-closet was a part of his living room. In actuality, he only had a one-room apartment. So his entire apartment was not only his living room but also his bedroom, kitchen and walk-in closet. His bathroom was elsewhere. He had hats and ties all over the place. Whenever he walked around the room, he would trip all over them. His dogs also liked wearing them and tried them on quite often. They had a great fashion and design sense too. They regularly made alterations to his garments. The dogs shortened them, fringed them, made aerations and striations and neatly tore them to shreds. He thought *it was adorable my dogs liked to dress just like me and wear my clothes. Besides, it gave me an opportunity to buy new ties and hats.* Of course, he wouldn't wear his special clothes outside, who would want to get them dirty? If they got dirty, he would have to take them to the dry cleaners and everyone knows things shrink when you take them to the dry cleaners. The *height-*

challenged man from last night owned a chain of dry-cleaning stores. He had heard initially that man was bigger than the tall man. All those years in the dry-cleaning business, shrunk him due to his inhaling the noxious fumes. But, he also wondered *was this just another tall tale people tell?*

He couldn't be sure. So instead he would wear his ties in the house and occasionally take out a hat or two out for a walk. Hats don't shrink, and they also don't get dirty. He never washed his hats. *Have you ever heard of a dirty hat?* He thought *they were the cleanest articles of clothing anyone can own next to a leather jacket. No one ever cleans them also. Leather jackets are made of skin. As everyone knows, you don't have to wash anymore if you are dead. Leather jackets are dead, dead, dead: So why clean them?* Impeccable logic, "Yes?"

He felt bad for the little dry cleaner because he owned so many leather jackets and knew he would never clean them. The more he thought about it, the less he liked his neighbor. The guy made money on laundering other people's dirt. He knew dirty money was a bad thing. And, money laundering was even worse. He decided then and there never to let him back into his apartment. He didn't want to associate with obvious criminals and definitely didn't want the PBS (Peoples Benevolent Society) to be after him too. The PBS was a group of people who formed a club so they would have a place to be buried, like a funeral club. He figured the dry cleaner sent them after him because he had so many leather coats. He had overheard Shorty (the dry cleaner) say, "I want to clean him out of his house and home." He was surprised Shorty also dry cleaned apartments. He couldn't quite figure out, *how could Shorty manage to fit my entire apartment into the dry-cleaning machine?"* Perhaps a dry cleaner had a better organizational sense than he did. He knew this for a fact because every time he would take ten shirts to the dry cleaner he only got eight or nine back.

When he brought this up to the dry cleaner, Shorty would say, "Hey I'm the professional and know how to count better than you! You only brought me eight or nine shirts. If you would have brought me ten shirts, then I would be giving you one or two extra back for good luck."

The Lonely Mystic, being the trusting soul that he was, believed him and apologized for doubting him. But his shirt collection started dwindling and it was then The Lonely Mystic understood deceit and falsehood only feed off of themselves. In the long run, they eventually starve. In the future, Shorty was not going to make any more money on The Lonely Mystic: He would have fewer and fewer shirts to clean. The Lonely Mystic marveled at how the universe was taking care of shifty people like Shorty: People who live off of the unsuspecting. He felt good. He was dressed and ready to face the world.

He looked at his watch. He loved watches. If it was five minutes after 12:00. He had been asleep for only five minutes. But if it was 1:00, he couldn't tell the difference, he would have slept for an hour. He went back in his mind thinking about what he had dreamed of and started to do a *reverse sheep count*. A reverse sheep count is when you retrace your steps. He always ate in bed before he slept, so there were plenty of crumbs on the sheet: He was prepared. He stood up on his mattress and started to walk around picking up the crumbs. He hoped they would lead him back into dream state, allowing him to retrace his dreams. He hoped this would reveal if he had dreamed much or little. As he circled around on the mattress, he started getting tired and lied down. Upon closing his eyes, he fell sound asleep.

He woke up and looked at the clock again. Now it was ten after twelve or two o'clock. So, *had I slept for two hours or ten minutes?* He still couldn't tell how long, nor could he remember any of his dreams. Luckily for him, he had left a timer on the stove to remind him his pot needed to be turned off. He didn't want the water in it to boil over. He raced over to the stove and realized: *there wasn't any water in the pot*. Now it was clear: *I had two hours of restful sleep*. That is until he thought *how could I be sure I had put water into the pot at all? How could I tell if the water in the pot had boiled over, or was never in there in the first place?* It wasn't like he could stick his finger into the pot and see if it was still wet. He had been burned once before, and lightning doesn't strike twice in the same place. He looked out and it was a raining. He wasn't taking any chances and tempt Mother Nature. His pot was made of metal, and metal attracts lightning. *No soirée Bubba*, he was going to take the safe road.

He decided despite his various theories, he had only slept ten minutes. *No wonder I feel so tired.* He thought *it must have something to do with the food I ate earlier.* The bed was very, very crummy. No wonder he couldn't sleep more than a few minutes at a time. So he undressed, but his dogs started to bark. They needed to go out again. He rapidly dressed, again. He quickly looked into the mirror and noticed his shirt didn't match his socks, so he undressed and put on another outfit. He had a firm motto, "Since you never know when love or lightning is going to strike, you had better be wearing clean underwear and a wash and wear shirt."

66   I AM 4 U – DREAM LOVER

La, La Land, Dream State, USA
Dream Lover
"Is this for real, or am I dreaming?"

LIFE LESSONS
1 Always dress for the occasion.
2 Inert substances also possess intelligence and have a sense of humor as well.
3 Dream girls can be found in your dreams so dream well.

MYSTIC POWERS
73 **Optimysiticus:** The ability to remain positive even amidst a multitude of disappointments and contrary circumstances. The ability to dress up when there is nowhere to go, to dress down and still stay up, and to stay up when down. The ability to discern the one amidst the many. The ability to be amidst the many and still be one. The ability to be still when shook, to be moved but not shaken, and if shaken, not stirred. The ability to tell time, you have no time for its nonsense. To tell nonsense you have no interest in it. And to take interest in only that which deserves your time.

The Lonely Mystic always slept in a suit. This way, if he met his dream girl during the night; at least he would be dressed for the occasion. He wouldn't have regrets about not having polished his shoes for his first date. Dressing up for sleep had its advantages: You didn't have to worry about stubbing your toes. And most importantly, when you ate while you are dreaming you never, ever spoiled your best shirt and tie. *Just try eating when you're awake and not spot them!* He was convinced food is not as unintelligent as most people believe, for many reasons:

First, it knows how to grow. All you have to do is plant it and it thrives. Let it age and it matures. It does all of this by itself without us having to do anything. Eat it and it turns itself into nourishment, nutrients, and life-sustaining substances. All without our intervention. So he was convinced some of it also has a wild streak as well as a humorous bent. Like shoelaces, when you aren't looking they undo and do their damage. *Just try to look away for just one split second when you are eating soup and your best tie is gone forever! Go ahead; heap that hot dog with mustard.*

You will have a souvenir tie for life. But none of this happened if you properly dressed for your dreams, He also dressed properly when he was awake. *I knew I would meet my dream girl only when I was asleep, right? Otherwise, why would she be called a dream girl?* He knew *the right one was only for me and she would give me a sign so I would know for sure.*

He loved going to sleep dreaming about the hundreds of women who were in his life. He was great with figures and kept track of all the women he dreamed of. After all, you never knew when they would pop up in your dreams again. The worst thing would be to have forgotten their names. *Who wanted nightmares? And everyone knew no one wanted to experience a woman's scorn,* "Right?" It always amazed him how the women he met in his dreams were never the ones he encountered during *waking state.* OK. Occasionally he would encounter some of the ones he had met and was attracted to. He would then test the waters to see if they were attracted to him. For the most part, they were complete strangers. Sometimes he would meet them in restaurants. Sometimes in open spaces like a mall. Sometimes on trains or buses. Sometimes in groups and sometimes other people he had never met would introduce him to them. With the ones he had met and was attracted to, clichés would often indicate whether he should further pursue them during the day. One time, in a dream, he was lying on the table next to a woman he was attracted to, but she was walking away. From that he knew he should *table it.*

He was wandering around in his dream one night when he saw her for the first time. She was sitting on a ledge, separated from all of the other women he had dreamt about. His heart skipped a beat; it just may have been two. She was holding a sign that clearly read *I AM 4 U*. He was joyous beyond words. He approached her and as he held out his hand to touch the sign, he woke up.

He looked at his watch. He couldn't believe what he saw. He had actually slept for a whole twenty-four hours. This wasn't unusual for him because if you remember, he is a mystical fellow. What was unusual was *I don't remember what I did in my dreams. Was I blacked out for this entire length of time?* For all he knew he could be leading multiple lives and the other lives were dreaming dreams of him dreaming dreams. But it dawned on him perhaps he hadn't slept a whole twenty-four hours or even twelve hours. Perhaps he had just fallen asleep and woke up right away. Sometimes he got really, really deep.

67   Knee Deep – Can You Hear Me Now?

Ubirdehcup, Ubirdehyam—1999
The Tourist
"No, I can't wait a minute,
All my free minuets are used up!"

LIFE LESSONS
1 Unusual circumstances sometimes bring unexpected outcomes.
2 What's worse for you may be better for someone else.
3 Relatively speaking, relativity is relative unless it is from your mother's side.
4 What's old to you is new to someone who is younger.
5 Even poverty has politics.
6 Cardboard is the sheetrock of the poor.
7 If your cell phone doesn't work, get a new one that does.

MYSTIC POWERS
74 **Touristical:** The ability to travel to remote locations and participate in local rituals without letting them go over your head. The ability to commune with the local wildlife, animals, and vegetables. The ability to dress the part and fit in. The ability to interact with dignitaries with dignity, with locals loquaciously and with wireless providers without penalty.

UBIRDEHCUP, UBIRDEHYAM—1999

    During his visit to the capital of Ubirdehyam The Lonely Mystic's depths reached new heights. He found himself in dire circumstances. His cell phone had accidentally fallen into the local communal dump as he was performing his morning rituals. Bathrooms were a scarcity. When traveling to fifth world countries he had learned, *what we take for granted, they need a grant for taking*. Newspapers were the new toilet paper. Holes were the new toilets. Cooking was the new radiant heat. TV was drinking a cup of tea while watching poor people walk around begging for money. Bottled water was empty soda bottles filled with rainwater, which had dripped down from some gutters. Pencils were some charred remains from burned out wood fires. Refrigerators' only existed in the winter, when it snowed. *Talk Radio* was a husband yelling at his wife and his wife yelling at her girlfriend next door, who was yelling at her daughter, who was whispering to her new boyfriend. *Hot Rods* were what the blacksmith used. *Go-karts* were what the horse and buggy driver drove. *Penisellin* was what the local stationery store merchant sold. *Tablets* referred to a religious item. A *computer* was a guy who was able to add three numbers in his head without using his hands and feet. *Poverty* was the new affluent class and *destitution* wasn't a word, but a communal categorization.

He was amazed in this day and age, with billions being donated, there still existed billions who needed to be donated to. He wiped whatever he could off his pants and phone and made his way up to dry land. The mayor of Ubirdehyam promptly greeted him.

The mayor was a jovial fellow. He had a little red thread pinned to his torn shirt. It was a mark of distinction. Colors were a rarity there. Even a thread was a luxury. The mayor welcomed him to the capital, which was called *Ubirdehcup*. Every city in Ubirdehyam had the same first eight letters and the last three were varied to indicate the characteristic of the city being designated. The mayor was honored he came to visit them and offered him some *TV* at the *TV station*.

He asked the mayor, "Is there somewhere I can wash up before we have some TV?"

The Mayor responded, "Oh. OK. We will go back to where you just came from and you can clean your hands in there."

He declined and told the Mayor, "Nah, it's OK. Let's just go to the TV station."

They had to walk through several *cornfields*. They were called cornfields, not because you could see hundreds of stalks of corn, but because the man and wife who owned them had corns on their feet. The land was barren and filled with rocks. Every time the owners walked to the TV station they developed corns on their bare feet since they didn't have any shoes to wear.

As they continued walking, they walked past a strange looking house. It was strange looking because it was a type of architecture he was unfamiliar with. It consisted of structures built out of cardboard boxes that had been combined with mud and had hardened. It was like *papier-mâché*. It consisted of several stories. He thought there was only one story, but when they approached, everyone in them ran over and started telling him all of their stories. He was overwhelmed. The mayor apologized for both of them having to leave. They finally made it into the town square, which was a slab of 12" x 12" concrete.

A wooden table sat at its side. A cart and a horse called a *drushek*, was parked alongside it. Its *balguleh*, who was the driver, stood next to the drushek. A slab of rock resting on another slab of rock served as the table. The top slab was table-shaped, sort of. Two sawn-off tree trunks sat at opposite sides of the rock slabs. At the side of the table, a burning outdoor fire was roaring. It had a metal teapot propped up on the surrounding rocks. On the table, there were two metal cups and a small box in the center, which opened. It had the letters "TV" embossed on the cover. Using his coat sleeve, the mayor took the pot in his hands and put it on the table. He then poured both of them a cup of hot water. He wasn't going to ask where the water came from. The Mayor then opened the small metal box and pulled out some herb like substances. He put them into the cups for himself and his guest. The Lonely Mystic bent over and smelled the brew.

Oddly enough it didn't smell too bad. They clanked cups and before he was able to take a sip, his train pulled into the station. It was located right behind the town square. He abruptly thanked the mayor and as he headed over to the train, the mayor stopped him and insisted the balguleh drive him to the station with his drushek. He thought of saying *no*, but he couldn't. He hopped onto the drushek and at a snail's pace the balguleh crawled to the train, which was only one hundred feet away. It reminded him of taxis he had taken to trains and how he had to hop out because walking was always way faster, given the usual traffic. Here, there was no traffic, but walking was still faster. He figured *it was a universal handicap for hired land transportation, advanced technology or not*

He barely made it to the train on time. If the balguleh hadn't whistled to the conductor to hold up, then he would have missed it for sure. Who needed a cell phone if you could whistle as loud as the balguleh did? He, unlike the balguleh, was able to usher only a whimper of a whistle that sounded like an albino teakettle in need of massive steroids. As he boarded, he thought *I needed to "PP." Before my visit here, I needed to "P" but after my visit here I need to double it.* Of course, for him, "P" stood for *piece*, but as he matured, it grew into a passion. He then changed it to *peace*. He wanted to make a contribution to the world to help achieve it. But now, after seeing all this poverty, he added another "P" to his "P" and hence… "PP". Somehow he wanted to be in a position to help achieve both peace and prosperity.

His depth didn't end there. He spent many a moment analyzing himself and his many, many different aspects. Although you would be surprised, he even named each and everyone one of them. He didn't find this to be a strange procedure. He had always been taught *to know one's self* is to be *in touch with the goodness inside*. He knew he was a "good person" because Mom had always told him so. Every time he did something for her, she would tell him how good he was. He thought *this might have something to do with obedience training*. Although he tried hard remembering what one of his buddies in Ubirdehyam had told him about this kind of conditioned response, it escaped him. He thought *I should call him*, but his *why doesn't it work when you want it to work* cell phone *wasn't working at that moment*. The thought *toss it back into the muck and mire of Ubirdehyam* did cross his mind.

He always made it a point to keep abreast of current technology. Accordingly, he would buy a new phone every month. No one was going to keep him stuck on a yearly plan. Nope, not him. He switched carriers regularly. They give you thirty days to switch, so he would buy a phone, use it for twenty-nine and a half days and then switch to another carrier. He constantly had a new phone, and as everyone knows the service is great for the first thirty days. Then it begins to degenerate sporadically and subsequently becomes progressively worse. They know how to market it to you, but he was light-years ahead of all of them. He knew phones had *built in adolescence* that started on the thirty-first day. From then on it was downhill. Whatever worked fast became the slowest piece of tech there was.

Once he accidentally kept his new phone for thirty days. On the thirty-first day, in February (Yes the thirty-first day he owned his phone occurred in February, and it wasn't even a double leap year.) on that thirty-first day, it took him exactly fifty-one minutes for his phone to connect to his voice mail. He clocked it. He pushed the "1" key and waited, and waited, and waited. Nothing happened.

Finally, he became impatient after patiently waiting for those fifty minutes and said, "Hello?"

Although he didn't expect it, Shorty, the dry cleaner answered the phone, "Hey, LM. How come you haven't come by to pick up your shirts yet?"

"How many are there?"

"None."

He knew it. Shorty had finally lost *all* of his shirts and had nothing more to cheat him on. Now Shorty was resorting to stealing the minutes from his phone plan. He tried hard to figure out how Shorty could be calling him when he was dialing his voice mail. Then he realized, *Shorty must have planted a bug in my phone the night I was unconscious*. He frenetically completely took his phone apart. Not just removing the battery, but disassembling the entire unit. He had learned how to do this on the internet.

They said if you want to disassemble your phone because you are fed up with poor service or reception, all you need to do is throw it against your neighbor's wall. Doing so, you can get rid of *two birds with one stone*. He felt bad about hurting one bird let alone two, but since he was sure he didn't have any stones in his phone, he did it anyway. So after throwing his phone against the wall, he looked around for chirping birds and held his hand out to catch some falling stones. Neither of which occurred. He did hear his dry cleaner calling him from the door. *How strange* he thought *first Shorty had planted a bug in my phone, and now Shorty had planted a bug in my doorknob?* He reached for the door but tripped over the broken pieces of the phone. His head started spinning and he felt like he was separating into more than one.

68 MORE THAN ONE – JUGGLE MY BALLS

All Over the Place, Up and Down—1974
Multiple Man
"Being Multi-dimensional
Doesn't make me a scatter brain."

LIFE LESSONS

1 If you are all over the place, then pull yourself together.
2 It's OK to say:
  "I can't make it."
  "God comes first."
  "I'm not into threesomes."
  "I'm OK where I am."
  "Who cares if it's gone?"
  "I'm allergic to wool."
3 Use all your body parts separately or in unison.

MYSTIC POWERS

75 **Monodualistical:** The ability to simultaneously be different and the same. The ability to come together, pick one's self up, be united and be one and at the same time be unique.

SOHO, NEW YORK—1974

The Lonely Mystic felt like he was separating into more than one *him*. This was not an unusual experience for him. He often felt like he was all over the place. On occasion, he actually was in more than one place at the same time. This was a skill he had learned during his foreign travels, numerous studies and from Pop. Different cultures, religions, and societies had different names for this phenomenon. Eastern Mystics called the capability of being able to be in two places at the same time as being able to bi-locate. Jewish Mystics also had an expression for this ability, which was formulated a bit different. Loosely translated it went *you couldn't dance at two weddings with the same* tuchus. Of course, anyone who has many young friends already knows it is feasible to dance at several weddings with the same *tuchus*. These youngsters are skilled in time-travel, which is the ability to drive their car swiftly without getting a ticket.

Russian Mystics looked at it differently. Their version was, you couldn't serve God and Country at the same time, so get rid of the country since you can't get rid of God. French Mystics said, "Two isn't enough, let's do a ménage á trois." Italian Mystics were convinced any location was a good location whether you were there with yourself, by yourself or with neither. Greek Mystics felt it was always necessary to be in two places at the same time otherwise how would you be able to find yourself? To do so, you would have to have been lost first? "Right?"

Polish Mystics, contrary to their neighbors, didn't find any of this relevant. They knew if they lost themselves they would be gone forever. So they kept a close watch on whom they were for fear of it running away. A discordant branch of their following did, however, deviate and went in search of their virginity. When it couldn't be found, they returned home to report this and the main *tour-de-force* gloated at having been right!

Irish Mystics knew if they ever found that pot of gold, they could buy their lost pot back. Not that they went looking for it, in the first place, or it had even ever left. Still, it was prudent to have a *Plan B*. When, however, confronted by their wives about their nocturnal escapades, they always exclaimed, "It wasn't me!" This led their wives into believing they had other selves that somehow, in the night, mysteriously separated from their bodies and went off in search of *Pot and Pub*. To perpetuate, for their spouses, this notion, they pulled up bunches of clover with four leaves and wrapped them in wool fleeces. They gave them to their spouses as proof of extraordinary events being able to occur. Of course, their wives didn't buy it and would tell them, "Stop handing me a bunch of clovers and trying to pull the wool over my eyes!"

The Lonely Mystic, *on the other foot,* would often find himself cooking dinner, only to be interrupted by the doorbell ringing. As he would rush for it, at the very same exact moment, his phone would ring causing him to lunge for that too. All of this occurred simultaneously to him letting the dry cleaner in; picking up a call from Mom on the other phone; turning down the spaghetti pot, which had come to a boil, while using his legs to separate the eleven fighting dogs. He felt God had given him two legs, two arms, two ears, two noses, two eyes, and two heads so he ought to use all of them at the same time. Of course, one of them was private, but he didn't mind proudly displaying the other ones.

He was an excellent *jugular*. When he was in Ubirdehyam he had joined the circus and was expertly trained there. One night, he needed a place to stay. *They had a train, and they had balls. So what more could I ask for?* He thought *juggling was in my genes and destiny.*

69   CIRCUS, CIRCUS – DANCING WITH ANIMALS

The Big Top, Ubirdehcup in Ubirdehyam—1999
Circus Man
"I'm so high, I need to come down."

LIFE LESSONS

1 What goes up must come down, unless it never left the ground in the first place.
2 If an apple never fell, would gravity still exist?
3 Uncertainty and gravity both didn't exist before their discovery.
4 Turkeys do not like cowboy outfits.
5 Check your turkeys for vanilla before you cook them.
6 Don't eat turkey on Halloween because they may come back to haunt you as gobblens.

MYSTIC POWERS

76 **Levititus:** The ability to rise above your limitations and safely return to your plateaus. The ability to rely upon friends in time of need and accept their help. The ability to inherit qualities and abilities and know how to use them to raise oneself up and even stay there when necessary.

UBIRDEHCUP, UBIRDEHYAM—1999

    The Lonely Mystic loved his days with the circus. In another life, he must have been a performer. He had the distinct feeling of being a French acrobat with a contrary sounding name. These feelings often drifted in and out of his daily thoughts, especially when he was on his throne. In this life he had a *one-of-a-kind* act that was especially in tune with the nature of his mystical being. It consisted of him jumping high up while on a trampoline and then coming back down. Due to this significant ability, you, the reader, must be beside yourself with admiration for him. At an early age, he learned *what went up usually doesn't stay there forever*. He unequivocally knew when he went up off of the trampoline, he would descend. There wasn't a single element of fear in his body to stop him from attempting to do so. He called it *my leap of faith*.
    Very spiritual, "Don't you think?" He would leap up and have great faith

this mysterious force, we call *gravity* would eventually bring him back down to earth. But, he also had a secret weapon in the event gravity was planning on playing some tricks on him. In both pockets, he kept an apple. Yes, he knew *an apple was the cause of gravity.* This was no ordinary mystical person. This was an educated mystic. He knew if he had an apple, then gravity could never fool him because it was the apple that first caught gravity by its tail and revealed its secrets to the world. Before then, no one had ever believed if you dropped something it would fall, or if you didn't hold on tightly, you would float up into outer or inner space. He figured *if I had two apples (since everything good came in pairs) then I could be doubly sure and secure about having to come back down.* He also figured *if I got hungry on the return trip, I could land on them and make applesauce,* which was one of his favorites, next to club soda, of course.

Sometimes, but only on wild nights, I would take out both apples and toss them into the air. On my return trip up, I would catch them. The crowd went wild when they saw me doing this. He would alternate two red apples with two green apples and even mix them up. Mom had always said, "Better to have two apples in the air then two apples nowhere." She inherited her poetic ability from her mother Hitou. Creativity ran rampant in his family.

CANARSIE, THE BROOKLYN—1961

Mom was a bit of a mystic herself. She had prognosticatory and visionary abilities: She would always know when he was hungry. She prepared food for him three times a day at just the right moments when his stomach started sending out distress calls. She knew when his clothes were dirty and washed them. She knew he would wake up all happy and shiny since she told him to "Sleep tight, wake up bright and…" The last part he didn't get until there was an actual crisis in New York. She would add, "Don't let the bed bugs bite."

When it got cloudy and stormy, she would prognosticate, "It was going to rain." When it snowed, she told him, "Put on your galoshes or you will get soaked." But most importantly, when he did something wrong, she would announce, "Wait until your father gets home!" How she knew his father would be upset was still a mystery for him. *My father didn't even know I played hooky yet. How could he already be upset with me?"* He must have inherited his *clairvoyance* from her. This is what made him able to jump up and down so adroitly. He could see how to bounce in color, none-the-less. Her uncanny ability to come up with *aprotoe* one-liners while she was standing on one foot must have been inherited from her father Zen Ben.

UBIRDEHCUP, UBIRDEHYAM—1999

The apple thesis, for him, was a close second to Newton's gravitational propositions. He considered it to be one of his loftier theorems. For him, it was a work in progress. He was really trying to disprove the *Certainty Principle*, which incidentally he had helped write. (Somehow he didn't get the credit for having done so.) He was very certain as to why that was. He felt, *if I didn't look at the apples when I was descending, they would still change. They always moved anyway?* Not even an i-Diot could figure that out. *If you weren't looking at them, how come they had changed anyway?* Somehow that thought sounded French to him, but since he didn't see any people talking about "horseys" he figured *it must just be my imagination.*

He surrounded himself on both sides of the trampoline with two huge stuffed animals. He did so just in case he remained suspended without coming down. He could always call upon them to help him descend. He knew stuffed animals were your best friends and in times of trouble, you can hold the animal close to you for comfort. As a child, he never had stuffed animals. The closest he ever came to having such a wonderful companion was a stuffed turkey.

CANARSIE, THE BROOKLYN—1961

Each year Mom would buy a turkey, dress and then stuff it. Mom dressed everything. She even dressed him up in costumes. His favorite one was a cowboy outfit. Of course, she didn't call it a cowboy outfit; she called it an, "Oh Boy Outfit." She named it so since every time he would put it on, she would always say, "Oh boy, do you looking good." She would then pick up the turkey by its drumsticks, suspend it in the air and dance around the kitchen with it: Quite a sight. He was sure that a movie, *Dancing with Turkeys* was named after this event: He also caught a glimpse of a TV show, *Dancing with Animals* this might have inspired.

His mom would stuff the turkey with whatever was at hand in the refrigerator. Each year, the turkey tasted different. There were always different things in the refrigerator to stuff it with. Last year, he swore he pulled out one of Pop's socks from it. Another year, he found a wad of dollar bills in there, a bit crisp, but still recognizable and usable. From that, he realized America is a strong and resilient country that can take the heat.

Two years ago he was eating some of the stuffing when Mom's engagement ring fell out of his mouth. She was so, so overjoyed when Pop had given it to her. Then she realized, "Wait an hour, your father never gave me this engagement ring?" She then took the turkey by the leg and started chasing Pop around the room yelling, "You good for nothing!"

That was all he had to hear. It immediately prompted him to enter a deep trance, meditating on the Mantra *You good for nothing* his mother had just given him. When he awoke, his father had stuffing all over him and his mother was wearing the ring.

He looked at her quizzically. She said, "If it is good for nothing then, it is just as good for me since I am definitely better than that *nothing* he swears he got it for."

Pop swore he bought the ring to surprise Mom with after eating the turkey and somehow it had fallen into the stuffing. The whole thing smelled fishy. He thought that might have been due to the *creamed herring* that was in the fridge right before Mom started to stuff the turkey. But he couldn't be sure. Since Mom liked the ring, she forgave Pop and we now move on to *Dressing the Turkey*.

Mom took his *Oh Boy Outfit* and dressed the turkey with it. It fit perfectly since she had purchased it when he was a young child. It looked so cute; she decided not to allow us to eat the bird. That was the last time we dressed and stuffed a turkey. Subsequent to that, the Cooking Police put out an edict, "You are never allowed to stuff turkeys again. Doing so would cause the turkey to make you very sick due to *vanilla poisoning*."

He loved vanilla. *How could that poison me? Not to mention, how could a dead bird ever come back from the dead and make me sick? Were they telling the public, as well as me Turkey zombies were invading the USA?* He believed in alien zombies, but not feathered ones. He thought *perhaps I was having some sort of weird nightmare?* He believed in reincarnation, so he did believe people came back from the dead. He had heard quite a few ghost stories in his day. That being so, he had never heard of turkey ghosts vengefully dumping vanilla all over people and making them sick. "Did you?"

One fine Halloween night, he had a revelation. Turkeys go, "Gobble,

gobble." "Right?" Although in actuality he had never heard a turkey go, "Gobble, gobble" or for that matter ever even say, "Hello, I'm a turkey. How are you?" He had read they do make that sound. Well, now that you mention it, *I might not have read it*. He may have heard it, somewhere. Nevertheless, his revelation, one of many, assuredly convinced him: Turkeys were the *Gobblens of Halloween*. Otherwise, why would they call them *Gobblens*? This realization made him feel good. And when he felt good, of course, he felt closer to God. Good always made him remember God. It was like a pneumonic, post-hypnotic trigger mechanism for him to connect to the Divine within himself and everything.

UBIRDEHCUP, UBIRDEHYAM—1999

His previous thoughts returned back to him while being suspended in midair. *I never had an opportunity to see if my stuffed animals would comfort me. Although I can't explain it I never ever got stuck up there. I figure this was due to me being a grounded fellow. Not having sufficient frequent flyer miles to stay high in the sky permanently may also have been a contributing factor.* For his act, he also had two helpers. They were foreign fellows and permanent resident of Ubirdehyam, their names were Mish and Mosh. When he wasn't up to his normal self, then they would grab him by his armpits and raise him up and lower him down: This emulated his trampoline act. The people loved this as well. They were kind and generous folk and always wanted to see good people being given a helping hand.

One day Mish and Mosh, each took out an apple from his pocket and when he got up, he just stayed there. He was frozen, in midair, without coming back down. This marked an additional time that he levitated, but it was not his last. He was just as amazed as all the people who were looking at him were. Surprisingly, the people started yelling at him, "Do something, do something!"

He thought they were worried about him falling, so he assured them he was all right and as soon as he could, he would come back down. When they started yelling at him, "Go up!" He was totally confused until he realized he was standing on the trampoline and hadn't jumped up yet. It was then Mish and Mosh first grabbed him by the armpits and raised and lowered him. The people were gay. Mish and Mosh were gay. And more importantly, his stuffed bear had somehow moved over to the stuffed lion and was pulling his tail. Both of them. The lion had a big grin. It was one of the happiest days of his life. So, he couldn't understand why the circus master told him to vacate the premises. He was only there for two weeks and was already being given a vacation? He thought *it was a dream job.*

SOHO, NEW YORK CITY—1974

He looked at his watch again, and it was time to walk the dogs. He didn't want a repeat performance with the Dry Cleaner, the Accountant, and the Ruler Man, so he walked them without a moment's further hesitation.

70 ALL WET – A MIDNIGHT SWIMMER'S SONG

LIFE LESSONS
1 Always have a backup plan.
2 The universe is on your side, although at times it may appear as if it isn't.
3 Some respond to what they understand, which isn't necessarily what you said.
4 You are more valuable to yourself then you give yourself credit for.
5 A lint brush works on clothes, not self-esteem.
6 Always wear socks in the winter.

MYSTIC POWERS
77 **Estimus:** The ability to raise one's self-esteem regardless of one's financial and monetary status. The ability to give oneself more credit than credit bureaus would have you believe you have. The ability to overrate yourself rather than do the inverse. The ability to wash away negative particles that have adhered to your aura's layers and return them to the Source of All.

The East River, the Middle of Winter—1974
The Swimmer
"This water is not only cold,
But it's also very, very wet!"

SOHO, NEW YORK—1974

When The Lonely Mystic's shower wasn't working; he often went for a swim in his very own private body of water. Not everyone in New York City could claim that! Since, to say the least, the plumbing in his building was antiquated, he had to do so quite often. He thought *how amazing. Exactly when I would turn the shower on. And it's working just fine. Then, at the very moment, I step into the basin and my foot touches the bathtub, the shower starts to dribble water out in spats and spurts.* He would look around to see if his bathroom contained a hidden camera. He thought *perhaps the doorman was playing* cranks *on me?* His doorman was so, so nosy.

Every morning the doorman would have the nerve to ask him, "How are you doing?" *Can you imagine such an invasion of privacy? Why was what I was doing the doorman's business? It wasn't his concern. Did he think he was my father or my best friend? Only Shirley and Irving, and my other acquaintances could have the privilege of asking such direct personal questions.*

He would always answer him with, "It's none of your business." Now the doorman was hard of hearing and swore he had heard, "I'm doing some business." From that he induced The Lonely Mystic was a dog breeder. He wondered *although The Lonely Mystic left with a specific group of dogs, why would he always come back with different ones?* He never could quite understand it.

That night, the doorman followed him. He saw him take the dogs down to the river; all eleven of them. He stood there speechless as he watched all of them jump into the water. The event fascinated him and kept watching. It was even better than the *suds operas* he often wound up watching. The Lonely Mystic loved that no one else had thought of jumping into the river. He figured *at night, no one wants to jump in the river so not to wake up the fish.* He knew better. He knew fish sleep during the day otherwise their light-sensitive eyes would start tearing. Nature takes care of itself. He knew if the fishes' eyes started tearing, then because there were so many of them, the river would have to overflow. He thought *it was remarkable how everything is so interconnected.*

He wasn't afraid of swimming alone in the water. He knew if he happened to need help, his dogs would take care of it. If they could pull him out of a manhole, they could surely pull him out of the East River. The Lonely Mystic had to walk five miles to get to the river, but he didn't mind, time was not an issue for him. He felt time was free. Whoever charged for time? He wouldn't say to himself, *Hey, The Lonely Mystic, I'm going to charge you for walking five miles to take a swim in the East River.* He wasn't stupid enough to do that. He knew he would soon go bankrupt if he billed himself for all the time he took to do all the things he did. Instead, he let his accountant, and lawyer bill him for those things. At least if he was spending quality time, he wanted to spend it with professionals and not with himself. He hadn't developed the high self-esteem he was to develop later on in life. Then he would feel he was worth the time he spent on himself.

He knew this was a sad, sad state of affairs. It started when the guy on the train took his money. He felt the universe was somehow telling him he was worth less than he had thought he was. At first, he brushed it off. He went to the drug store and purchased a lint brush and rolled it all over him making sure he caught ever iota of self-contempt and self-recrimination. But he obviously didn't get them all. The lint brush only had a few sample sheets. He was devastated and knew he needed to find another way to recapture and regain his self-worth. He was on a quest. He was on a mission. He knew he would travel far and wide, no matter what the distance and elevation would be. He would find a way to once again feel whole and substantial, to feel worthy of his own self-respect, but first, he needed to dry off. Icicles had already started forming all over his body.

It was ten degrees outside. It was the middle of winter. He had left his wool socks home. Normally, he would put his wool socks on when he came out of the river. They would make him feel warm and tingly all over. As everyone knows, if your socks are wet, then your whole body feels chilled. He did the next best thing. He put his feet into his shirtsleeves and his hands into his pants. He figured *if I confused my body, then it wouldn't know how cold it really was outside. Without that knowledge, my body would think it was really much warmer, perhaps even toasty.* So, there he was with his hands in his pants and his feet in his shirt when Irving and Shirley happened to come walking by.

71 Strung Out – All Hung Out to Dry

All Washed Up, Lah, Lah Land
Saved
"How could it be a dream,
When my leg is all wet?"

LIFE LESSONS
1 How long is a long time anyway?
2 Where does time run to when it runs away?
3 Do good times all congregate in the same place?
4 Were good times always good, or were they bad once and then converted?
5 The rainbow grows fruits when it isn't busy *rainbowing*.
6 Why do doctors. recommend apples? If everyone ate them then, they would go out of business.

MYSTIC POWERS
78 **Chronistical:** The ability to make time. The ability to find time. The ability to utilize time to one's advantage. The ability to be on time. The ability to view time and to never waste time since it is used in the making of diamonds. To be able to have enough time and adequate time. The ability to be able to spend time when needed and to save time when necessary. To have all the time in the world and have no time at all.

Upon seeing Irving and Shirley, The Lonely Mystic felt as if he had been reunited with long, lost old friends. Of course, this was only partially true. He hadn't seen them for a long time since he had only met them the other night. Plus, their real names were Cynthia and Bob.

He often pondered, *how long time really is? Where did time live? Where did time go when it flew away? Where was it vacationing when it was slow as molasses? When people said, "they didn't have any time," did that mean their watches were broken or did they mean someone had stolen their moments from them like the dry cleaner did to me? When someone was running out of time, if they stopped running would time catch up with them or even come back? Why would they run out of time anyway? Time had always been good to me.*

He knew some people had bad times. Others had difficult times and some had easy times. He actually tried to catch time one time, but just in the nick of time, time had its way. He thought *perhaps time had something to do with sand or* shadows. Perhaps it had something to do with hands and ticks. *If you look around you can't see time, but it took time to look around even though you couldn't see it. Perhaps time was invisible and if you put some lemon juice on it, it would appear like invisible ink does.*

He tried to put lemon juice on his watch one time and it made time stop. He was ecstatic. He was making progress, but this time, the watch never started working again. He had read it was waterproof so he figured it was also lemon-juice-proof. Then he realized perhaps the watch was just a *lemon*. Since it was already a *grand complication*, dousing it in its own fluids was just over-the-top for it. He figured *it got so overwhelmed with being in its own element it just gave up the ghost and died.* He tried it on another watch that didn't even say it was waterproof. He figured this way there would be no confusion as to it being or not being able to withstand the tests of time. And, as he half expected, the lemon juice has stopped time yet again. He figured I must be *on to something*. He thought *if lemon juice stops time, it must also stop aging.* He figured *people drank orange juice because they never had sufficient time in the morning for a real meal. As well as because orange came before lemon yellow in the color spectrum.*

First, of course, were red apples. Apples have been the cause of many problems for people since antiquity. Take Eve's apple, hand it over to Newton and then take a paring knife out and look for that worm the early bird is hunting for. Lemons have gotten sour grapes over the millennium. If you have problems, make lemonade, which won't help you if you are a yellow-bellied coward or a sourpuss. Of course, as you progress on the color spectrum the problems get worse. Sour turns to depression when yellow becomes blue, and depression turns to envy when blue changes to green. Then envy becomes indifference, which progresses to withdrawal and eventual dissolution. Not that the color spectrum is biased, but nature's colors have a natural evolution. Time starts out nice and easy with red. Then as it moves toward the opposite end of the rainbow, it speeds up and compresses.

He thought *perhaps the way to prolong time from disappearing was to eat apples and oranges, lemons sparingly, blueberries infrequently and stay away from plums and eggplants. Perhaps that is why doctors always recommended apples.* You never heard one say, "Please have a lemon a day and you will stay happy and healthy." Of course, after a long swim on a warm summer's night, he loved sitting down with a cool glass of lemonade pondering this and other mysteries of the universe. But tonight was not a warm summer's night and he was in for some really sour purple grapes, which right about now was the color of his lips.

He had swum along the East River and wound up at the South Street Seaport. He was almost frozen solid by now, so Irving and Shirley lifted him by the armpits and hung him up to thaw out. They weren't really Irving and Shirley. They were EMS rescue workers. The doorman saw The Lonely Mystic was starting to go down and before returning to the building he had called them. The Lonely Mystic had a vivid imagination, he wasn't hung up to thaw out, but he was put into a sleeping bag to warm up. EMS considered putting him into a straight jacket since the only thing missing from his outfit was having his head up his you know where. Who else would be walking around in ten-degree weather wearing his pants on his arms with his head sticking out of his zipper and his shirt on his legs?

His dogs enjoyed the ride home in the ambulance. His neighbors, however, were beside themselves when in the middle of the night the sirens started to roar as they approached his apartment. He started feeling warm and toasty and couldn't wait to have some of the health food in his freezer.

He was glad he had gone for a swim. Soon he would go out on a date with his dream girl. He was already thinking about what outfit to put on for her tonight when he fell out of his bed. He had been dreaming the whole time; except for the part about the icicles forming on his legs. The heat in his building was broken and one of his dogs just couldn't wait.

72 ALL ABOARD – NIGHT LADIES & MR. PICK

The Pits, the Shady Side of Town
A Good Time
"No, I don't want your money,
I'll kiss you for free!"

LIFE LESSONS
1 A shoebox is a poor man's castle.
2 A dream is a poor man's fortune.
3 A slice of bread is a poor man's banquet.
4 One day at a time is a poor man's thirty-year mortgage.
5 Lonely train rides to nowhere can be a good escape since you aren't actually going anywhere.
6 Open an account in the Cosmic Bank and deposit there regularly.
7 When you least expect it, the universe will heap you rewards for your good deeds.
8 Running or walking around in circles only gets you back to where you began in the first place.

MYSTIC POWERS
79 **Theoretical:** The ability to formulate opinions and explanations for things one has no idea about at all. The ability to create explanations about events without prior knowledge. The ability to understand the ramifications and implications of circumstances without experiencing them previously.

The Lonely Mystic lived in a hotel. He only pretended it was a rental apartment. After all, what was the difference between a hotel room and an apartment? An apartment was made up of rooms. He had *a* room, so it was part of an apartment. For him, this was a very economical way to live since he only had to worry about paying rent for one *day* at a time. People who rented apartments had to worry about one to two *rental years* at a time. How would they afford to continue living there if they were robbed on the train or other possible mishaps that might occur during the course of the lease? He had none of these concerns. He only had to worry about paying for that one day.

Imagine someone who buys a house and has to worry about all thirty years right up front! That was incomprehensible to him since he knew time didn't exist. So why worry about thirty years. He couldn't even handle worrying about thirty minutes, let alone thirty years! He was proud of thinking about the financial ramifications of his long-range planning, which in actuality was a twenty-four hour plan. He didn't think there were any disadvantages to this. He never had to pay for a maid. *Everyone knows how expensive they are.* He never had to worry about redecorating. If he truly wanted to make a change, he could switch rooms. *Now, who could do this if they own a house?* And more importantly, *if I didn't want to cook, all I had to do was fast. Everyone knows if you own a house you can never fast since you are too busy cooking for all the people who want to visit and stay forever.* Not him. Even Mom wouldn't set foot in his apartment. She would tell him it was because of where it was located. He never understood, he always knew where it was located. *It never moved?* He thought *she had it confused with a trailer park or someone who sleeps in their car.* He didn't own a car or a trailer and definitely never parked a trailer next to the car.

He felt safe in that hotel since it was located on a safe and a friendly block. Only once did he see a strange looking guy? The guy happened to be walking around outside of the hotel carrying a pickaxe. Although he didn't see any *construction work going on,* he figured *there must be some nearby.* He wasn't worried. The guy had a hat on, and he figured the man could keep a lid on it. Of course, *it also could have been the conductor waving to the train, and the pickaxe was an optical illusion.* He figured *I would look at it this way.* He always tried seeing the brighter side of things. But then, *why was there a target over one of the women's head? Was it a target or was it a hat?* His depth perception sometimes played tricks on him. He knew he was deep and was able to perceive depth, but when he looked at some things, they appeared to be all there at once.

This problem started when he was a little boy. He and his buddies decided to take optical illusion photos. The kind where you held out the palm of your hand and positioned it under a distant house or a person. Once the picture was taken, it looked as if you were actually holding up the house or person. He figured *somehow my brain got stuck in that mode and it got locked into perceiving things in two-dimensions instead of in three-dimensions.* So to combat this, he always looked at things from as many angles as he could. This sometimes led him to go around in circles. People would ask, "Hey LM, are you running in place?" He would check. He didn't have his sneakers on, so he responded, "No, I am not running in place, I'm running in circles." He told them he was deep in thought. And obviously, he was engaged in *circular reasoning.* Scientific, methodical and absolutely accurate communications were a core value.

His hotel was right under the train. When he approached, the women usually outside of the hotel always took him by the arm. They just loved calling him

"Honey." They always asked, "Do you want to have a good time?"

"Of course."

Surprisingly they then would say, "OK Tiger, a hundred bucks a squeeze, please."

He would tell them, "Sorry, I never accept money from strangers, even if you are polite and say, 'Pretty please.' " He was hard of hearing. He guessed they were all French. After he responded, they spoke French to him and started naming what sounded like all sorts of animals and making animal sounds. He figured *they all belonged to a foreign animal rights organization since they wore furs and lots of leather.*

Leather and furs would be the typical things animal rights people wear, "Right?" After all, an animal has a right to be worn. *I never understood why all those people wanted to prevent others from infringing on an animal's rights by not allowing furs and leather to be worn.* But times have changed, and just like the Turkey Police stopped turkey stuffing, the Fashion Police prohibited fur from being worn except at special *Fur Balls.*

These Fur Balls were held once a year during *Fashion Week* on Eleventh Avenue in the Manhattan. You could see all of the beautiful, scantily clad ladies lining up there. A constant parade of cars came to pick them up. It was similar to a Hollywood premiere. The difference was the ladies didn't go anywhere. They just stayed in the car for a while and then came out with money in their hands and a handkerchief on their lips. *Maybe they all had a snack and won the lottery?*

When it passed, the train would shake his entire building. It wasn't a regular train; it was one of those freight trains that took a whole thirty minutes to pass by. He always imagined himself on one going nowhere, slowly, without a care or worry. He didn't have to worry about his dogs since they weren't actually his dogs. He was a *dog walker* by trade. It was a skill he developed in Asia. The hotel would send dogs up to him, and he would walk them. He really had no responsibilities at all. He was a free man. No mortgage or rent, no spouse or family to support and Mom took care of herself.

She always told him, "Don't worry about me, take care of yourself." She would then hand him three pages of chores to do for her. He figured this was her gift to him. By taking care of her; he was taking care of himself. He knew *Mom knew best,* and *who was I to argue with my mother's nature?* Although he had to admit, at times it got a bit confusing. *By fulfilling her needs, what was I getting out of taking such good care of myself?* He hoped *whatever good deeds I had accumulated in my Cosmic Depository account would eventually result in an abundant return: At some point, in some way, at some time, maybe, hopefully, and perhaps.* He eagerly awaited those special series of moments that would allow him to reap the benefits of selfless giving.

Mom didn't look at it that way. She gave him opportunities to give to her and by doing so; she was, in turn, creating a return of such goodness to him. He was amazed at how the Cosmic Depository worked and was very happy to have opened an account. He was even luckier there was a branch located not far from his hotel. Coincidentally, it was that very same bank he had walked into the other day. The day he wanted to safely deposit his gun into their vault. During that thought, he had a *perspiration*.

He realized *I had received a whole bundle of money from that bank for doing nothing! Wow,* he thought *what good swarma was that!* He loved swarma, especially when it was covered with *whomiss* and *technica*. He didn't care for the *pits*. When they asked him whether he wanted *whole-wheat pits* or *white pits*, he would always say, "Hold the wheat, put it in right here." He then pointed to his palm with his left hand. He was hard of hearing. They would spread the whomiss and technica onto his palms. He then would go off and have a delicious meal. No need to have to clean his hands afterward. He licked them clean. He was a good boy and ate up all the goodies. But, he did wonder, *do I have more points in my account, and if I went back to the bank, would I score more money?*

Money wasn't everything to me. How could it be? For the greater portion of his life, he only knew how to spell it and not hold on to it. But even without money, he was absolutely free to do anything he wanted, while dreaming of course. *Dreams are a poor man's fortune. Now, who else could make these swarmic claims?* He considered himself quite special. "Don't you agree?"

73 LA TUB – MUSIC TO MY EARS

The Lavatory, Vacation Paradise, NY
Ooops!
"I see you're naked,
But my eyes are closed!"

LIFE LESSONS
1 If you have sand, then make whomiss.
2 Even sand can be a marketable commodity.
3 One person affects the whole of humanity.
4 Knowing where you are going sometimes helps.
5 Exit gracefully and quickly when you have gone through the wrong door.
6 Better to walk through the right door then to walk into the wall.
7 Not all high pitched women are opera singers.

MYSTIC POWERS
80 **Circumstanceulus:** The ability to quickly act in the event of unforeseen circumstances. The ability to regroup, retrace and retain one's composure amidst unplanned events. The ability to respond instead of reacting. The ability to instantly size up and play down accidental occurrences. The ability to maneuver around, through and in random or generated scenarios that unexpectedly occur in one's life.

The Lonely Mystic finally got out of bed. He broke the icicles off his pants, dried his foot, and shook his finger at the one dog who somehow had remained hidden under his bed. He then wiped the whomiss from his eyes. He was always happy when he touched his eyes in the morning and felt *sand* since he knew *who* had placed it there. Of course, you do too. If you don't then here is the explanation: It was the *Sand People*. See, you knew it. "Right?" He has known this since childhood: The Sand People got sand, and everyone else got oil. Since it was such a major luxury item there, he knew they had to find ways to export it. They wanted to accumulate good swarma and boost the economy. Everyone knew if you hoarded things and didn't share them, they only built up and came in on you. So, who wanted to be covered with sand, "Right?"

The Sand People came up with a plan, which would enable them, to distribute sand worldwide. After exhaustive and exhilarating deliberations coupled with counter-arguments back and forth among splinter groups and factions (as was the way of the people) they all decided the most economical way to do this was to export. And what more economical a way to export this? "You guessed it again!" *Ship it while you sleep!* The Sand People had cornered the market on sand and overnight delivery. It was a future technology.

Their marketing strategy was so prevalent little children were taught about the Sand Man. Personally, he collected his *sand* every morning and kept a stash of the stuff: He valued anything from the Holy Land. For him, this was a gift from *above*. For him, it was his very own personal Mana. He never ate the sand; he may have tasted it once or twice when he was very hungry, but still, he valued it highly next to other things that come out of his orifices. After all, he was made in his maker's image and anything he created or that somehow came from him was to be revered. But he never could quite understand *why didn't the Sand Man ever put whomiss or technica on my eyes?* Next to sand, those were the next big exports. At least if he woke up with whomiss on his eyes he wouldn't have to call up for breakfast, he could just slurp it down and shower. But he understood: From a marketing perspective *Sand Man* sounds better than *Whomis Man*.

He truly appreciated how the stealthy Sand People were able to sneak into everyone's house, place some sand on everyone's eyes and then disappear. He knew they all belonged to a special branch of the elite culinary services called, the *Habaganoosh*. They were taught how to dish out the swarma so only good could come to them. It was a religious offshoot of a larger organization. Their leadership answered to a supreme and higher authority. He knew that from the TV he watched as a child. It was a huge philanthropic organization bent on feeding the world. His grandmother, Hitou was a card-carrying member. She would constantly remind him of their motto by saying, "Eat. Eat. Eat."

He would respond, "But Hitou, I'm not hungry, hungry, hungry."

She would retort, she loved to *retort* since it was a food word She made incredible apple retorts. They were delicious. She would retort and say, "The world is starving and you aren't hungry? What kind of person are you? You are separating yourself from the rest of humanity by not wanting to eat?" She always spoke in three liners. But occasionally and very rarely she got some extra words in.

Her husband, Zen Ben, would chime in at the end of all her three liners and say his characteristic one-liner, "If you eat, there will be one less hungry person in the world to feed."

He was truly lucky to have such wisdom and support around him while he was growing up. "Don't worry" from his mother, "Eat, eat, eat" from his grandmother, "Feed the world and save the self" from his grandfather and "Turn a deaf ear" from his father. Pop couldn't take all the altruistic gobbledygook that was being dished out by the other three and just *vacated*.

Even though his Pop came from Europe, Pop swore he was from Missouri. This was the basis for The Lonely Mystic's conjecture that somehow, he was an *Ecstatic Concoction*. How else could someone who always said, "I'm from Missouri, prove it to me," have met his mother on the other side of the ocean and have created him? He didn't want to call his father a liar; *how could I?* But it was a problematic enigma for him: *How could my father be in two places at the same time?* Then he realized *I had inherited my bi-location abilities from Pop!* At that very moment, he understood how his *Ecstatic Concoction* had occurred.

Pop must have said to Mom, "I'm from Missouri."

She must have said, "Prove it to me."

So Pop did and there ya' go! He was concocted and everyone was ecstatic. "Remarkable!"

He was rubbing the sand from his eyes and placing it into his dentures cup while he was walking around with his eyes closed. He reached out to feel for the bathroom door. His studio suite had so many doors; he never knew which the closet door was, or which one was the bathroom door, or which one connected to the always locked adjoining room. Well, it was always locked until this morning. Somehow, by a freak accident, he had opened it and walked into the bathroom of the adjoining room.

There she was, a naked woman, without any clothes none-the-less! *What a beauty* he thought. The second thought that came to mind; *was this a dream? Was I underdressed and did I have pee all over my leg?* But then he thought *why wasn't I wearing my suit? The first night I go to sleep without it I just happen to meet a woman in the morning?* He was so upset with himself. He thought *she must have been an opera singer in her former life. She had such a high voice.* It felt like he was in a front row seat at the Opera House. He knew it was an opera since she kept speaking in French and contradicting herself over and over. Why was she asking for those sausages and at the same time asking him to help her get out of the bathroom? It was so, so confusing for him.

She kept yelling, "i-Diot. Help me. Get out of here!"

The other man in her apartment came running over to her. Now he knew he was dreaming. He recalled when he had joined the Polyandrists in Tibet, every woman he met after that, even when he returned to the US of A, had always had another man in their life. He was so fortunate these two complete strangers honored his religion, the religion that allowed a woman to have multiple lovers. He wondered *how they knew this about me? I always kept the religious part of me to myself.* He thought *my skills of thought transference and telemytzuris was exponentially growing. They must have grown to the point of me being able to influence someone without even having to tell them my problems.*

He didn't understand. *Why did the women never admit to having a second lover? Why did they always make up one reason or another as to why I was projecting this on myself?* Why did they say this was my problem and not theirs? It wasn't until he had a dream about a woman being caught in a time warp with two lovers that he understood he must be experiencing multiple dimensions. Although he thought he knew the women he was with; in reality, they were not the same people. Otherwise, how could they deny something he saw with his very own eyes? Namely, that *other* man.

For example, right now he had just met his dream girl, in a dream and there she was with another man in her bathroom. She couldn't deny that. "Right?" But why was she speaking French to him in his dream? Why was she yelling for him to leave? Why was she telling the other man to throw him out of his own dream? He figured *perhaps if I walked back out into my own room I would wake up and figure it out?* Luckily, he walked back just at the right time; the other man had just thrown a bottle of shampoo at the door. He thought *the loud bang would wake me up*, but then he realized *wait a minute, I am awake!* He spasmodically locked the door from his side of the room, put his back against it. He thought *wow that was more exciting than any dream I had ever had! Perhaps I ought to stay awake more often than not?*

74   ALL BOXED IN – REPEAT OFFENDER

LIFE LESSONS
1 If you dream, make sure you are awake before you daydream a nightmare.

MYSTIC POWERS
81 **Imobilus:** The ability to wait, wait and wait. The ability to endure the passage of time without noticing it passing.

Deep Within, Cerebellum
Two Too
"Wake me if I'm up
While I'm sleeping."

The Lonely Mystic was very upset about having walked through the wrong door. Some events, which occur in one's life, can appear to be completely out of one's control. Then there are events one accidentally generates. Some people are easy on themselves. They have a *laisez-fairé* attitude of *hey, mistakes happen, I'm only human.* He found this a difficult sweaty acorn to hold onto, let alone swallow. *I should have wiped all the sand from my eyes before I went looking for the bathroom. I should have looked in to see whether I was in the right room. I should have, should have, and should have...*

And so it went on with him in his head. Over and over until he remembered when one door closes, another one opens. So he sat around his room staring at all the doors waiting for one of them to open. He was used to sitting and waiting; it was part of his training in Asia. He knew how to wait and fast at the same time. Fasting made waiting go even slower, which to him was a contradiction in terms: *How could fast be slow?* He knew *time didn't really exist. Whether I waited fast or slow wouldn't make a difference.* He was curious what the outcome of his last wrong door experience would be. He waited and waited. Several long minutes went by.

He then started having visions. Fasting and waiting often visited these upon him. He started seeing himself as different people, from different eras. He even saw himself as a child, as well as being all bones standing in a coffin. He saw himself supported on two platforms, each with different heads on them. He decided to reach out and walk through one of the doors in his vision. He walked right through it. He was a truly brave soul. He felt no matter what happened he was ready and well prepared to deal with it. He felt confident and felt strong. He was ready, willing and able to accept his new destiny. So he walked on. He then heard that very vocal, loud screeching, and operatic French voice. Again!

    This time the man who was in the room grabbed him by his hair; he still had five of them on the left side of his head. He was thrown back into his room. *Oh boy. What a morning I'm having and it isn't even ten o'clock yet.*

75 ROOM SERVICE – ORIGIN OF A SPECIES

The Mystic Arms Hotel, State of Confusion
Squeaky Clean
"Yes, I want everything cleaned,
That's what you are here for!"

LIFE LESSONS
1 Vindication sometimes catches you when you are least prepared for it.
2 Speaking the same language is not necessary for effectively communicating your needs to another.
3 A cat to you may be a hat to another or vice versa.
4 Mom isn't the only one who knows best. Pop may know a thing or two, too.

MYSTIC POWERS
82 **Emaculus:** The ability to be squeaky clean. The ability to stay squeaky clean. The ability to have your place squeaky cleaned. To know just the right amount of laundry detergent to put into your washer. To know just the right amount of dishwashing liquid to put into your dishwasher. To know just the right amount of antifreeze to put into your car. To know just the right amount of toothpaste to put on your toothbrush. Being skilled and well versed in ascertaining finite measurements mitigated with infinite possibilities and being able to quantify and compartmentalize such so proportionate and proportional balances exists.

    The Lonely Mystic needed to shower. He needed to wash off all of the bad swarma the man in the woman's bathroom had just dished his way. He did so. This time he walked through the right door. He had just come out of the shower when the cleaning woman opened the other door. *See,* he knew it! He knew a door would open after he got kicked out of the last one. He felt vindicated. He was always able to predict the future. It was part of his mystical training. Time after time, he was given exemplary proof of his uncanny abilities. Of course, this cited example was but only one small example of such.

    There he was, standing in the corner of the room. He watched the cleaning woman come gliding in on her vacuum cleaner. Her name was Ima. It was a common name. Once, he had asked her for her name, she said, "Ima Clean." Coincidentally her name, actually, was just that. How appropriate! He didn't take it that way, although he never doubted she was clean. With some people, you can tell they haven't cleaned themselves in quite a while. For example, crumbs hanging from their eyebrows or from nostril hairs were often a dead giveaway. Shredded collars were another. If they had a type of perfume you couldn't recognize and it made you gag: Well, take a wild guess. You could definitely assume it wasn't perfume at all.

Ima had none of those qualities. On the contrary, she was immaculate. There wasn't a speck of dirt or foul smelling odor on, or about her. It was quite surprising as she was busy cleaning a whole day. He had various theories as to how this was possible. One was *a rolling stone gathered no schmutz*. She moved so swiftly dirt (schmutz – a slow element) didn't have the time to adhere to her. Liquids are svelte and swift. Dirt is grungy and dawdling.

For example, if dirt were fast, would you let your bed sheets stay on your bed for a few days without changing them? Absolutely not. You would run to the shower in the morning because you're filthy from sleeping. But, "No." Your sheets are immaculate; otherwise, you would wash them every day, "Right?" Sheets are inorganic, but your body is organic. Dirt is attracted to organic substances first. It knows it can find food there. What kind of food is it going to find on a clean bed sheet? Nothing. But on your nice, juicy, silky, hairy skin it will find billions of eatable microbes to feast upon.

Intuitively you know this. Bedbugs know this too. That is why they populate your sheets. "Do you think nature is stupid?" Could you imagine nature holding a class for bed bugs and saying, "Hey guys and gals, if you want to eat go wait on the side of the wall and floor. Perhaps in a week or so, some dirt will come your way. Then you could attach yourself to it and eventually find your way to the bed." No Siree! Nature tells the bugs to go directly for the jugular and "Head for those sheets." First, of course, no one has yet realized where bed bugs get their travel orders from. How they manage to wind up on the sheets and pillowcases in the first place is the second biggy. Well, be forewarned now. Perhaps this subtle, single piece of info merits the big bucks you paid for buying this book.

The bed bugs come from your local water. They infiltrate your washer. They get a free ride. They are immune to chlorine. They love chlorine. Chlorine, for them, is like vodka for others. Give them chlorine, and they will start repopulating their species. So they swim into your washers and dig deep into your sheets. They have nifty little crab-like claws. Next to chlorine, they love bleach and heat. Give them all three and they thrive and multiply. By the time you throw that nice *clean* sheet onto your bed, it is filled with the little buggers. So what does the chief accomplice of bed bugs say the moment she enters your domicile to *clean* it for you?

She says, "Do you want me to change the sheets too?" Of course, that is always extra. Of course, it's extra. It's extra aggravation for you. Now you have to go to the pharmacy and buy all kinds of stuff for things you can't see. You call the exterminator and tell him you know there are *things* crawling around, but you haven't seen *them* yet. He gets very happy inside since now he can charge you for doing nothing at all. What kind of proof do you have he sprayed your place for anything? For all you know he walked around spraying water tinted with some stuff he bought in the local hardware store. What are you going to do? Call the Bureau and complain you didn't know what you had, but the exterminator didn't kill it? They would laugh you off of the phone.

You could, of course, ask the cleaning woman to wash your sheets and pillowcases in bottled water and use vodka and maraschino cherries instead of bleach and soap. This way the bugs would get inebriated and the red dye in the cherries would definitely kill them off. See how happy you are you bought this book just for this info alone. "Right?"

Following close behind Ima was a crew of three helpers. He could never figure out what country they came from, but he knew they were definitely not from around these parts. They were also definitely not from The Brooklyn. He could tell this from their vocabulary. They only knew one letter. Everything she said to them would prompt "C, C, C" in sequential elevated tones as an answer.

Ima also always brought a cat along with her. At least he thought it was a cat. It did look something like her hat. Stranger things have happened to him; in any event, it was a very, very selfish cat. All it ever did was talk about how it was doing; "Me-how, me-how, and me-how." That's all he ever heard come out of its mouth. The cleaning woman had a verbose vocabulary, which consisted of four words. He knew the cat belonged to her. She too would use the same word, "Me" quite often. He knew she was very polite and educated. She always called him by his proper title, "Mr." but he didn't understand why she thought he was an obstetrician.

Pop had always wanted him to become a doctor. However, he didn't think his father knew this cleaning woman. But then again, Pop had passed on and he didn't know what Pop was up to now. Maybe he told the cleaning woman his son was a doctor. Maybe he told the cleaning woman he knew how to make babies. One of the ladies outside of his hotel had once asked him if he wanted to make babies with her too. This was right after she had told him it would only cost him two hundred dollars. This totally confused him: *Everyone knew you could get a baby for free. You just need to call the adoption agency. Why would someone want to pay two hundred dollars to make one?* But the cleaning woman didn't want him to make a baby. It was very obvious she already had one inside of her: She went around telling everyone she was ready to deliver.

All he ever heard her say was, "Mr., me due now?" She pointed to everything before she cleaned it and said the same thing over and over. It was quite noisy on those mornings with the cat "me-howing," the little men running around going "C, C, C," and Ima, in a very low voice saying, "Mr., Mr. Me due now?" He was glad when the whole troupe finally vacated his room. This didn't take long. She worked like a whirlwind, swirling around like a bunch of leaves in an autumn wind. It was like a hurricane had swept through his room. Before he could say, "C, the cat's meow, your done," she was finished. Now he could finally dress and start the day. It was exhausting doing nothing, even early in the day!

76   STIFF UPPER LIP – ALL AROUND TOWN

Taken For a Ride, Any Place, USA
All That Glitters...
"If it's 'Such a bargain,'
How come it ain't sold yet?"

MANHATTAN,
NEW YORK—1974

LIFE LESSONS
1 Physiognomy, precious metals, and astrology can affect your emotions.
2 Beware of woozy plastic surgeons.
3 Not all that glitters is solid gold.
4 Not all people who offer help have your best interests at heart.
5 Some broken things aren't worth being fixed.
6 Silence is golden if you don't pay for it through the nose.
7 Just because you don't see something doesn't mean it isn't bad for you.
8 Your life can change in a matter of seconds.

MYSTIC POWERS
83 **Extemporaineist:** The ability to utilize unplanned events to one's advantage and capitalize upon them. The ability to cull bits and pieces of random knowledge and synthesize them into a conglomerate philosophy and didactic which explains common events in uncommon ways. The ability to camouflage sight and sound in ways that are normally heard or seen. The ability to create circumstances that unknowingly contribute to one's greatest good and benefits.

The Lonely Mystic had often heard, "If you keep a stiff upper lip, then you can even overcome depreciation and feelings of low self-esteem." He had also read in the tabloids; *investing in gold is the best vanguard against depreciation.* From his parental warnings, he knew, "The sun was bad for you and if you don't listen to people, then they can't influence you negatively." Utilizing these gerbils of wisdom, he was determined to overcome his low spirits. He formulated a game plan to overcome his recent misfortunes.

His first stop was the plastic surgeon: Someone who straightens things out. You know, someone who smoothes out all of the wrinkles in your life. As a result of these thoughts, he asked him for a *stiff upper lip*. The night before this particular surgeon had been playing a bit too much hanky-panky with his receptionist. As a result, he was a bit woozy that day. A needle intended for The Lonely Mystic's upper lip instead hit his lower one. An allergic reaction to the injection occurred immediately. His lip swelled up big time. He wasn't upset. He had a firm belief *all that happens, happens for the best.* Even though this *best* might be unobvious at first. The doctor's name was Dr. Voltaire.

Next, he went shopping for some gold. He traveled into Manhattan by hailing a taxidermist. It was rush hour. He figured it would take lots of time to get into the city. Four hours later he arrived at the jewelry district in Manhattan. For those of you who have never visited there, you would be pleasantly surprised. A one-block area houses more jewelry stores and jewelry business than some countries. You must wear sunglasses on the street: The reflections coming from the gold and diamonds in the windows could cause permanent damage to your wallet. You also need coming prepared by wearing protective earbuds plugged into your favorite player. This may mitigate street hawkers hawking you until you succumb to enter their infamous den of wares. Should you be unfortunate enough to fall prey to their repetitive song, you'll leave having purchased something you didn't want in the first place.

Of course, he wasn't one to fall prey to such shenanigans. He walked into his favorite pawnshop only after the hawker in front of it had touted its merits for fifteen minutes. He had never been in a pawnshop before. The suspicious looking individual told him as soon as he entered, he would feel comfortable in it again and again.

His philosophy on purchasing used items was: *If you buy new things, you never know whether they are good. If you buy old things then for sure they are good. Who would want to pawn something if they didn't want it back again?* He felt *if you wear gold it would depreciate less because if you and other people saw it, it would be appreciated. Everyone knows appreciation is the opposite of depreciation.* He purchased a few gold necklaces and rings. Well, at least some of the rings and necklaces were gold. The owner explained the dynamics and chemistry of gold to him. He was amazed. The owner, whose name was Justa Cruk, (He was foreign.) said:

> You don't want to buy a solid piece of gold jewelry. If you did and gold went down in value, you would then lose a great percentage of your investment. If you purchase a plated gold-filled piece of jewelry, then if gold went down in value, you would lose only a small portion of your investment.

Justa was perfectly willing to sell him a gold filled or plated pieces of jewelry for the same price as a solid gold piece. This way he wouldn't be subject to the fluctuating prices of the metals commodities market. He was ecstatic about the sound value of his purchases. He put all of them immediately on so they could start being appreciated and start increasing in value.

Next, he walked to the electronics district. There you could buy watches, electronics and everything else, even if it hasn't even existed yet. He bought a pair of *noise-canceling* headphones. The shop clerk explained these were a special pair of headphones. Noise-canceling headphones needed batteries to work for the electronics to filter out background sounds. You constantly had to purchase batteries for them to keep out the noise. These were special since they didn't need batteries; this allowed them to work forever.

These didn't need batteries because they were *broken-in*. The clerk explained since they were broken-in already, they kept all the noise out. If you put them on and plugged them into your player, you would absolutely hear nothing! *What more would anyone want out of a noise-canceling device* he thought. They sounded perfect! He put them on and heard absolutely nothing. He loved the silence. It sounded so soothing and peaceful. He especially liked the lows of silence. He struggled very hard to hear its midrange and highs. Since he had problems with his hearing before he figured his hearing was degenerating further when he heard nothing now. The clerk had told him to hear music, someone next to him had to have their player turned on very high. He figured *the clerk was half right. And everyone knows half a truth is better than a whole lie.*

He listened carefully. Then he heard *the sound of one hand slapping*, over and over. He had finally figured out Zen Ben's Kohan. He was slapping his face to stay awake because the silence and quiet surrounding him were putting him to sleep. He then realized *if I put on really, really dark sunglasses, I wouldn't be able to see the sun. If I can't see the sun, then, of course, it isn't bad for me.* "Out of sight, out of mind" was one of his favorite theories.

Outfitted with his new gear, he went walking and looked like a new person. He was on his way back to The Brooklyn and momentarily stopped for a traffic light. It was such a long light he managed to catch a few winks during the pause. He knew *catnaps* were good for cats, otherwise, *why would they have them? They must also be beneficial for me, especially in the middle of the day.* He always liked taking good care of himself. Of course, when he awoke a whole three seconds later, he was *robbed blind*. With those dark glasses on, some despicable someone must have thought he *was* blind. They took his gold, his earphones, and his glasses. When he opened his eyes, he saw the robber trying to take his hat too! So he reached out to him. He had learned to confront your fears and learn to embrace them. Wouldn't you know it? The robber punched him directly on his upper lip!

It stiffened up immediately. He was beside himself with joy! He thought *finally, I got what I wanted. Now I can overcome my feelings of misfortune, which arose and permeated my being, from the last time I was robbed.* He thought *God truly worked in mysterious ways.*

77 AU NATURALÉ – FATHER T AND BI BI

Prospect Park, the State of Brooklyn—1974
Smell the Daisies
"I have time for everything,
But everything will take too much time."

PROSPECT PARK, THE BROOKLYN—1974

LIFE LESSONS
1 Time alone lasts longer and goes by slower.
2 If you want to know what hunger feels like, then don't eat.
3 You can't figure out how hunger feels on a full stomach.
4 Knowing the reason for something happening doesn't preclude having the experience of it.
5 Strangers can become friends, and friends can affect our lives significantly.
6 Always exhale after an inhale or you may get confused.

MYSTIC POWERS
84 **Temporial:** The ability to position oneself in another time and place at the same time and place. The ability to move from here to there and back without having left. The ability to transverse the known into the unknown without knowing how. The ability to pull rabbits out of pockets as well as hats. The ability to smell daisies as well as roses. The ability to walk on the grass even when it clearly says the opposite. The ability to realize one's elders are just babies who have lost their youth and gained their age.

The Lonely Mystic decided to head out to Prospect Park for a long walk. Of course, he had to take three trains to get there. That didn't matter since it was the park of his childhood. He loved visiting it. He also loved long walks, especially without the dogs. It wasn't he didn't love his dogs; he did, but everyone needs spending some quality time alone. For many reasons, some people find that a difficult thing to do. Perhaps they can't find the time, to take the time, to have the time, to spend the time on themselves, by themselves and for themselves. This, for some, of course, isn't by choice, but is circumstance based. Others always find reasons never to be with themselves. Then some of those have the means and prowess to spend the time alone. Those are the *lonely ones*, the ones who have lost their families or the ones who have lost their friends. Perhaps they never knew their families or ever made friends. Perhaps they chose to be apart or were forced to do so. They were the ones, who due to destiny, fate, choice or what have you, walk the path of life spending more time with themselves than with others. Zen Ben used to say, "A *hungry* man doesn't know how a *full* one feels." Those who have not experienced the *Solitary Way* don't know it and really can't judge it. Even though they think such judgments could easily be made. Opinions are not only free, at times; perhaps more often than not, they may be ill-founded and incorrect.

He didn't set out to be a lonely mystic. It was just life had created opportunities based upon decisions he made. Of course, we all make our own decisions to move forward, backward or stay at rest. These are our *Horagummies* and based upon those decisions; certain paths unfold; our personal *Auragummies*. These are transformational opportunities provided by our Soul. If you asked him, he would say,

> Everything I have done has brought me to the point of unfolding this tale, my MoREgummy, the story of my life. As a result, I am the right person, in the right place and at the right time. I live my life seeking to choose the best and highest choices I can make for the greatest good in the service of God. This is my *Quantum Cubit*. It is at the forefront of modern knowledge and uses ancient means of transformation, change and being: It is *QuantumREotics*. The multi-universe is a synchronistic, synergistic, multi-dimensional spiritual metropolis of possibilities and probabilities and I consider myself to be truly fortunate for being where I was, where I am, where I am heading to and who I am being.

When the owner of the hotel asked him to vacate the premises right after he had walked into the opera singer's room for the second time, he accepted it with grace. He wasn't due a vacation, but who was he to fight with his boss? He didn't plan on being on vacation so soon, but you can't look a gift horsey in the mouth. Some people would beg to differ and say he did so every morning when he looked in the mirror. He often wondered *why that was. Perhaps a horse's mouth is so long, you would never see the end of it?* This was just one of those mysteries he aspired to understand.

The head of the hotel came up to his room shortly after the housekeeper left. And told him about his *vacation*. He was instructed to take his belongings with him and had until the end of the day to do so. He was a little confused about the *belongings* part. He knew what *leggings* were and knew what a long shirt, or pants were. He never quite understood, why he was wearing a pair of pants? He only had one pants on, *why were they a pair? Was each leg called* a *pants?* And more importantly, *were they "a" long or "b" long?*

He finally understood the manager wanted him to take all of his clothes that "b-long" to him. *I didn't have any* b long *pants or shirts? All my shirts were short sleeve, and my jacket was also thirty-eight short, so where the manager got a* b *long from was beyond me.* He was about to ask the manager, but the manager walked out and slammed the door after him. He figured *my vacation started at day's end but I didn't mind starting it sooner. Plus the park was a good place to start it with.*

He met an Asian man in the park who seemed to have appeared as if out of nowhere. The man had a little boy with him, and the little boy had two pairs of rabbits, one pair at each side of him. The elderly man approached and asked, "Have you ever been to Paris?"

He answered, "Yes, only once, when I walked into a door, and I didn't even have to pay for the ticket!"

The old man looked him in the eye, and said, "Ly My." (pronounced Lee My) "It is important to be able to time travel."

The rabbits were hopping up and down and the young boy smiled a lot. The Lonely Mystic found the old man's statements interesting. He loved his new name: *Lee My* (short for Lone*LY My*stic). He figured *now I was on vacation.* Since vacations usually lasted two weeks, he agreed with the old man and was ready to time travel.

He asked the old man, "Kind sir, what is your name?"

"You may call me Father T."

"Is your name also abbreviated?"

"Yes, T is for *time*. Are you ready?"

Lee My was always ready, willing and able, so he said, "Yes."

For his first trip, Father T decided to send Lee My to a distant past. The young boy handed him a daisy he had picked and the two rabbits jumped into each of Lee My's short jacket pockets. He didn't even want a long jacket. *Was that hotel manager wrong!* Somehow he remembered seeing those two rabbits before. Then Lee My picked up the daisy and smelled it.

No sooner did he inhale deeply, when a wind came and started to blow all the leaves, bushes and trees in a circular manner. At first, it was slow, then, it became increasingly stronger and swirled faster.

He could hear the young boy yelling "Bi, Bi."

He figured *it was his name,* so he said, "Bye, bye, Bi Bi."

Father T kept telling him, "Remember to return! Just exhale when you are ready."

Lee My thought *that was strange? Who would wait to exhale?* But no sooner did he finish his in-breath of daisies that he found himself elsewhere. He was no longer in Prospect Park, The Brooklyn.

78   IT'S GOOD TO BE KING – SMALL FRY

The Royal Palace, Herminia—1974
King for a Day
"So what if I'm short,
I'm the King!"

LIFE LESSONS
1 It's always good to get the full picture before jumping to conclusions.
2 Height is relative, but short is short and small is small.
3 If you don't feel the rain, then you might be standing in-between it.
4 Experience deeply, it may leave you before you know it.

MYSTIC POWERS
85 **Regressionist:** The ability to regress to past lives, recall certain events and then swiftly return to the present with some goodies.

THE ROYAL PALACE, HERMINIA—1974

The Lonely Mystic looked around and noticed, things looked a lot different after inhaling the scent of the daisies. He saw things from a different perspective. Not quite putting his finger on it, he still continued looking around. Then he understood why: *The men around me were quite large.* He thought perhaps I wound up in some strange *Giant Land*. A place where people were bigger than they should have been. Upon looking at his hands he immediately understood. He was a young child. Something pointy was poking his head. Taking it off he realized it was a golden crown. He thought *boy that explains why I like to use the word* boy, *as often as I do and why I like wearing gold so much.*

The man standing next to him, on his right looked just like a younger version of Father T. That man was holding a rounded abacus shaped device. The man standing next to his left was wearing a beautiful multicolor shawl with little string-like balls hanging from it. The man standing farther to his left, who was also the one to the right of Father T was only a little bit taller than him.

Father T started speaking and said, "You are in the land of *Herminia*."

At least that was what he thought he had heard. His head felt a little cloudy and his sinuses were stuffed up since he was allergic to flowers. He did just breathe in a daisy.

He asked Father T, "Where is Herminia?"

Father T answered, "It resides in between the raindrops."

Lee My looked up to see whether it was raining. He tried hard seeing the rain. He didn't think Father T was lying to him. He even held his hand out to see whether it got wet. Needless to say, it didn't.

When he did this, the shorter man on his left slapped it and said, "Hi-five."

Lee My was happy since at the very least; one of the men had introduced himself to him. He slapped him back saying, "Me too." He was also happy to meet Hi Five.

The short man on his right then grabbed his hand and said, "Me too, too," while pointing to himself.

Lee My was very confused. He figured that man was trying to tell him he *too* was happy, but the man kept shaking his head sideways saying, "Me Too, too, Me Too."

Lee My figured *his name was Me Too* and thought *what an odd coincidence?*

Father T began speaking to him saying,

> Lee My you are king of your destiny and you have all the time in the world to be who you want to be and explore yourself. You will find you in yourself and in others. Everyone you see is a REflection of who you aRE. Everything you hear is the sound of you speaking to yourself. Everything you know you have known before and are REmembering it. Every place you visit; you have visited before and aRE REexperiencing it. Do you REmember now?

Lee My was about to say, "No." Instead, he started exhaling a deep breath. Before he could answer, he was back in the park. The Prospect Park, that is.

It was a very sunny day, and Father T was gone, Bi Bi was gone, but more importantly, he still had two rabbits in his pockets. When he took a closer look, the rabbits had multiplied. A whole slew of rabbits started jumping from his short jacket down some hole they found next to a tree. He could swear he saw one of them holding something metallic and yelling something... He couldn't quite make it out.

He started walking home, not realizing he had none. He was more than a little bewildered by his recent experiences. As he continued walking, he saw a field of daisies. He smiled and although he had a flower allergy, he decided to pick a bunch of them. He figured he didn't' know when he would want to vacation again and so he had better be prepared. This vacation was so much better than the ones before. This time he didn't have to choose; all he had to do was breathe. And only once. so he didn't have to worry about his breath stopping either. It was *i-Diot* proof. This way he was very careful not to inhale the flowers scent. Now he knew how potent they were. As he continued walking, he saw a bunch of people surrounding something. Being a curious fellow, he walked on over to take *a-look-see.*

79   THE READER - I MADE IT UP

Out of the Blue, Grassy Knoll—1974
Fortuno Smiles
"How can my future
Fit into those small cards?"

LIFE LESSONS
1 If you can't read it, then make it up.
2 Start your own language; some billionaires didn't even graduate college.
3 If words don't work, use your hands.
4 Not all cards are for playing poker.
5 Not all coins are there for the taking.

MYSTIC POWERS
86 **Kinesiologist:** The ability to use movements to communicate. The ability to utilize kinetic energy to convey complex concepts that can't be verbally expressed because no one else understands what it is you are trying to say. The use of specific motions to convey specific concepts to specific people at specific times about specific things. Being able to control one's movement and motion so one doesn't trip all over what is being said.

CENTRAL PARK, NEW YORK CITY—1974

The Lonely Mystic was no longer in Prospect Park. He easily recognized he had somehow returned to Central Park, in The Manhattan. He didn't think it odd. After all, he had just returned from a place that existed between the raindrops. He thought *perhaps one of them got blown a bit too hard and landed up in The Manhattan.* There was a small crowd of people up ahead. He tried edging his way in front of them. So he could see what was going on. He pushed gently and then obviously a bit too much.

Looking up, he was in front of a table, face to face with a bald-headed man.

He asked the man, "What are you doing?"

The man said, "I am Reader."

Lee My was happy. He finally had found someone he had something in common with. He also considered himself as being a reader.

He had learned to read when he was a small child. He spent lots of time in a stroller and made it a point to read all the store signs during the long walks Mom had taken him on. Of course, he made up his own words for the signs he saw. His parents were to busy loudly discussing. They didn't have the time to teach him what the signs really said. Once he asked them. They responded in a strange language, which he didn't understand. It didn't at all sound like the baby talk he was used to.

All these things didn't faze him even one iota. To this day he still reads the same way he did as a child; by making up his own words. Of course, later on, he realized everyone else, as children, had similar problems. They too had made up their own words. Most of the time he didn't understand what they were saying when they spoke to him. He was glad this was a universal issue. He would have hated being the only one who had a personal language. If that were the case, how would he be able to communicate? He called his language *sign language* for two very good reasons: Primarily because he had learned to read from signs. Second, because he used to point to each of the letters when he was trying to figure out what they meant. This resulted in him using his hands a lot when speaking to others. People seemed to understand him. They always patted him on the back and had such, sad pitiful little smile on their faces. He felt bad for them.

Reader motioned to a deck of cards on the table and then pointed to Lee My. Since Lee My was proficient in sign language, he understood Reader wanted to play cards. So he lifted the deck, shuffled it and put three cards in front of Reader, three cards in front of him, and one card in the middle for good luck. He felt especially lucky, so he put one card on the left for him and one card on the right for Reader. He saw there were some coins in a bowl. He figured they were there as part of the card tricks Reader was going to do. He picked them up and waited for the reader to direct him. He smiled looking at Reader.

The people were cheering and laughing so hard they couldn't stand up straight. Reader lit the four incense sticks on the table and started to rub the beads that were all over his jacket. He began speaking to Lee My. Lee My thought it strange he was able to understand Reader but figured Reader's parents must have been friends with his parents. As a result, Reader had learned sign language too. Reader proceeded to tell Lee My the following tale. A tale which would change his life.

80 THE READING – THE TROUPE

Another Time, Another Place
What a Bunch of Characters
"I know how to bait a hook,
But how do you bait a breath?"

LIFE LESSONS
1 Is last year considered a past life?
2 There are so many characters in my past my future is stuck in my present.
3 One can feel lonely even in very crowded places.

MYSTIC POWERS
87 **Exhibitionist:** The ability to be part of a very large public display and feel very private. The ability to be on display and yet be invisible to those watching. The ability to delve deep within and extricate oneself from where one is. The ability to disappear into a crowd even when millions of millions have all eyes upon you. The ability to backtrack, even into other lives, whether they have or haven't yet existed.

Reader asked The Lonely Mystic, "Do you remember having been in the circus once?"

Lee My answered:

Of course, I've been to the circus twice, not once. When I was in Ubirdehyam, I joined the circus. But only briefly, since the owner sent me on a vacation soon after I had joined. I also remember Mom taking me out of school one day and the whole family going into the city to see the Big Top. It was one of the best days of my life!

He didn't realize Reader was referring to a past life of his. Reader continued:

In the lifetime I'm looking at, you had many positive experiences. These experiences have influenced many of your present and future lives. You modeled several of your lives, past, and future, after personages you met in that lifetime. There were four in particular who were special to you. I would like to tell you about those with your kind permission. Yes?

Lee My was speechless, something which didn't often happen to him unless he was sleeping or eating. He managed to squeak out a very, very faint "OK." He never knew what that word meant, but since he always heard it being said, he used it too. He thought *it had something to do with a place out in the Old Wild West.*

The first person Reader told him about was *Swingsta*, who was a trapeze artist. The second person he told him about was *Mage*, a magician. The third person he told him about was *Au Contrairé*, a contortionist, and the fourth person he told him about was *Shif T*, who was a shaman.

The people had now started to camp out in the park around them. The hot dog vendors had pulled their carts closer. The balloon man was selling balloons like hotcakes. People didn't mind spending fifty dollars for a balloon. The price had gone up because the world's helium supply was escaping into thin air. You could even see ticket scalpers on the periphery charging ten dollars a ticket for empty grass spots for people to sit down on. Some out-of-towners were so gullible at times. The police came and started to barricade the area. The crowd was growing so large it started inferring with traffic.

That day there was a parade on the avenue. When it was over, all the parade attendees came over to see and hear what the commotion was about. Someone brought a boom box over to Reader. They plugged in a microphone, so everyone could hear what was being said. Soon media trucks arrived with reporters surrounding the event. Someone began streaming the reading to the Internet. Before you could say Lee My, billions of people were tuned in, turned on and were ready to hear what Reader had to say.

The Lonely Mystic looked around and said, "I am glad it's a quiet morning." He was used to *paparazzi*. It was his favorite pizza topping. He would always order paparazzi pizza with double sauce. He needed double sauce since everyone knows sauce evaporates. Then the cheese remains with small spots of make-believe sauce under it. He was no fool. No one was going to jip him out of his money. He looked around for the pizza delivery guy. He was surprised he couldn't find him. He could almost smell the pizza.

Instead, he smelled cigarette and cigar smoke and a little of some other stuff. There were so many people crowding around now. He loved it when that happened. He valued his privacy and with so many people there, *who would be concerned about me?* He felt lost amidst a sea of drops in an ocean of water. He was just one lonely droplet swimming around in a universal pool of swoosh. He felt the cool waters around him. He heard the sound of the waves, the swoop of the seagulls, and the pitter-patter of fish jumping in and out of the water. He felt the seaweed glisten across his body as the salt tightened his skin. Then he abruptly came back to reality.

He was thankful for his mini-vacation. Since it was in a wet climate; he brushed some of the seaweed out of his five hairs, some of the sand off his skin and shook the saltwater out of his shoes. He turned to Reader and said, "Hi-five me too, let it rip!"

Reader looked at the cards one more time. He looked all around and noticed the huge audience that had formed. The interested bystanders paused and held their breath; less the noises of their breathing interfered with what was to occur next. Reader closed his eyes and dove deeply into the recesses of his innermost being. He inhaled and smelled the fresh cut grass and daisies. His lips parted ready to speak. The crowd waited with baited breath…

TO BE CONTINUED...

Epilogue

Of course our tale doesn't end here. Stay tuned for the next volume of **PORTRAITS OF A LONELY MYSTIC IN 3D: Double Talk**. Guaranteed to be twice as good!

THE LONELY MYSTIC
AS DELIVERY GUY, THE SAGA CONTINUES...

"I like a good *pop,*

Every once in a while."

EXCERPTED FROM

PORTRAITS OF A LONELY MYSTIC IN 3D:

DOUBLE TALK

LIST OF ILLUSTRATIONS

A Good Time 221
All That Glitters ... 235
Animaal 153
Attitude Dude 11
BaH D 118
Calypso Kid 40
Captain Cosmos 45
Circus Man 209
Cool Cat 70
Cool Dude 48
Cosmotician 96
Crew Cut Cutie 73
Crypto Man 66
Deep Dude 62
Ding-Ah-Ling 25
Do D Dude 114
Dream Lover 200
Farm Boy 12
Fortune Smiles 246
Frenchie 189
Hi Roller 2
Ice Cold Kid 30
ICMEUCUWECUS Dude 125
Incogmento Man 135
King for a Day 243
Mr. Collegiate 155
Mr. Directions 38
Mr. Metalico 170
Mr. Singularity 161
Mr. Supplemental 167
Mr. Vacation 33
Mr. Wardrobe 197
Multiple Man 207
Mustache Man 60
Ooops! 225
Pieceman 51
Quizator 144
Ring-A-Linguist 108

Runaway Kid 7
Saved 218
Serious Dude 110
Shades 93
Sherpa Boy 14
Shirley 177
Smell the Daisies 239
Squeaky Clean 231
Star Man 43
Super Sonarist 102
Tears of Joy 1
The Black Cap Kid 9
The Community 88
The Contortionist 182
The Do Do Man 55
The Exacerbator 141
The Excersist 74
The Fool 27
The Hitch Hiker 187
The Intermediary 146
The Listener 84
The Lumanist 139
The Man 133
The Meditator 172
The Messenger 86
The Mystical Mystic Mystic 91
The Naked Truth 81
The Neighbors 192
The Plumbing 148
The Socialite 158
The Soda Pop Kid, 5
The Space Cadet 174
The Swimmer 215
The Taxidermist 128
The Tourist 202
The Vigilante 78
The Wise One 53
Ting-A-Ling 105

Two Too 229
Wall Street Dude 121

Misha Ha Baka / Portraits of a Lonely Mystic in 3D 254
What a Bunch of Characters 248
Wise Guys 20

ADDITIONAL BOOKS BY MISHA HA BAKA

www.habakabook.com

Visit www.mishahabaka.com, www.habakabook.com, www.mikeigh.com and www.quantumreotics.com for more Misha Ha Baka.

MiKeigh Music

Available for purchase at www.mikeigh.com.

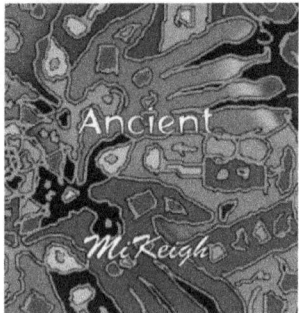

ABOUT THE AUTHOR & ARTIST

Misha Ha Baka has worn many hats during his professional career. He has penned several other works including Confessions of a Lonely Mystic small talk, Confessions of a Lonely Mystic short talk and the Print Opera series. He holds a BA in English Literature, an MA in Asian Studies and has studied healing and mystic thought in Asia, England, Israel, and the United States. He is an ordained spiritual healer and ordained member of the clergy. He is a fine artist, a graphic artist, a musician, and a composer with dozens of albums of original music such as *Passion*, *Miracle* and *Ancient* by MiKeigh. Contact www.mikeigh.com for additional information.

Contact www.mishahabaka.com for permission requests or other inquiries.

For my beloved wherever she may be…

www.ingramcontent.com/pod-product-compliance
Lightning Source LLC
Chambersburg PA
CBHW080534170426
43195CB00016B/2555